A Practical Guide to Usability Testing

Joseph S. Dumas
Janice C. Redish

intellect™

EXETER, ENGLAND
PORTLAND OR, USA

Revised Edition published in Paperback in Great Britain in 1999 by
Intellect Books
FAE, Earl Richards Road North, Exeter EX2 6AS, UK

Revised Edition published in USA in 1999 by
Intellect Books
ISBS, 5804 N.E. Hassalo St, Portland, Oregon 97213-3644, USA

First Published 1993, Reprinted 1994.

A catalogue record for this book is available from the British Library

ISBN 1-84150-020-8

Printed and bound in Great Britain by Cromwell Press, Wiltshire.

Table of Contents

Part I

Part II

Part III

Conducting and Using the Results of a Usability Test

Preface to the First Edition

This is an exciting time for people who are interested in usability, usability engineering, and usability testing. The community of people who are actively applying usability engineering methods is expanding rapidly.

The Community is Growing

It's an exciting time because the community is doing much more extensive networking and sharing, thanks in large part to the efforts of Janice James of American Airlines. Since 1991, usability specialists have gathered in "birds of a feather" sessions at the annual meetings of SIGCHI and the Human Factors Society. In 1992, the Society for Technical Communication started a Professional Interest Committee on Usability; and a new group, the Usability Professionals Association, held its first annual conference at WordPerfect's headquarters in Orem, UT. Common Ground, a newsletter of usability testing professionals, has been published quarterly since August 1991. ~you'll find more information about all of these groups in Appendix B, "Relevant Organizations and Journals.")

Ideas About Usability are Evolving

It's an exciting time because usability engineering and usability testing are concepts that continue to evolve. Interesting research studies and new ideas come out almost every month. Our own thinking about these concepts has evolved considerably since we first began helping companies develop and test products in the early 1980s—and it continues to evolve. Questions remain, and, at places in the book, we raise issues that deserve further research. One of our goals for this book is to stimulate your thinking about how to define and do usability engineering and usability testing.

Usability Brings Many Fields Together

It's an exciting time, because the people in many technical fields are coming together. People who now see themselves as usability specialists come from training and work in human factors psychology, technical communication (document design), functional quality assurance, total quality management, software engineering, and probably many other areas. This is both a source of strength and weakness.

This diversity is a strength if we can learn to talk and work with each other. People from different backgrounds bring complementary perspectives to testing and discussions about usability, yet they all share the same primary goal: to focus on users and make products usable.

This diversity is a weakness if each specialist thinks that he or she can cover all the areas in which usability is relevant. It is also a weakness in that many people are learning to be usability specialists on the job. We know usability specialists and test laboratory directors whose training was not in empirical data collection or human-computer interaction. Many of these people are competent professionals who improve the usability of the products they work on. The best of them understand their limitations. When they need help, they ask for it from people who can supplement their skills.

We have written this book for the broad audience of people who are interested in usability testing. You do not need an advanced degree in a behavioral science discipline to understand what we say. We do, however, point people who are new to testing to information about human-computer interaction and document design and urge them to build their knowledge and skills in these areas. We also expect the book to be useful to the increasing number of university faculty who offer courses that cover usability issues and usability testing.

About the examples we use in the book

As we'll discuss in Chapter 2, usability engineering and usability testing are relevant to all types of products. Anything that people use or read has an interface that can and should be developed with usability in mind, tested iteratively with real users, and improved based on test results before it is marketed or given to users. Although most of the examples in this book come from computer-based products, including hardware, software, and documentation, issues of usability are not confined to computers, and our definition of "computer-based" is very broad. For example, we consider the testing of a TV set with menus or an oscilloscope with software-based controls or an anesthesia workstation with multiple displays or a user's guide for a business telephone to be within the scope of this book.

About Terms: People as "Participants"

We had to decide what to call the people who come to a usability test. We call them participants, a neutral, plain English term.

Subjects may be appropriate for behavioral science research studies, but we believe that it is inappropriate in usability testing. As we point out in the last section of Chapter 2, usability testing is not the same as a research study. Most people who participate in usability tests are not familiar with the vocabulary of behavioral science research. They are likely to associate subject with being subjected to something, which has unpleasant connotations. If the people who conduct the test think of the participants as subjects, they may also inappropriately treat the situation more like a research study than like a usability test.

Calling them users would be accurate and convey the important point that these people must represent at least some segment of the eventual users of the product, but we wanted to distinguish between users, the entire population that interests you, and participants, the user representatives who come to a test. Some groups call test participants evaluators or co-evaluators, which emphasizes their role, but that may confuse other groups who use evaluators to mean the people who are observing and recording, that is, the test team.

About the Scope of this Book

Although the title focuses on usability testing, about a third of this book is about usability engineering: building usability into products (and documents as part of products) from the beginning. The goal of usability specialists and of product teams must be to make more usable products, not to conduct usability tests. Usability testing is only one of several techniques in the tool kit of usability engineering.

We stress this critical point throughout the book. In Part 1, we describe how testing works with other usability tools within the entire context of human-computer interaction and document design.

Preface to the Revised Edition

This revised edition of *A Practical Guide to Usability Testing* includes this new preface and new back matter: a list of relevant books published since 1993 and updated appendices on relevant organizations and on usability labs, both permanent and portable. The body of the book is unchanged. Almost everything in it is still true and relevant.

The field continues to draw in new people from a variety of backgrounds. We believe that they will still find this the most comprehensive and useful introduction to usability and usability testing, as so many others have in the past. We wrote the book knowing that people would adapt the methods to their own situations and needs, as they indeed have. The flexibility that we included in the first edition continues to make the book serve its purpose well.

Our own thoughts about usability, usability engineering, and usability testing and our own practice have continued to evolve over the years since we wrote the book. New challenges and opportunities have made us adapt our own methods. In lieu of rewriting the entire text, we have added comments later in this preface to explain how the field has changed. Read those comments to give yourself an overview of the field as it exists today. Return to specific comments, which are keyed to chapters and pages of the text, as you read the body of the book.

When we wrote the *Preface* to the first edition of this book, we said it was an exciting time for people who are interested in usability and that the community of people who are actively applying usability engineering methods was growing rapidly. As we approach the year 2000, both of those are still true.

The Community Continues to Grow

The community of usability specialists continues to grow – at an even more rapid pace. The Usability Professionals' Association now has 1,000 members. Almost half (about 450) attended the eighth annual meeting in 1999. The Special Interest Group on Usability of the Society for Technical Communication has more than 1,500 members. Jobs for usability specialists abound.

The Community Continues to Come from Diverse Backgrounds

The continued growth of the community means that this book is still needed. Many people enter the field of usability each year, and they continue to come from a wide variety of disciplines and experiences. We wrote the book with this diversity in mind, with the goal of helping a broad audience understand the value and role of usability and the specific technique of usability testing.

The Practice of Usability Continues to Evolve

In the first *Preface*, we said that it was an exciting time because usability engineering and usability testing are concepts that were still evolving. Five years later, that is also still true. When we consider the major changes that have taken place in the field since the first edition of this book, we find three themes in that evolution. We might label them with the adjectives:

- informal
- iterative
- integrated

Usability Testing Has Become More Informal

Many specialists are doing more active intervention (a technique that we describe on page 31) than they were doing five years ago. Even when they do not actively intervene while the participant is working with the product, many specialists now stay in the room with the participant. Many are relying more on qualitative data than on quantitative data – more on identifying problems and less on justifying the existence of those problems with counts of time and error. Many are doing little or no videotaping. Some are taking notes without logging every action the user takes. Most are doing evaluations with just one or two people conducting each test session. Reporting has become much less formal, often just a memo of the major findings and recommendations.

We see several reasons for the evolution to less formal testing. Certainly, one reason is the pressure to do more with fewer resources.

Another is the need to get results that can be used in ever more rapid development and release cycles. However, a third reason is that both usability specialists and those who must act on the results of the testing have more confidence in the process now than they did in the early years. There is not as much need to justify the methodology or the results of a particular usability test. There is more acceptance of the fact that the value of usability testing is in *diagnosing problems* rather than in *validating products* and, therefore, a greater realization that you do not need large numbers of test participants to feel confident that you have seen problems that need to be fixed.

No matter how formal or informal an evaluation you want to do, a usability evaluation requires planning, preparing, working with test participants, analyzing the data, and communicating the results. That's what this book is about. The templates and examples can help you with rapid planning. Although we describe usability labs and logging software, we said even in the first edition that neither is necessary to a successful usability evaluation. You can easily scale down the analyses and reports that we describe in the book.

Later in this preface we describe specific changes that we might make today to several chapters of the book to help you use the process in the even more rapid pace and informal atmosphere of today's typical testing.

Usability Testing Has Become More Iterative

From the very beginning, even in the first edition of this book, we urged you to involve users throughout the process and to do small usability evaluations throughout the process rather than just once at the end. Iterative testing has become a major theme of the profession. Many usability specialists have found that they can evaluate products with very small samples (typically 3 to 6 people in a round of testing) because they are getting to involve users earlier and more often in the process.

Usability Testing Has Become More Integrated

The first third of this book is about bringing usability into your company and putting usability testing as a technique into the context of an entire usability engineering approach. Table 3.1 on page 40 is a list of 16 techniques that you can use in a usability engineering process. We are pleased to note that many design and development teams are including more of these techniques as well as more usability evaluations in their development process.

In fact, the lines among the techniques are blurring. When a team goes on a site visit to observe and interview users in the context of their home or work and takes along a few scenarios to ask the users to try, is that a contextual inquiry, a user and task analysis, or a usability evaluation? When a team includes a user in paper prototyping and has the user try scenarios with the prototype as part of the session or brings in other users to try scenarios with the prototype, is that prototyping or usability evaluation? It doesn't really matter what we call the techniques. We are excited to see the overlapping and integration of these techniques because the goal is to involve users, to have them do real work with emerging designs, and to observe and learn from our observations, so that we continually improve the product.

Our three themes are interrelated. Integrating usability more deeply into the design and development process has allowed for more iterative evaluations and more informal evaluations. When design and development teams include usability specialists, when the project includes pre-design user and task analysis, prototyping with user involvement, and other early usability activities, the product that comes to usability evaluation is likely to be in much better shape than the products for which usability specialists were arranging usability tests even five years ago.

There's Room to Grow Even More

Over the next decade, we predict continued growth in the community of usability specialists and continued growth of interest in usability from users to CEOs. The growth will be both through expansion of existing usability groups and through the introduction of usability into yet more companies. There are still many who have not heard or heeded the usability message. And usability testing remains an excellent catalyst for getting usability into a company. There are still many designers, developers, writers, and managers who have never seen their users working with their products. It is still most often those first observations of an actual usability test — or of videotaped highlights of a test — that break down the barriers between those who make the product and those who use it.

Our Brief Comments on Sections of the Book

If we were writing a new book on usability testing, we would keep most of the original material in this book. It is still relevant today.

But there have been changes in the variety of ways testing is practiced. What follows are our comments on specific issues. In same cases, we list changes we see, while in others we re-emphasize the position we took in the first edition.

Related to Part I, Chapter 2, page 22: What is usability testing?
In the list of the five characteristics of every usability test, the first characteristic we listed was, "The primary goal is to improve the usability of the product." That characteristic still applies to most usability tests, tests that we would now call "diagnostic." But there are other kinds of tests in which the goal is not diagnosis. For example, in a comparison test, the primary goal might be to see which product is most usable; and, in a baseline test, the primary goal might be to gather a set of measures of a product's usability. In all of these types of tests *the focus is on usability*, but the primary goal may not be diagnosing problems.

Related to Part I, Chapter 2, page 26: Questions that remain in defining usability testing
We say, "Would a test in which there were no quantitative measures qualify as a usability test? Probably not." We still believe this assertion is correct, as long as "quantitative" includes simple measures such as counting the number of participants who have the same problem or counting errors. There are, however, more testers who are comfortable with qualitative measures and who use them more frequently than quantitative measures such as average task time. Some usability specialists focus only on qualitative measures and problem lists, in part because they are testing early designs and prototypes. They are doing more active intervention and less formal usability testing.

Related to Part I, Chapter 2, page 27: Testing applies to all types of products
We re-emphasize that any product that people use has an interface, whether it is software, hardware, documentation that goes with software or hardware, a document by itself — from product labels to patient package inserts to government regulations —, a mechanical device that has no computer connection, etc. etc. And every interface can benefit from usability testing.

   In the first edition, the list of products we described did not include web pages or web sites. Now and for the foreseeable future, web pages and web sites may become the most common products we usability test. In a new book, we would probably devote a chapter to testing web products. The process needed to test on the web (planning, preparing, conducting, analyzing, using) is the same as the process this book describes. However, we would add information about new possibilities for remote testing and for capturing data while testing web sites. In lieu of a new chapter, here are three web sites with useful information:

- on remote evaluation:
    http://hci.ise.vt.edu/~josec/remote_eval/
- on metrics for testing the web and visualizing results:
    http://zing.ncsl.nist.gov/~webmet/
- on web development and usability in general:
    http://www.useit.com/alertbox/index.html

Related to Part I, Chapter 2, page 26: Comparing usability testing to research studies

It is still critical for usability testers as well as others to recognize that diagnostic usability tests are not research experiments. A diagnostic usability test is a type of formative evaluation in which the goal is to identify problems in time to fix them.

The distinction between usability tests and experiments is even clearer now than it was when we wrote the book. For example, Shneiderman (1998, page 128) says:

> While academics were developing controlled experiments to test hypotheses and support theories, practitioners developed usability-testing methods to refine user interfaces rapidly. Controlled experiments have at least two treatments and seek to show statistically significant differences; usability tests are designed to find flaws in user interfaces. Both strategies use a carefully prepared set of tasks, but usability tests have fewer subjects (maybe as few as three), and the outcome is a report with recommended changes, as opposed to validation or rejection of hypotheses.

Related to Part I, Chapter 3, pages 40-44 and 46-47: Identifying users' jobs and tasks and interviewing and observing users in context

These pre-design usability activities have become much more widespread and important over the last several years. This is an exciting and extremely useful change in product design and development. We re-emphasize our original point that usability evaluations are only one technique in the toolbox of the usability specialist (usability engineer). The more that is done with usability from the very beginning of thinking about any type of product, the fewer problems will emerge in later evaluations of designs and of developed products.

We would point out that, in addition to doing job and task analysis as we briefly discuss on pages 40-44, product development teams should be doing user analysis and environment analysis. That is they should begin by identifying and understanding different users, developing profiles of their relevant characteristics. They should visit users in their homes or work places and understand the physical, social, and cultural environments in which the users do their work.

In fact, contextual inquiry, which we describe very briefly on pages 46-47, has been adopted and adapted by many usability specialists and their design and development colleagues to gain this type of information.

Many more resources are now available to help usability specialists with these other techniques. From the additional bibliography in the back of this revised edition, you might look at these books for more on starting with usability techniques other than usability testing and for designing from the data you gather with these usability techniques:

Beyer & Holtzblatt, 1997

Hackos & Redish, 1998

Nielsen, 1993

Wixon & Ramey, 1996

Wood, 1998

Related to Part I, Chapter 3, page 48: Conducting usability tests of competitors' products

Comparison testing has become much more common than it was in 1993. These tests place special demands on testers to be fair and unbiased. In fact, comparison tests often require behavioral science research design skills and the application of inferential statistics. They are more like research studies than other types of usability tests. In a new book, we would probably devote a chapter to comparison test methods. For a brief introduction to some of the issues in comparison tests see:

Dumas, J. S. (1998), "Usability testing methods: Using participants as their own controls." *Common Ground*, January, 3-5.

Related to Part I, Chapter 5, pages 63-77: Evaluating usability throughout design and development – especially pages 69-75. Having users work with prototypes

Just as much more is now being done to bring usability into the process before design, usability is infusing the design process to a much greater extent. In fact, new methods have blurred the lines between design and evaluation. As more teams are doing early prototypes, including users in the prototyping sessions or bringing in users to do walkthroughs and usability evaluations of the prototypes, design and evaluation become intertwined as a joint method.

Related to Part I, Chapter 5, page 75: Comparing paper versus interactive prototypes

On the basis of the research available at the time, we said in the first edition that interactive prototypes were preferable to paper prototypes. While some people still believe this and believe that it is easy with current tools to create working simulations, others believe that paper prototypes have numerous advantages, from ease of creation to the democracy of everyone being equally familiar with the prototyping tools (that is, paper, pencils, and sticky notes). Developing paper prototypes has become a common early design method and usability specialists have become creative in making paper prototypes interactive. Thus, some usability specialists prefer paper-based to software-based prototypes for early testing. Paper is a medium that makes it easy to change design elements and avoids the commitment to a design that instantiating it in software sometimes brings.

Related to Part I, Chapter 6, page 92: Building a usability laboratory
The settings where usability testing occurs have increased. Tests are still conducted in usability labs and more labs are built every day. But tests are also conducted in settings in which the tester and the test participant are not in the same location. Generically known as "remote" usability testing, these tests have stretched the bounds of where tests occur. Remote tests typically use some combination of special software and a telephonic connection. The tester can see what the participant is doing by looking at a video feed or seeing the screen the participant sees. The tester and the participant have some way to communicate, most often a voice telephone connection. These testing methods have made it possible to conduct a usability test when the tester and the participant cannot be in the same room, in adjacent rooms, in the same building, in the same city, or even in the same continent.

Related to Part I, Chapter 6, page 96: How to build a lab, and what it costs
The list of usability lab equipment in Table 6-1 is still a useful guide. The one addition we would make to the list is a scan converter for displaying what is on the test participant's screen. The cost varies widely, from about $2000 to $10,000, depending on the quality of the image it provides and its capabilities, such as the ability to zoom in on a portion of the screen. New types of cameras are available, including tiny ones that can be mounted directly on the computer, and ones that allow change in direction or zoom with much less noise than earlier ones.

Furthermore, many people are now choosing to use portable labs instead of building separate spaces. A portable lab not only saves the cost of building but allows usability evaluations to take place in a variety of settings including the user's home or work place. Appendix A contains a list of five vendors we are aware of who customize and sell portable usability labs.

Related to Part II, Chapter 7, page 100: How long does usability testing take?
There has been a major shift in the time it takes to conduct a typical usability test. In the book, we describe a range for a typical diagnostic

test of 4-12 weeks. We do describe an example showing that experienced testers can test part of a product in one week. With the current trend toward shorter, iterative tests, an elapsed time of 2-3 weeks for a test is more typical and one-week tests are much more common.

Related to Part II, Chapter 9, page 127: Deciding how many people to include in a test
The values we report for the number of participants per group are still accurate. If anything, the numbers have become smaller as testers do more iterative tests. We still believe that the minimum number of participants in a diagnostic test is three per group.

Related to Part II, Chapter 10, pages 144-150: Planning how many calls it will take to find a participant
Our advice on recruiting has not changed. The typical no-show rate is still 10%. One more rule of thumb we would add is that when we plan a test, we assume that we will be able to recruit about *six participants a day*. When we do tests for clients, we suggest that they pay participants about $50 an hour for being in a test in order to keep the no-show rate low. Some companies have been successful with other incentives, such as free software, which is more cost effective for them.

Related to Part II, Chapter 13, page 191: What should you consider in building or buying a data-logging program?
While we have not conducted a survey, we believe that fewer test teams are doing formal data logging, in which a test team member tries to capture as many events as possible with data-logging software. Using a stop watch for task times, when they are recorded, and keeping notes is more common. This is part of the trend toward less formal testing methods. Perhaps testers feel more confident that they can use informal methods and still capture what they need.. There are more commercially available data-logging programs for those who want them. The companies that we list in Appendix A who sell portable labs also sell data logging products.

Related to Part II, Chapter 16, page 234: How many people do you need to run a test?
We start out this section by saying, "Three people make a good usability test team." While that statement is still true, it is much more common to have teams of one or two people. It is still true that there are two essential roles in a test team, (1) interacting with the test participant and taking notes, and (2) knowing the product. In cases where experienced testers are evaluating their own company's products, having a one-person team is common, but that one person should not be the developer or writer. One final point, the role of narrator that we describe on page 141 has disappeared from testing.

Related to Part III, Chapter 20, page 310: Tabulating and analyzing data
The concept of "triangulation" - diagnosing usability problems with a combination of quantitative measures, qualitative measures, and a problem list is still the most used data analysis method.

Related to Part III, Chapter 20, page 191: Using statistics
It is still the case that most usability testers use descriptive statistics to describe the usability strengths and weaknesses of a product and only use inferential statistics for special occasions, such as in a comparative usability test.

Related to Part III, Chapter 22, page 339: Communicating the results
Part of the trend toward informal testing methods is the way test results are reported. Instead of writing formal test reports, testers are more likely to have a meeting with developers or give an informal briefing of test results, followed by a group discussion. Confidence in the testing process has made more informal reporting methods possible. Developers are less likely to question the validity of the testing method because usability testing has become the method of choice to evaluate the usability of products.

Related to Part III, Chapter 23, page 356: Why make a highlight tape?
Highlight tapes are still an effective way to communicate test results. Our impression is that highlight tapes are used less often as a way to communicate test results, but are still important. In earlier days, highlight tapes were prepared for almost every test. More recently, they are used selectively. Highlight tapes are still needed when the developers and/or their managers are not sure that usability testing methods are accepted as valid and reliable ways to evaluate a product. When the audience is less skeptical about the value of the method, testers are less likely to need a highlight tape.

Related to Part III, Chapter 24, page 367: Changing the product and the process
We still believe that the most important benefit of testing is that it can uncover flaws in the development process itself. We again urge usability testers to look for the most basic causes of usability problems, especially when the problems point to a development process that creates or sustains usability problems rather than prevents them.

Acknowledgments

This book comes from our many years of working to make products and documents useful and from almost a decade of usability testing. Our approach to testing, our thoughts about its place in the design process, and our understanding of what can be learned from a usability test have all evolved—and continue to evolve—through our work on specific clients' products, the workshops that we give, and the colleagues with whom we talk.

In particular, we would like to thank these clients and colleagues:

People who helped us create and refine our ideas

- Janice James, Manager of the Usability Design Center and the Automated Decision Center at American Airlines, with whom we developed the workshop that made us put so much of this on paper. Many of the ideas in this book come from our close collaboration with Janice over the last several years
- our colleagues in the AIR Usability Laboratory, Marilyn Coleman, Brian Philips, Jackie Schrier, and Mike Wiklund, with whom we have developed, tried out, and changed our procedures over the years and who contributed to and reviewed parts of the manuscript
- our professional colleagues in other companies, especially, Charles Abernethy, Marybeth Butler, Judy Ramey, Jeff Simmonds, Anna Wichansky, and Jack Young, who shared the information in Appendix A with us about their usability laboratories

People we conducted usability tests with

- our former colleagues, including Leslie Carter, Sally Cummings-Ewalt, Virginia Diehl, Tom Eissenberg, Jean Harris, Carol Mills, and Tyson Rose, who helped us get started in usability testing
- our many clients who prefer to remain unnamed, who have given us the opportunity to test their products and documents, and, thereby, to not only improve what they were doing, but also to learn and improve what we were doing

People who reviewed drafts of the book

- Sheryl Hansen, who provided insightful comments on the material about starting a usability program

- David Schell, who worked with us in years past and who reviewed early drafts of this book with keen insight
- the anonymous reviewer whose excellent suggestions made us rethink some of our substantive points and aspects of our style

People who helped us prepare and edit the manuscript

- MaryAnn Gleezen, whose assistance with style sheets and transferring files from Mac to PC and back again was invaluable
- Carol Davidson of Ablex, who shepherded the book from manuscript to printed copy
- Marianne Tarczal, who, with unfailing patience, edited and produced endless drafts and facilitated the collaboration of two authors who were first 500 miles and then 3,000 miles apart

People who provided encouragement and support

- Ben Shneiderman, whose enthusiasm is sustaining, and especially
- Martie Dumas and Joe Redish, our respective spouses for their support and encouragement and for being patient through many working evenings and weekends. Over the past two years, the four of us have been closely connected despite the distance and look forward to continuing our friendship.

How To Use This Book

We have divided the book into three parts:

Part I
Concerning Usability

This establishes a context for usability testing. These six chapters define the concepts of usability, usability engineering, and usability testing. The central theme of this part is that usability and usability testing are best viewed within the context of research and practice on human-computer interaction. Usable products are built on a foundation of understanding about users and the tasks they want to accomplish. We describe how usability testing is one of several techniques you can use to design and evaluate the usability of products. Chapter 6 closes this part with a discussion of how an organization that develops products can establish a usability program.

Part II
Planning and Preparing for a Usability Test

This comprises Chapters 7 through 17. It starts with "Planning a Usability Test" and ends with "Conducting a Pilot Test." These chapters describe all of the activities that happen before the test begins. As you can see, testers will usually spend more time planning and preparing than they will conducting a test. Well-run tests don't just happen. They are the product of a systematic approach to testing.

Part III
Conducting and Using the Results of a Usability Test

This comprises Chapters 18 through 24. In it, we describe how to interact effectively with test participants, observe and record events during a test, analyze data, recommend changes, communicate test results, and make changes in the product and the process of design.

At the end of the book there are two appendices. Appendix A discusses how to build a usability laboratory. It describes the layout, equipment, and special features of a sample of existing labs. Appendix B lists the names and addresses of organizations and professional journals concerned with usability and usability testing.

xxii • *How to use this book*

We have written this book for three audiences, each with its special interests and needs:

1. You may be a person, perhaps a software or electrical engineer, a writer, or a student, with a modest knowledge of human-computer interaction who is interested in knowing how to do usability testing and how testing fits into the product development cycle. You will want to read all of the chapters, and we suggest that you read them in order. You may also want to read some of the literature we list in References.
2. You may be a person, such as a human factors specialist, with a good understanding of the literature and research on human-computer interaction who is interested in knowing how to do usability testing. You will want to focus your attention on Parts II and III, but we suggest that you at least skim the chapters in Part I.
3. You may be a person, such as a product or marketing manager, with a need to understand enough about usability testing to make decisions about when and whether to conduct a test, or you may just be curious about testing and want to see what it is all about. You will want to read the short opening of each chapter, which tells you what is in the chapter. You can then decide to look more closely at the chapters that interest you most. We suggest you read Part I because it defines usability and usability testing and places testing in the context you may not be familiar with, the context of human-computer interaction.

As the title suggests, we have tried to make this book "practical" for those of you who will be conducting a test. We give examples throughout from our experiences conducting tests. Near the beginning of each chapter, we include a paragraph describing what is in that chapter. We call these paragraphs "signposts," because you can read them like signs on a highway that tell you whether you are heading where you want. Skim through these paragraphs if you are unsure whether the information you are looking for is in that chapter.

At the end of many chapters, we have included forms that are examples of the materials we describe in the chapter. We encourage you to use these forms in your own tests. You will almost certainly have to tailor these forms to meet your needs, but we have included them to make it easier for you to begin testing quickly.

Part I

Concerning Usability

In this part, we set the context for usability testing. We define usability, usability engineering, and usability testing and describe how testing fits with other tools that help you design and evaluate the usability of computer-based products.

Chapter 1, "Introducing Usability," defines usability and places it within the process of usability engineering, which is a systematic approach to usability. We also describe the benefits of focusing on usability.

Chapter 2, "Introducing Usability Testing," defines usability testing and discusses the testing of parts of a product, different types of user interfaces, and documentation. We describe the benefits of usability testing and compare it to laboratory research studies.

Chapter 3, "Uncovering Usability Needs Before You Design," discusses the need to understand users, the audience(s) for a product, and the tasks users want to accomplish. We describe techniques that can be used before designing a product and introduce a wide variety of techniques that you can use throughout design.

Chapter 4, "Basing Designs on Expertise in Human–Computer Interaction," discusses some principles and practices of human–computer interaction. We describe literature and research about what makes a usable product and where to find the guidance that experts who have been studying human–computer interaction provide for us.

Chapter 5, "Evaluating Usability Throughout Design and Development," discusses methods, including usability testing, for evaluating usability throughout design. We compare the advantages and disadvantages of usability testing with other methods for assessing usability.

Chapter 6, "Establishing a Usability Program in Your Organization," discusses how to introduce usability testing and usability engineering to an organization and how to decide whether to build a usability laboratory. We describe the need for a team approach to product design and how to fit usability testing into organizations with different management styles.

In Part II, we go on to describe how to plan and prepare for a usability test.

1

1

Introducing Usability

At the social hour of a recent business meeting, talk turned to "which word processor are you using now?" As people expressed their joys and frustrations with different products, someone said, "I wish I could do envelopes with [my word-processing software]. It's silly to be doing everything on a printer and then going to the typewriter to do the envelope." Other users of the same product agreed. Someone complained, "We're still addressing envelopes by hand."

The developers would probably be shocked because you can address envelopes with the product. The functionality exists. *Building functionality into a product, however, doesn't guarantee that people will be able to use it.* Although some of these business people had been using the product for years, they weren't using this function. They were convinced either that they couldn't address envelopes with this product or that if the product let them do it, learning how would be too difficult.

Usability is an attribute of every product—just like functionality. Functionality refers to what the product can do. Testing functionality means making sure that the product works according to specifications. Usability refers to how people work with the product. Testing usability means making sure that people can find and work with the functions to meet their needs.

The right functionality—working correctly—is critical, but not sufficient, for a product to be successful. A product by itself has no value; it has value only insofar as it is used. *Use* implies users. Therefore, the way that users will work with the product is a basic issue for product designers and developers, whether they wish it were or not.

In this first chapter, we consider these questions that you or your managers may be asking:

- What is usability?
- What does usability affect?
- How do you ensure usability?
- Who benefits from a usability focus?
- Is a usability focus cost-effective?

What is Usability?

Usability means that the *people who use the product* can do so *quickly and easily* to accomplish *their own tasks*. This definition rests on four points:

1. Usability means focusing on users.
2. People use products to be productive.
3. Users are busy people trying to accomplish tasks.
4. Users decide when a product is easy to use.

Usability Means Focusing on Users

To develop a usable product, you have to know, understand, and work with people who represent the actual or potential users of the product. No one can substitute for them.

Other developers only represent users if the product is a tool for developers. The writer down the hall only represents the users of a manual if the manual is for writers.

Even managers, supervisors, or others who might be asked to speak for a group of users cannot substitute for the actual users. Managers may be too far removed from the actual tasks that users do and from the words in which the users represent those tasks to themselves.

People Use Products to be Productive

People consider a product "easy to learn and use" in terms of the *time* it takes to do what they want, the number of *steps* they go through, and the *success* they have in predicting the right action to take. They use the interface and the documentation to help them achieve their own performance goals.

To develop usable products, therefore, you have to understand users' performance goals. You have to know the users' jobs and the tasks that the product is automating or changing or embellishing.

Users Are Busy People Trying to Accomplish Tasks

People connect usability with productivity, because no one gets paid for time spent just sitting at a computer. They get paid for processing invoices, or for noticing and resolving alarms on the computer network, or for analyzing samples in a laboratory machine.

Hardware and software are *tools* to help busy people do the work they get paid for. Documentation is a tool for helping people use the hardware and software tools. People's tolerance for time spent learning and using tools is very low.

Users are concerned with productivity and with accomplishing their own goals at home as well as at work. You may want to use your VCR to record a program so that you can watch it later. Your goal is to watch the program; the VCR is the tool you are using to achieve that goal.

Many VCRs fail a test of usability for this function. Users cannot program their VCRs in the time and effort that they are willing to spend on this task. The VCRs may have high functionality (the feature works as it was designed to work), but they have low usability (people cannot use them quickly and easily to accomplish their tasks).

Users Decide When a Product is Easy to Use

Users, not designers or developers, determine when a product is easy to use. We are all so busy that we are constantly balancing the time and effort we think that something is worth for the benefit we think we will gain from it.

How many functions of your word processor, spreadsheet, voice mail, or microwave are you *not* using that you might use if they were easy enough to learn, use, and remember next time you need them? To develop usable products, you also have to understand how much time and effort typical users are willing to spend figuring out how to do a task with the product.

The learning curve for many products is so difficult that most users quickly reach a low plateau of knowledge and stay there. They use only a small percentage of the available functionality. Figure 1-1 shows what happens with many users and many products.

If a product is consistent, predictable, and easy to use, people will be able to learn much more quickly, better remember functions they use infrequently, and use more of the product. Figure 1-2 shows the learning curve that you would like to see.

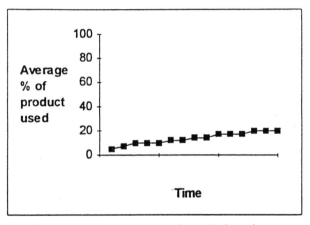

Figure 1-1.   Learning curve for typical products

What Does Usability Affect?

Usability is an attribute of the entire package that makes up a product—the hardware, software, menus, icons, messages, manual, quick reference, online help, and training. Changes in technology have blurred the lines among these product pieces, so that it is no longer useful to think of them as separate entities.

The line between hardware and software has blurred. Products that we used to think of as machines have become computers. Telephones, televisions, and medical equipment now have displays with menus. Functionality that used to be obvious because it was controlled by switches or dials on the surface is now buried in the

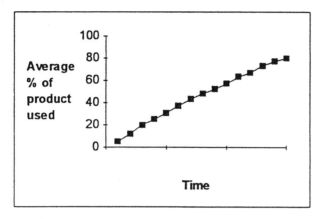

Figure 1-2. Learning curve you would like to see

product and reached only by knowing the right pathway through the menus and prompts (Dumas, 1990).

The line between documentation and the rest of the product has also blurred. More and more of the documentation is embedded in the software. Designers creating new products have to ask questions like: What are the best words and symbols to put on the screen? What order should they be in? Is there a useful metaphor? How consistent can and should the wording be?

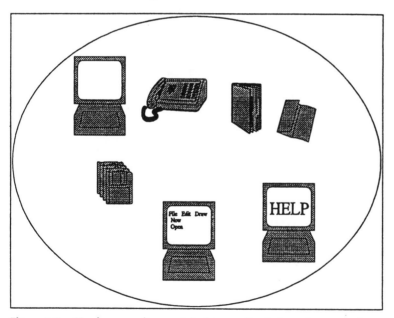

Figure 1-3. Hardware, software, interface, online help, print manual, and training materials are all part of the product.

Products now communicate with users in many ways. As Figure 1-3 shows, the interface—icons, menus, messages, prompts, and the way these elements are organized—as well as the information that we more traditionally think of as documentation—print manuals, tutorials, and online help—are all part of the way the product communicates with users. They must all be consistent and work together to be usable.

How Do You Ensure Usability?

Usability is not a surface gloss that can be applied at the last minute. Usability is deeply affected by every decision in design and development. Therefore, usability has to be built in from the beginning.

You ensure usability by:

- engineering it into a product through an iterative design and development process
- involving users throughout the process
- allowing usability and users' needs to drive design decisions
- working in teams that include skilled usability specialists, interface designers, and technical communicators
- setting quantitative usability goals early in the process
- testing products for usability, but also integrating usability testing with other methods for ensuring usability
- being committed to making technology work for people

Engineering Usability into Products

Gould and Lewis (1985) give us four principles for developing usable products:

- Focus early and continuously on users.
- Integrate consideration of all aspects of usability.
- Test versions with users early and continuously.
- Iterate the design.

An early and continuous focus on usability has many benefits, including

- creating functionality that is likely to be used
- making changes before they become too expensive
- making documentation and training easier to develop
- reducing the need for updates and maintenance releases

Building usability in is sometimes called *usability engineering* (Good, 1988; Whiteside, Bennett, & Holtzblatt, 1987) to emphasize the parallelism to software engineering. Usability engineering starts with identifying users, analyzing tasks, and setting usability specifications, moves on through developing and testing prototypes, and continues through iterative cycles of development and testing.

(Chapter 3 starts with a list of several techniques for usability engineering. Chapters 3 through 5 offer brief discussions of each of the techniques on that list.)

Involving Users Throughout the Process

A focus on usability requires users. If you follow the techniques for usability engineering that we discuss in this book, you'll be working with many different users over the course of the project—interviewing and observing users before you design, conducting early usability tests as you have users try out prototypes, conducting usability tests with other users as you develop the product further, and so on. Although each of the techniques we discuss includes only a small sample of users, one advantage of the iterative usability engineering approach is that, by the end of the project, you may have worked with a fairly large and varied sample of users.

For many groups, taking a usability focus includes having representative users on the design team. That can be a tremendous advantage. If the user on the team has actually been a user very recently, that person can help define users' jobs and tasks, keep the team focused on users' needs, and give daily input to design decisions.

Having a user representative on the design team is an excellent step, but it is not sufficient to ensure the product's usability for all its users. The person who is brought in as a user representative is often more knowledgeable and experienced than most users both about the job and the technology. If the person has recently been in a supervisory position, he or she may no longer be attuned to all the users' concerns and needs. And over time with the project team, the user representative may become too knowledgeable about the product and forget that it will all be new to the other users. No one individual can represent all users. You must still plan on usability testing with more users.

Allowing Usability and Users' Needs to Drive Design Decisions

Any design and development effort involves numerous problems and decisions. In many cases, a problem can be solved in many different ways. Do you change the hardware, the software, the documentation, the training materials, or any or all of them together? There are always constraints and tradeoffs.

What should be the driving force in deciding how to weigh constraints and balance tradeoffs? The driving force must be helping users to accomplish their tasks. Unless that is the goal of the effort, the product is likely to fail.

If the product is for users inside the company and it doesn't help those users do their job more quickly and easily than they did before, they won't want to use it. They'll find ways around it, ways to avoid it. If they are forced to use it and it decreases their productivity, the company will suffer because lost productivity means lost revenue.

If the product is for the public market, and it isn't easy to learn and use, it won't sell well. If some people buy it and then don't like it, they are likely to tell others. Word of mouth is a powerful force in the marketplace, for or against a product. In short, to have a successful product, the design must be driven by the goal of meeting users' needs. The focus must be on usability.

Working in Teams that Include Skilled Usability Specialists, Interface Designers, and Technical Communicators

Building a usable product requires a team effort, including specialists who understand usability, interface design, and technical communication.

. . . *because users expect more today*.   Yes, products were developed for a long time without specialists like these. In earlier times, usability was most often left to chance, and the products varied in their ease of use from poor to acceptable. If the product was particularly simple or the group was lucky enough to have someone who could see the product from the users' point of view, they may have avoided the disasters others fell into. All too often, however, none of the developers understood the users' tasks or could take the users' point of view, and the products were very difficult to use.

Usability may have been less important when personal computer products first appeared. In the early stages of any developing technology, products differ widely in the functionality they offer. Users put up with difficult products to get the benefits of functionality that isn't available elsewhere.

The first spreadsheet programs were very cumbersome to use, but users bought them and accepted the products' quirks because they had no choice. As soon as they had a choice, usability became one of the attributes they considered in buying spreadsheet software.

Today, users have many choices in most product lines. Differences in functionality are no longer sufficient to overcome poor usability. Ease of use has become a major point of competition.

. . . *because developing products is a more complex job today*.   As more products become computer-based, companies are asking employees to do new and much more complex jobs for which they have neither experience nor training. The human–computerinterfaces to new versions of devices like telephones or chemical analyzers are harder to use and harder to create than were the simpler products of the past. Old-style documentation no longer works for products with so much more functionality in a world in which users are even busier than before.

Old approaches no longer work. Expecting engineers who were very good at making keypads for telephones to learn, on the job, not only how to program a microcomputer chip to control a telephone answering machine, but also to create useful screens, menus, messages, and online help by themselves is not reasonable.

To make a top-of-the-line product that is easy to use requires skills in interface design, technical communication, and usability as well as skills in engineering and programming. One person cannot be a specialist in all of these areas. Cross-skill teamwork is the way to success in the 1990s.

Setting Quantitative Usability Goals Early in the Process

A key component of usability engineering is setting specific, quantitative, usability goals for the product early in the process and then designing to meet those goals.

Decisions on design have always been made. The issues are who should make them and on what basis. For many designers, the idea of thinking about these decisions in terms of usability and of measuring usability is revolutionary.

Many managers still think of the phrase "easy to learn and use" as just vague marketing words. Many product designers still focus on what the product can do instead of how users will work with it. Setting quantitative usability goals puts usability into concrete terms and forces the design team to consider the product in terms of users' tasks and users' tolerance for time and effort.

Setting quantitative usability goals means that instead of one vague goal like "let's make this product user-friendly," you have *many* specific goals that lead to specific design decisions on exactly how it will be user-friendly. Here is just one example of a specific goal and some plausible design decisions for it:

Usability goal:
- Users will be able to install and set up this software program in less than 10 minutes.

Design decisions:
- Put the instructions for starting the installation on a separate 1-page card. Put them in numbered steps.
- Create an interactive installation program where users

answer simple questions at the appropriate time for each choice they have to make.
- Help users make appropriate decisions by having a short message on the bottom of the screen telling users the implications of each choice for the questions.
- Indicate on the screen how much of the disk has been copied.

With vague goals, you have no basis for evaluating how well you've done with the product. How will you know whether it is "user-friendly"? With specific, quantitative usability goals, you do have a very clear basis for evaluation. With a prototype based on these design decisions, you can have real users try to install and set up the program and see if they can do it in 10 minutes or less.

Setting quantitative usability goals isn't an armchair exercise. If the "10 minutes" comes from system requirements rather than from knowing about users' expectations and needs, you could meet the goal and still not have a product that people will want to buy and use.

Having a rational, usability-focused basis for these goals means using the other techniques in this and the following chapters, such as identifying users, observing and interviewing users, doing job and task analysis, and conducting usability tests of existing versions of a product. We'll have more to say about these techniques in Chapter 3, "Uncovering Usability Needs Before You Design."

Setting quantitative usability goals and making design decisions to achieve them isn't a solitary exercise. To be done well, it requires the same type of cross-skill teamwork that we talked about in the last section.

Furthermore, it requires *all* the skills we talk about there. In the early literature on usability engineering, only software engineers and human factors specialists were thought to be needed for setting goals and making design decisions. That isn't true. Technical communications specialists are also needed. As we pointed out in a 1991 paper (Redish & Dumas, 1991), many of the design decisions made at this early stage are about how the product communicates with users. Also, documentation works with the rest of the product as a way to meet the goals. Writers need to be part of the team.

Testing Products for Usability, But Also Integrating Usability Testing With Other Methods for Assuring Usability

Usability testing is a systematic way of observing actual users trying out a product and collecting information about the specific ways in which the product is easy or difficult for them. When usability testing was first introduced in the 1980s, the model for it was function test-ing, and, therefore, it usually occurred once at the end of the develop-ment process. The assumption was that, for the most part, the test would verify that everything was fine, and any minor problems that showed up could be easily fixed.

The first usability tests of products shocked people. Everything wasn't fine, and more problems showed up in these usability tests than could be fixed at that late stage of development.

Over the course of the last decade, the models for both function testing and usability testing have shifted. Usability testing is best used to *diagnose problems*, not to verify that all is fine. Usability testing is best used *early and often*, not once at the end when it is too late to make changes. Usability testing is best used as part of a *process that focuses on usability throughout design and development*, not as the sole time when users are considered.

Usability testing is but one technique in the tool kit of user-centered designers. In the rest of this first part of the book, we focus on the entire process of usability engineering and put usability testing into that context.

Being Committed to Making Technology Work for People

All of us are surrounded by computers, from the machines on our desks at work and at home, to our household appliances, to the devices like cameras and exercise equipment that we use for our leisure time. The number of personal computer applications is enormous. Each upgrade of these products offers an ever-increasing array of functions to an ever-increasing number of people. The trend will continue. In the near future, television sets will become interactive computers, bringing more choices—and more opportunities for enormous frustration—into even more people's lives. People are suffering from "feature shock." The amount of functionality that is developed but never used because it is too difficult to find or figure out has become a critical problem.

Usability engineering and usability testing were developed in part to address the problems of feature shock and unusable functionality. A usability test focuses attention on individual users as they struggle with a particular interface. A usability test also makes the importance of usability obvious to those who watch. Usability testing has in many cases been the catalyst that makes designers and developers change their attitudes about users and usability.

Being a usability tester carries a commitment to making technology work for people. It also carries the commitment to making others change their focus from the technology for its own sake to making that technology work for people.

Who Benefits From a Usability Focus?

Everyone benefits from usability. Users obviously benefit from a product that reduces the learning curve and allows them to use more functionality with less effort.

Companies benefit by

- selling more of the product
- selling other products
- enhancing the company's reputation
- saving money on internal products
- reducing support costs
- reducing training costs
- reducing the need for updates and maintenance releases
- making documentation and training easier to develop

Selling More of the Product

Customers care about usability. Look at the lists of buyers' concerns that accompany product reviews in *PC Week*. Figure 1-4 is just one typical example.

Usability is more important to buyers than either price or performance. In Figure 1-4, note that access to support is tenth on the list. Buyers would rather be able to use the interface intuitively or find what they need in the documentation themselves than call the support line.

Showing that you care about usability can increase sales. The manufacturer of a software-driven laboratory machine found from customer surveys that their professional-quality documentation was a major factor in customers choosing their machine over its competitors. It wasn't only that the documentation made the machine easier to use. Customers felt that they could *trust* machines from a company that cared enough to put the time and effort into good documentation.

Selling Other Products

Users' experiences with a product can have an impact far greater than sales of that one product. If users are productive with the first product they buy from you, they're likely to buy your next product. If they have a difficult time with the first product, they'll be reluctant to try the next one. Long life for a company depends on repeat business, and letting a poor product out the door can have disastrous effects on repeat business.

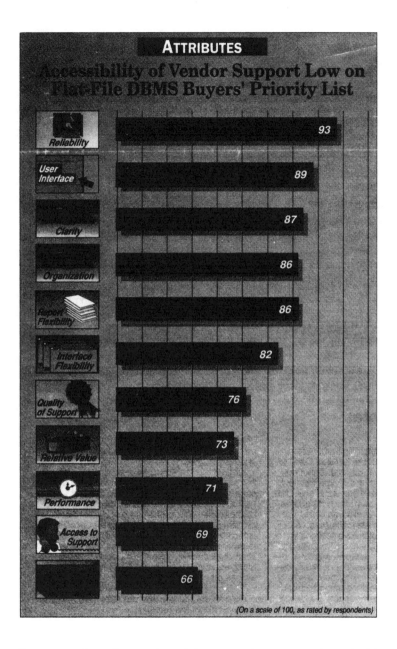

Figure 1-4. Ease of use and good documentation are more important to buyers than price or performance. (Reprinted with permission from *PC Week*, 1/9/89, p. 81. Copyright © 1989 by Ziff Communications Company. Respondents rate concerns from 0 to 100.)

Enhancing the Company's Reputation

Some benefits are intangible and hard to quantify, but nonetheless very real. Selling by reputation (by word of mouth) is a cost-effective strategy—but only if the words are positive. Satisfied customers sell your products. Dissatisfied customers can kill a product.

Saving Money on Internal Products

If you are developing a product that will only be used within your company, don't dismiss usability as irrelevant. Usability is *doubly* valuable for internal products. If an internal user has to call the support line for answers, the company pays both for the support person's time and for the user's nonproductive time. Moreover, the internal user's learning time and any loss of productivity are also company expenses. If an internal product is easy to learn and use, the company saves training time and reaps the benefit of the users' increased productivity.

Reducing Support Costs

Many companies spend enormous sums supporting users with help desks, customer-service centers, installation, and maintenance. A major usability goal for many product development teams might be to reduce these support costs. Users would rather that you spent that money up front to design and deliver a product that they can use without having to call for help.

Reducing Training Costs

Similarly, a major expense in acquiring new hardware and software is training, whether that is paid for by the developers or by the users. For many companies, reducing training costs is a powerful incentive, and an intuitive, easy-to-use product should reduce training time and cost.

Formal training has become less common as hardware gets less expensive and software proliferates. When only a few people in a company needed to be skilled with a particular program and the costs of the computer and programs were high, companies often invested in training for those few people. The ratio of training cost to product cost was low.

Now, software is relatively inexpensive, and one program may be used by thousands of people. The ratio of training cost to product cost is very high. Most companies do not routinely send all users to training.

We are skeptical when developers tell us that they do not need to be overly concerned about a difficult or inconsistent interface, because "training will take care of it." The assumption that everyone will be trained is seldom valid. Budget cuts later in development may mean less time and money spent on creating good training materials. Customers may choose not to send their people to training, especially if they have to pay for it. Even if the training is "free," customers pay the cost of time lost from people's jobs.

Most training, moreover, happens only when a new product is first introduced. Job turnover can rapidly negate the effectiveness of that initial training. People hired after the product first came into the company don't usually get any training, but they still have to use the difficult or inconsistent product.

Reducing the Need for Updates and Maintenance Releases

Users are less tolerant of buggy software, unusable features, and incorrect documentation than they might have been years ago. They expect products that work and are easy to use right away. That may be because they know it can be done; they have other products that meet that expectation. It may be because the market has changed. Most users today are not software engineers who know how difficult it is to get a bug-free, easy-to-use product out the door. By focusing on usability before putting the product on the market, you can save the time, cost, and embarrassment of sending out fixes for problems that could have been found in usability testing.

Making Documentation and Training Easier to Develop

A product that is consistent, predictable, and organized in users' language and by users' tasks is much easier to document than a product that was developed without a focus on usability. The more that writing a task-oriented manual requires reinterpreting and reorganizing the product's structure and metaphor, the more difficult it is to develop a coherent and concise manual or a logical tutorial.

Is a Usability Focus Cost-effective?

You may need to build a business case to convince managers that this new approach is worth the money. Usability engineering does have costs associated with it. It takes people's time to conduct activities like studying users before design, creating prototypes, and conducting usability tests. The benefits we have been discussing in this chapter, however, should yield savings that are greater than the costs.

Balancing Cost and Savings Both Before and After Release

In making the business case for building usability into products, however, don't just count the extra costs on the development side. Balance new costs with potential savings both before and after the product is released.

Here's a before-release example. If two development groups are arguing about what an interface should look like, consider this: What is it costing for the person/hours spent in rival development efforts and in meetings about the interfaces? A usability test might cost less and would give you better answers.

The following are two after-release examples:

- Does your company keep a log of calls to the customer support lines? How much is the company spending on support costs when a test could have found the problems that customer support representatives are solving on the phone?
- How much productivity is being lost because users are taking up a colleague's time figuring out how to do something or are hunting in documentation instead of doing their work? Observe what happens in a few departments over the course of a week and work out the cost of lost time.

$	$$$$
Build usability into products **from the beginning.** Test and fix iteratively **before** release.	Spend money **later** • on fixing problems • on support calls • on training Get poor reviews. Deal with unhappy and unproductive customers or employees. Lose customers or employees.

Figure 1-5. Focusing on usability may cost money, but *not* focusing on usability is likely to cost a lot more.

Measuring Savings Through Iterative Testing

Several authors have analyzed development projects for the costs and benefits of usability engineering (Brown, 1991; Gould et al., 1991; Karat, 1990, 1992; Mantei & Teorey, 1988). In these projects, it is fairly easy to estimate the *cost* of items such as usability tests. Measuring the *benefits* is more difficult. When a product has been improved through usability engineering, the organization does not release two versions, one improved and one not. How then do we measure the benefits of usability engineering?

One approach to measuring benefits is to conduct iterative usability tests with the same tasks. After each test, the product is improved on the basis of the findings from the test. If you assume that the product would not have been improved without the tests, you can attribute any improvement in users' productivity to usability engineering.

Using this approach, you would

- conduct an initial usability test, recording times for a set of tasks
- change the product based on the results of the test
- conduct a second usability test, recording times for the same tasks
- subtract the times for the tasks in the second test from the times for the first test (The difference is the time saved because of improvements that are due to the usability engineering approach.)
- multiply the time saved by the number of people who use (will use) the product
- convert the time saved to dollars saved in terms of the users' average salaries

You can see that this method is very conservative. It does not consider savings from reducing customer support or reducing the (much greater) cost of making changes to the software after it is released.

This approach was applied to several products developed by IBM for internal use as reported by Karat (1992). In all cases, the benefits of applying usability engineering were substantial. For a small product, which is used by a few thousand people, the cost of the usability engineering activities was $20,700; the benefit was $41,700. For a larger product, which is used by over 200,000 people, the cost of usability engineering was $68,000; the benefit during the first year of implementation was $6,800,000.

These initial studies show that designing for users does pay off. Over time, we expect that additional studies and new approaches to measuring the benefits of usability engineering will give even more support to the fact that the benefits of usability engineering far outweigh the costs.

2

Introducing Usability Testing

We begin this chapter by defining usability testing, examining both what is and is not required for a usability test and reiterating the important point that you should test early and often—not just once at the end of the development process. We then look at how our definition of usability testing applies in a wide variety of situations. We also add two more benefits to the list we began in Chapter 1; these two are benefits that come more from usability testing than from other techniques in the usability engineering approach. Finally, we end the chapter by comparing usability testing with two quite different techniques with which it is often confused: beta (or field) testing and research studies.

What is Usability Testing?

While there can be wide variations in where and how you conduct a usability test, every usability test shares these five characteristics:

1. The primary goal is to improve the usability of a product. For each test, you also have more specific goals and concerns that you articulate when planning the test.
2. The participants represent real users.
3. The participants do real tasks.
4. You observe and record what participants do and say.
5. You analyze the data, diagnose the real problems, and recommend changes to fix those problems.

The Goal is to Improve the Usability of a Product

The primary goal of a usability test is to improve the usability of the product that is being tested. Another goal, as we will discuss in detail later, is to improve the *process* by which products are designed and developed, so that you avoid having the same problems again in other products.

This characteristic distinguishes a usability test from a research study, in which the goal is to investigate the existence of some phenomenon. Although the same facility might be used for both, they have different purposes. (See the section, "Comparing Usability Tests to Research Studies," later in this chapter.)

This characteristic also distinguishes a usability test from a quality assurance or function test, which has a goal of assessing whether the product works according to its specifications.

Within the general goal of improving the product, you will have more specific goals and concerns that differ from one test to another.

- You might be particularly concerned about how easy it is for users to navigate through the menus. You could test that concern before coding the product, by creating an interactive prototype of the menus, or by giving users paper versions of each screen. (See Chapter 5 for more on these types of tests.)

- You might be particularly concerned about whether the interface that you have developed for novice users will also be easy for and acceptable to experienced users.
- For one test, you might be concerned about how easily the customer representatives who do installations will be able to install the product. For another test, you might be concerned about how easily the client's nontechnical staff will be able to operate and maintain the product.

These more specific goals and concerns help determine which users are appropriate participants for each test and which tasks are appropriate to have them do during the test. (See Chapter 8, "Defining Your Goals and Concerns," for more on this topic.)

The Participants Represent Real Users

The people who come to test the product must be members of the group of people who now use or who will use the product. A test that uses programmers when the product is intended for legal secretaries is not a usability test.

The quality assurance people who conduct function tests may also find usability problems, and the problems they find should not be ignored, but they are not conducting a usability test. They are not real users—unless it is a product about function testing. They are acting more like expert reviewers.

If the participants in the usability test do not represent the real users, you are not seeing what will happen when the product gets to the real users.

If the participants are more experienced than actual users, you may miss problems that will cause the product to fail in the marketplace. If the participants are less experienced than actual users, you may be led to make changes that aren't improvements for the real users. (See Chapter 9, "Deciding Who Should Be Participants," and Chapter 10, "Recruiting Participants," for more about making sure that the people who come to your test represent the users.)

The Participants Do Real Tasks

The tasks that you have users do in the test must be ones that they will do with the product on their jobs or in their homes. This means that you have to understand users' jobs and the tasks for which this product is relevant.

In many usability tests, particularly of functionally rich and complex software products, you can only test some of the many tasks that users will be able to do with the product. In addition to being realistic and relevant for users, the tasks that you include in a test should relate to your goals and concerns and have a high probability of uncovering a usability problem. (Chapter 11, "Selecting and Organizing Tasks to Test," and Chapter 12, "Creating Task Scenarios," give more information about what to have users do in a test.)

Observe and Record What the Participants Do and Say

In a usability test, you usually have several people come, one at a time, to work with the product. You observe the participant, recording both performance and comments.

You also ask the participant for opinions about the product. A usability test includes both times when participants are doing tasks with the product and times when they are filling out questionnaires about the product. (For more on deciding what to observe and record while users are working with the product, see Chapter 13, "Deciding How to Measure Usability." For more on questionnaires, see Chapter 14, "Preparing Test Materials.")

Observing and recording individual participant's behaviors distinguishes a usability test from focus groups, surveys, and beta testing.

A typical focus group is a discussion among 8 to 10 real users, led by a professional moderator. Focus groups provide information about users' opinions, attitudes, preferences, and their self-report about their performance, but focus groups do not usually let you see how users actually behave with the product. (We discuss focus groups in more detail in Chapter 3, "Uncovering Usability Needs Before You Design.")

Surveys, by telephone or mail, let you collect information about users' opinions, attitudes, preferences, and their self-report of behavior, but you cannot use a survey to observe and record what users actually do with a product.

A typical beta test (field test, clinical trial, user acceptance test) is an early release of a product to a few users. A beta test has ecological validity, that is, real people are using the product in real environments to do real tasks. However, beta testing seldom yields any useful information about usability. Most companies have found beta testing to be too little, too unsystematic, and *much too late* to be the primary test of usability. (Because some people still believe that a beta test substitutes for a usability engineering approach and for usability testing during the process, we discuss beta testing in some detail later in this chapter.)

Analyze the Data, Diagnose the Real Problems, and Recommend Changes to Fix Those Problems

Collecting the data is necessary, but not sufficient, for a usability test. After the test itself, you still need to analyze the data. You consider the quantitative and qualitative data from the participants together with your own observations and users' comments. You use all of that to diagnose and document the product's usability problems and to recommend solutions to those problems.

As we will discuss in Chapter 20, "Tabulating and Analyzing Data," this is not a trivial task. Usability testing is distinguished from beta testing by both the quality and quantity of data that you have. The data are systematic, comparable across the participants that you saw, and very rich.

The Results Are Used to Change the Product – and the Process

We would also add another point. It may not be part of the definition of the usability test itself, as the previous five points were, but it is crucial, nonetheless.

A usability test is not successful if it is used only to mark off a milestone on the development schedule. A usability test is successful only if it helps to improve the product that was tested and the process by which it was developed. As we discuss in Chapter 24, "Changing the Product and the Process," part of your task as a usability tester is doing what you can to make sure that the results of the test are used appropriately.

Someone must use the results of the usability test.

What Is Not Required for a Usability Test?

Our definition leaves out some features you may have been expecting to see, such as:

- a laboratory with one-way mirror
- data-logging software
- videotape
- a formal test report

Each of these is useful, but not necessary, for a successful usability test. For example, a memorandum of findings and recommendations or a meeting about the test results, rather than a formal test report, may be appropriate in your situation.

Each of these features has advantages in usability testing that we discuss in detail later, but none is an absolute requirement. Throughout the book, we discuss methods that you can use when you have only a shoestring budget, limited staff, and limited testing equipment.

When is a Usability Test Appropriate?

Nothing in our definition of a usability test limits it to a single, summative test at the end of a project. The five points in our definition are relevant no matter where you are in the design and development process. They apply to both informal and formal testing. When testing a prototype, you may have fewer participants and fewer tasks, take fewer measures, and have a less formal reporting procedure than in a later test, but the critical factors we outline here and the general process we describe in this book still apply. Usability testing is appropriate *iteratively* from predesign (test a similar product or earlier version), through early design (test prototypes), and throughout development (test different aspects, retest changes).

Questions that Remain in Defining Usability Testing

We recognize that our definition of usability testing still has some fuzzy edges.

- Would a test with only one participant be called a usability test? Probably not. You probably need at least two or three people representing a subgroup of users to feel comfortable that you are not seeing idiosyncratic behavior.
- Would a test in which there were no quantitative measures qualify as a usability test? Probably not. To substantiate the problems that you report, we assume that you will take at least some basic measures, such as number of participants who had the problem, or number of wrong choices, or time to complete a task. The actual measures will depend on your specific concerns and the stage of design or development at which you are testing. The measures could come from observations, from recording with a data-logging program, or from a review of the videotape after the test. The issue is not which measures or how you collect them, but whether you need to have some quantitative data to have a usability test.

Usability testing is still a relatively new development; its definition is still emerging. You may have other questions about what counts as a usability test. Our discussion of usability testing and of other usability engineering methods, in this chapter and the next three chapters, may help clarify your own thinking about how to define usability testing.

Testing Applies to All Types of Products

If you read the literature on usability testing, you might think that it is only about testing software for personal computers. Not so. Usability testing works for all types of products. In the last several years, we've been involved in usability testing of all these products:

Consumer products

Regular TVs

High-definition TVs

VCRs

Remote controls

Cordless telephones

Telephone/answering
machines

Business telephones

Medical products

Bedside terminal

Patient monitor

Anesthesiologist's workstation

Blood gas analyzer

Integrated communication system for wards

Nurse's workstation for intensive care units

Engineering devices

Digital oscilloscope

Network protocol analyzer (for maintaining computer networks)

*Application software for microcomputers, minicomputers,
and mainframes*

Electronic mail

Spreadsheets

Database management software

Time management software

Compilers and debuggers for programming languages

Operating system software

Other

Voice response systems (menus on the telephone)

Automobile navigation systems (in-car information about how to
get where you want to go)

The procedures for the test may vary somewhat depending on what
you are testing and the questions you are asking. We give you hints
and tips, where appropriate, on special concerns when you are
focusing the testing on hardware or documentation; but, in general,
we don't find that you need to change the approach much at all.

Most of the examples in this book are about testing some type of
hardware or software and the documentation that goes with it. In
some cases, the hardware used to be just a machine and is now a
special purpose computer. For usability testing, however, the product
doesn't even have to involve any hardware or software. You can use
the techniques in this book to develop usable

- application or reporting forms
- instructions for noncomputer products, like bicycles
- interviewing techniques
- nonautomated procedures
- questionnaires

Testing All Types of Interfaces

Any product that people have to use, whether it is computer-based or not, has a user interface. Norman in his marvelous book, *The Design of Everyday Things* (1988) points out problems with doors, showers, light switches, coffee pots, and many other objects that we come into contact with in our daily lives. With creativity, you can plan a test of any type of interface.

Consider an elevator. The buttons in the elevator are an interface— the way that you, the user, talk to the computer that now drives the machine. Have you ever been frustrated by the way the buttons in an elevator are arranged? Do you search for the one you want? Do you press the wrong one by mistake?

With the configuration in Figure 2-1, impatient people might reach out to close the doors and make the alarm bell ring instead.

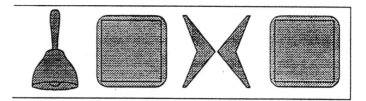

Figure 2-1.   Part of the user interface to an elevator

You might ask: How could you test the interface to an elevator in a usability laboratory? How could the developers find the problems with an elevator interface before building the elevator—at which point it would be too expensive to change?

In fact, an elevator interface could be tested before it is built. You could create a simulation of the proposed control panel on a touch-screen computer (a prototype). You could even program the computer to make the alarm sound and to make the doors seem to open and close, based on which buttons users touch. Then you could bring in users one at a time, give them realistic situations, and have them use the touchscreen as they would the panel in the elevator.

Any product or part of a product that people will use should be tested for usability.

Our point is that, with a little ingenuity, you can prototype any interface and have users try it out in a usability test.

Testing All Parts of the Product

Depending on where in the development process you are and what you are particularly concerned about, you may want to focus the usability test on a specific part of the product, such as

- installing hardware
- operating hardware
- cleaning and maintaining hardware
- understanding messages about the hardware
- installing software
- navigating through menus
- filling out fields
- recovering from errors
- learning from online or printed tutorials
- finding and following instructions in a user's guide
- finding and following instructions in the online help

You must also, however, test how the parts work together and support each other. Even if you are focusing on one aspect of the product, be alert to what you see and hear about other aspects.

When we first started doing usability testing, clients sometimes asked us to "just test the documentation," because another group "owned" the software. We learned very quickly that in any usability test, even if you are focusing on the documentation, you learn a tremendous amount about the software (and vice versa). We couldn't *not* report what we had learned—and our documentation clients also realized that their software colleagues had to know what we had learned about the interface. They also realized how futile it was to think of the documentation and software separately. Good changes to both products and processes came out of those tests.

Testing Different Aspects of the Documentation

When you include documentation in the test, you have to decide if you are more interested in *whether users* go to the documentation or in how well the documentation works for them *when they do go* to it. It is difficult to get answers to both of those concerns at the same time.

If you want to find out how much people learn from a tutorial *when they use it*, you can set up a test in which you ask people to go through the tutorial. Your test paticipants will do as you ask, and you will get useful information about the design, content, organization, and language of the tutorial.

You will, however, not have any indication of whether anyone will actually open the tutorial when they get the product. To test that, you have to set up your test differently.

Instead of instructing people to use the tutorial, you have to give them tasks and let them know the tutorial is available. In this second type of test, you will find out which types of users are likely to try the tutorial, but if few participants use it, you won't get much useful information for revising the tutorial.

Giving people instructions that encourage them to use the manual or tutorial may be unrealistic in terms of what happens in the world outside the test laboratory, but it is necessary if your concern is the usability of the documentation. At some point in the process of developing the product, you should be testing the usability of the various types of documentation that users will get with the product.

At other points, however, you should be testing the usability of the product in the situation in which most people will receive it. Here's an example:

> A major company was planning to put a new software product on its internal network. The product has online help and a printed manual, but, in reality, few users will get a copy of the manual.
>
> The company planned to maintain a help desk, and a major concern for the usability test was that if people don't get the manual, they would have to use the online help, call the help desk, or ask a co-worker. The company wanted to keep calls to the help desk to a minimum, and the testers knew that when one worker asks another for help, two people are being unproductive for the company.
>
> When they tested the product, therefore, this test team did not include the manual. Participants were told that the product includes online help, and they were given the phone number of the help desk to call if they were really stuck. The test team focused on where people got stuck, how helpful the online help was, and at what points people called the help desk.
>
> This test gave the product team a lot of information to improve the interface and the online help to satisfy the concern that drove the test. However, this test yielded no information to improve the printed manual. That would require a different test.

Testing with Different Techniques

In most usability tests, you have one participant at a time working with the product. You usually leave that person alone and observe from a corner of the room or from behind a one-way mirror. You intervene only when the person "calls the help desk," which you record as a need for assistance.

You do it this way because you want to simulate what will happen when individual users get the products in their offices or homes. They'll be working on their own, and you won't be right there in their rooms to help them.

Sometimes, however, you may want to change these techniques. Two ideas that many teams have found useful are:

- co-discovery, having two participants work together
- active intervention, taking a more active role in the test

Co-discovery

Co-discovery is a technique in which you have two participants work together to perform the tasks (Kennedy, 1989). You encourage the participants to talk to each other as they work.

Talking to another person is more natural than thinking out loud alone. Thus, co-discovery tests often yield more information about what the users are thinking and what strategies they are using to solve their problems than you get by asking individual participants to think out loud.

Hackman and Biers (1992) have investigated this technique. They confirmed that co-discovery participants make useful comments that provide insight into the design. They also found that having two people work together does not distort other results. Participants who worked together did not differ in their performance or preferences from participants who worked alone.

Co-discovery is more expensive than single participant testing, because you have to pay two people for each session. In addition, it may be more difficult to watch two people working with each other and the product than to watch just one person at a time. Co-discovery may be used anytime you conduct a usability test, but it is especially useful early in design because of the insights that the participants provide as they talk with each other.

Active Intervention

Active intervention is a technique in which a member of the test team sits in the room with the participant and actively probes the participant's understanding of whatever is being tested. For example, you might ask participants to explain what they would do next and why as they work through a task. When they choose a particular menu option, you might ask them to describe their understanding of the menu structure at that moment. By asking probing questions throughout the test, rather than in one interview at the end, you can get insights into participants' evolving mental model of the product. You can get a better understanding of problems that participants are having than by just watching them and hoping they'll think out loud.

Active intervention is particularly useful early in design. It is an excellent technique to use with prototypes, because it provides a wealth of diagnostic information. It is not the technique to use, however, if your primary concern is to measure time to complete tasks or to find out how often users will call the help desk.

To do a useful active intervention test, you have to define your goals and concerns, plan the questions you will use as probes, and be careful not to bias participants by asking leading questions. (See the section on "Interacting with Participants" in Chapter 19, "Caring for the Participants," for some useful hints on how to ask questions.)

Additional Benefits of Usability Testing

Usability testing contributes to all the benefits of focusing on usability that we gave in Chapter 1. In addition, the process of usability testing has two specific benefits that may not be as strong or obvious from other usability techniques. Usability testing helps

- change people's attitudes about users
- change the design and development process

Changing People's Attitudes About Users

Watching users is both inspiring and humbling. Even after watching hundreds of people participate in usability tests, we are still amazed at the insights they give us about the assumptions we make.

When designers, developers, writers, and managers attend a usability test or watch videotapes from a usability test for the first time, there is often a dramatic transformation in the way that they view users and usability issues. Watching just a few people struggle with a product has a much greater impact on attitudes than many hours of discussion about the importance of usability or of understanding users.

As Figure 2-2 shows, after an initial refusal to believe that the users in the test really do represent the people for whom the product is meant, many observers become instant converts to usability. They become interested not only in changing this product, but in improving all future products, and in bringing this and other products back for more testing.

Changing the Design and Development Process

In addition to helping to improve a specific product, usability testing can help improve the process that an organization uses to design and develop products (Dumas, 1989). The specific instances that you see in a usability test are most often symptoms of broader and deeper global problems with both the product and the process.

When we discuss analyzing the data in Chapter 20, we urge you to think about the breadth and depth of the problems. First, we urge you to ask how what you see affects the entire product.

To consider a simple example, let's say you've just completed a usability test in which participants sometimes got messages from the

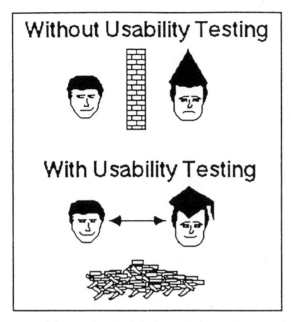

Figure 2-2. Usability testing can break down the wall between those who create the product and those who use it.

program, and they did not understand those messages. If you list just the messages that happened to come up during the test, the product team may be tempted to rewrite those specific messages.

A usability test, however, only samples parts of the product. You must ask, "What's wrong with the messages that users did not understand? What other messages are there in this program? Are the other messages like the ones that users saw and did not understand?" You would probably recognize a global problem with messages and recommend that all the product's messages be reviewed and rewritten.

Thinking globally about the product isn't enough, however. We also urge you to ask how the problems that you see came about. To continue with our example, if the messages aren't clear, you must ask, "How did they get this way? Who wrote them? If developers wrote them, what training did they have in writing for users? If there are technical writers in the company, why didn't they write the messages? If there aren't technical writers in the company, why not?"

"How" and "why" questions lead to discussions of process and ways to improve the process. Improving the process has much greater long-term impact on usability than improving the product. In Chapter 23, "Changing the Product and the Process," we suggest ways for you to stimulate changes in your organization to improve the process as well as products.

Comparing Usability Testing to Beta Testing

Despite the surge in interest in usability testing, many companies still do not think about usability until the product is almost ready to be released. Their usability approach is to give some customers an early-release (almost ready) version of the product and wait for feedback. Depending on the industry and situation, these early-release trials may be called beta testing, field testing, clinical trials, or user acceptance testing.

In beta testing, real users do real tasks in their real environments. However, many companies find that they get very little feedback from beta testers, and beta testing seldom yields useful information about usability problems for these reasons:

- The beta test site does not even have to use the product.
- The feedback is unsystematic. Users may report—after the fact—what they remember and choose to report. They may get so busy that they forget to report even when things go wrong.
- In most cases, no one observes the beta test users and records their behavior. Because users are focused on doing their work, not on testing the product, they may not be able to recall the actions they took that resulted in the problems. In a usability test, you get to see the actions, hear the users talk as they do the actions, and record the actions on videotape so that you can go back later and review them, if you aren't sure what the user did.
- In a beta test, you do not choose the tasks. The tasks that get tested are whatever users happen to do in the time they are working with the product. A situation that you are concerned about may not arise. Even if it does arise, you may not hear about it. In a usability test, you choose the tasks that participants do with the product. That way, you can be sure that you get information about aspects of the product that relate to your goals and concerns. That way, you also get comparable data across participants.

If beta testers do try the product and have major problems that keep them from completing their work, they may report those problems. The unwanted by-product of that situation, however, may be embarrassment at having released a product with major problems, even to beta testers.

Even though beta testers know that they are working with an unfinished and possibly buggy product, they may be using it to do real work where problems may have serious consequences. They want to do their work easily and effectively. Your company's reputation and sales may suffer if beta testers find the product frustrating to use. A bad experience when beta testing your product may make the beta testers less willing to buy the product *and* less willing to consider other products from your company.

You can improve the chances of getting useful information from beta test sites. Some companies include observations and interviews with beta testing, going out to visit beta test sites after people have been working with the product for a while. Another idea would be to give tape recorders to selected people at beta test sites and ask them to talk on tape while they use the product or to record observations and problems as they occur.

Even these techniques, however, won't overcome the most significant disadvantage of beta testing—that it comes too late in the process. Beta testing typically takes place only very close to the end of development, with a fully coded product. Critical functional bugs may get fixed after beta testing, but time and money generally mean that usability problems can't be addressed.

Usability testing, unlike beta testing, can be done throughout the design and development process. You can observe and record users as they work with prototypes and partially developed products. People are more tolerant of the fact that the product is still under development when they come to a usability test than when they beta test it. If you follow the usability engineering approach, you can do usability testing early enough to change the product—and retest the changes.

Comparing Usability Testing to Research Studies

In our experience, many people who are new to usability testing confuse it with social science research. Managers sometimes put too much faith in the fact that usability testing yields quantitative data. They sometimes reject recommendations from an expert reviewer because the reviewer, cannot provide quantitative data. They sometimes base major decisions on just a few of the numbers from a usability test without considering the range of data that a usability test provides.

Usability testing and scientific research are both "empirical" methods, that is, they both focus on observations of actual behaviors (Dumas, 1988; Gould & Lewis, 1985; Rubenstein & Hersh, 1984; Shneiderman, 1992). They are, however, also very different. Whether you are a tester or a user of test results, understanding the differences between testing and research should help you report and apply test results appropriately.

On the surface, a usability test looks like a research study:

- You often conduct tests in a facility, called a *laboratory*, that looks very much like a research laboratory.
- You sample participants who are representative of the population of interest.
- You often take some steps, in selecting or training participants, to control variables that might otherwise make interpreting the results difficult.
- You record measures, both objective and subjective.
- You analyze the data and write a report that uses empirical data to back up findings.

But the similarities are more apparent than real.

Focusing on Different Goals

The major difference between a social science research study and a usability test is in their goals. The goal of a research study is to test whether or not some phenomenon exists. To make that decision, the test must be done with a sample size large enough to detect the phenomenon if it is present. The ways to estimate how large the sample must be to make a proper decision fill large sections of statistics texts.

The goal of a usability test is to uncover problems, not to demonstrate the existence of some specific phenomenon. Experience has shown that you can uncover most major problems in a usability test with relatively few participants (Virzi, 1992). You cannot, however, then apply the same statistical tests to the data that you can in a social science research study.

Using the Same Laboratory

Usability tests and research studies may take place in similar physical settings. We and others conduct both usability tests and research studies in the same laboratory. Use of the same physical space, however, doesn't make the methods the same.

Selecting Participants Differently

Throughout this book, we stress that one of the criteria for conducting a valid usability test is to select participants from the population that will use the product. We do not, however, talk about this selection as "scientific sampling."

In research studies, the researchers often go to elaborate lengths to ensure that they have a *random* sample of participants from some relevant population. In fact, the statistical tests that are applied to research data assume that the participants were selected through some random process. In usability testing, you usually have a *convenience* sample—people from the appropriate population whom you happen to find and who are available to you.

Controlling Fewer Variables

In social science research, much skill and creativity go into isolating the specific variable or variables that you want to study and controlling for the influence of all other variables. In a usability test, you try to exert some control over confounding variables, such as level of computer experience, that might make the results difficult to interpret, but with only a few participants from a convenience sample, you cannot exert the level of control over confounding variables that you would work toward in a research study.

In a usability test, you also cannot usually isolate specific variables. The "independent variable" you want to study is usually the interface. Trying to isolate one specific variable within the interface will not give you the information you need to see how it actually works for users.

As a consequence, it is not always clear what is causing a problem. When participants select wrong menu options, is the cause a poorly organized menu hierarchy, poorly worded options, the participants' experience with a previous version of the product, or some combination of these possible causes?

In a usability test, in fact, the problems that you see often stem from multiple causes. To identify the problems and understand the causes, you must consider several measures together, not just the quantitative data. You bring your expert knowledge of human–computer interactions and document design to bear along with your observations, participants' comments, and the quantitative data. (We describe this process in detail in Chapter 20, "Tabulating and Analyzing Data.")

Weighing Observations More

Because a usability test is an empirical method, the test team carefully records the data of interest, such as the number of errors and the length of time it takes to complete a task. The participants typically also fill out questionnaires and give their opinions.

These are the same measures that are often recorded in a social science research study. In fact, the same performance measure could be collected in a research study and a usability test. In a usability test, however, the observations of the test team and the comments of test participants are often given more weight in diagnosing problems than they are in a research study.

Analyzing and Reporting Data Without Inferential Statistics

Most usability tests include descriptive statistics, such as means (averages), medians, ranges, and frequencies. In Chapter 20, "Tabulating and Analyzing Data," we discuss the use of inferential statistics, such as t-tests. For research studies, the results of inferential tests are frequently at the heart of the discussion of the data. Inferential statistics are, however, seldom appropriate for usability tests.

In summary, the greatest similarities between a usability test and a research study are in the physical setting in which they take place and in the types of data you collect. The other similarities are more apparent than real. The major difference is that they are serving different purposes.

3

Uncovering Usability Needs
Before You Design

Our focus in this book is on usability testing within the context of usability engineering. We want you to think of usability testing as one among a set of techniques for assuring usability. This book is built on two important principles:

1. Usability must concern any group developing any type of product that people are going to use.
2. Usability has to be thought about, planned for, and designed into the product from the beginning—as well as tested throughout the development process.

In Table 3-1, we list several techniques for building usability into products. In the rest of this chapter, we discuss the first group of techniques, focusing on planning for usability before designing the product. We discuss the other techniques in the next two chapters.

Identifying Users' Jobs and Tasks

Products that you are developing and testing exist to help people do their jobs. In order to make a useful product, you have to understand *what* those people's jobs are and *how* they do the tasks that are part of the job.

Table 3-1. Techniques You Can Use in a Usability Engineering Process

Some Useful Techniques for Planning, Implementing, and Evaluating Usability

Uncovering usability needs before you design
  Identifying users' jobs and tasks
  Convening focus groups
  Interviewing and observing users in context
  Conducting usability tests of existing versions
  Conducting usability tests of competitors' products
  Setting quantitative usability goals
Basing designs on expertise in human–computer interaction (HCI)
  Understanding the HCI and document design approach
  Using HCI and document design principles and guidelines
  Setting and using local rules
Evaluating usability throughout design and development
  Getting experts to review the design
  Having peers or experts walk through the design
  Having users work with static prototypes
  Having users work with interactive prototypes
  Getting user edits on early versions of documentation
  Asking users about their satisfaction
  Conducting iterative usability tests

As you plan and design a new product, you have to consider how well the product matches the users' job functions and how well the way they will do the tasks with the product matches the way they did the tasks before the product. It is not that computer products must parallel exactly what users were doing before. In fact, there would be no reason to build a product if it did not offer some new value, if it did not make the users' tasks faster or less burdensome or offer some other benefit that users could not have before. However, products that ignore what users do and how they do it are likely to be rejected because they do not help users meet their own needs.

When you analyze a job, you describe *what* a person in a particular role does. You list the tasks that the job comprises. When you analyze each task, you describe *how* the person does, can do, or should do the task (Drury, Paramore, Van Cott, Grey, & Corlett, 1987).

Analyzing Jobs

In organizations, each job has functions or tasks associated with it that the person who holds the job is supposed to fulfill. For example, the job of payroll clerk may have as one of its functions to "determine how much each employee should be paid for this period."

Sometimes these functions are written into a job description. Often, however, you will find that job descriptions are too vague to be much use in determining the users' job functions that are relevant to the product you are planning.

There are several methods for identifying job functions so that you can do a task analysis. You can work with an expert or group of experts to break down a job into its component tasks. This is one of the ways that user representatives can be integrated into a design team. One company that designs medical products for nurses has hired several nurses to work with designers. Other methods are to observe and interview users as they do their jobs or to walk through the tasks with a person who is doing the job.

Analyzing Tasks

Task analysis began as a method to study the efficiency of assembly-line operations (Mundel, 1970). Hence, early task analysis was one of the methods of time-and-motion studies. During World War II, task analysis was expanded as the focus changed to studying people working with complex electromechanical systems. For these systems, the task analysis had to include mental operations as well as observable actions. It also had to include following written instructions.

Task analysis is hierarchical. That is, each job can be broken down into a set of functions or tasks. Each of those tasks can then be broken down further into subtasks; subtasks can often be broken down further, and so on.

For example, one of us (J. S. D.) has been helping to design new equipment for anesthesiologists by observing and interviewing anesthesiologists and attending classes where they are being trained.

An anesthesiologist's major job function is to deliver anesthesia safely and effectively to patients in operating rooms. This major job function can be broken down into five tasks. One of those tasks, "Manage induction," can be broken down into at least eight subtasks as Figure 3-1 shows.

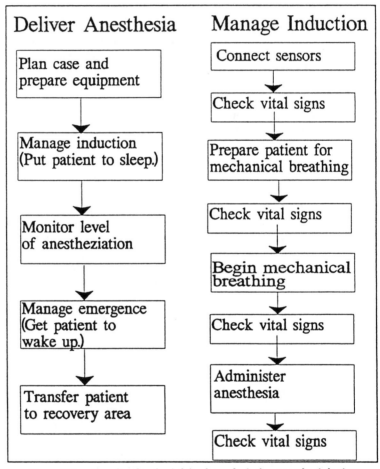

Figure 3-1. Two levels of a job/task analysis for anesthesiologists

Each task has

- an objective (goal) to achieve
- a starting point that initiates it
- an action or set of actions (These can be perceiving and

using information, making decisions, or performing an
observable action.)
- a stopping point when information is received that the
objective of the task has been achieved

Each of the anesthesiologist's tasks under "managing induction" can
be analyzed further. Consider the task, "Check vital signs," as an
example. The task analysis might look like Figure 3-2.
    Some task analyses also consider the knowledge and skills required
by the task and the displays and controls and other aids used to

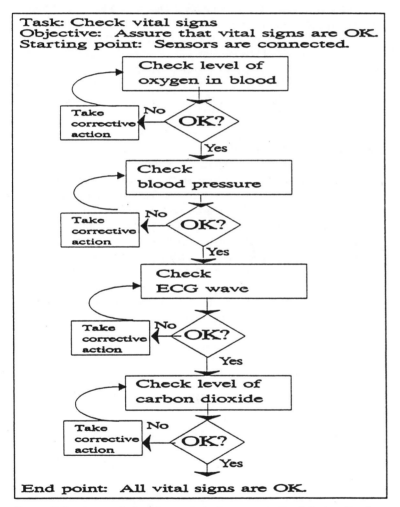

Figure 3-2. An analysis of one task for an anesthesiologist. Further
analysis would be necessary to understand subtasks like "'take corrective
action."

perform the task. For example, the payroll clerk may need employees' time sheets to "determine how much each employee should be paid for this time period." The anesthesiologist has to know what blood pressure is OK for each patient and type of surgery.

The specific data that you collect in a task analysis will depend on your purpose. When you are thinking about designing a product, you will be interested in a task analysis of how certain people now do their jobs. As you design the product, you will be interested in a task analysis of how people will accomplish their objectives using the controls, dials, menus, or other aspects of the interface that you are planning.

Doing a task analysis usually involves designing a form on which you list the information you need for each task, such as the task, its objective, its starting and stopping points, and the actions it requires. In addition, there should be a column or columns that show how the person will interact with the product or products to accomplish the task. (For a detailed description of task analysis methods, see Carlisle, 1986; Drury, 1983; Drury et al., 1987; McCormick, 1976; Wolfe et al., 1991; or Woodson, 1981.)

The Value of Task Analysis

An important value of task analysis is that it focuses attention on users' tasks. Product designers work so closely with the product that they must make a concerted effort to keep from becoming totally immersed in the functionality. It is all too easy to forget that the product exists because human beings are trying to accomplish tasks. Task analysis refocuses attention on users, and on their tasks and goals.

The emphasis in task analysis is on how the human and the product work together to achieve a goal.

Another important value of task analysis is that it gives you a rational basis for design decisions. A good task analysis tells you the objectives of each task, which tasks are most important to users, and which tasks depend on other tasks. You can then use this information to design the product. For example, task analysis can help you determine how to group icons and which to put on the main toolbar, or how to structure a menu hierarchy.

Convening Focus Groups

A focus group is a structured discussion about specific topics, moderated by a trained group leader. A typical focus group session includes 8 to 12 people and lasts for 2 hours. The people are carefully chosen, as in usability tests, to represent the potential users of the product.

If the potential audience is large, you would probably want to have several focus group sessions, possibly in different geographical areas. Having sessions with different types of users (executives and support personnel, forms users and data entry clerks, novices and experienced users) may be wise. In most cases where you can divide the user population into groups like these, you'll want to have separate sessions with each type of user so they can air their concerns and needs.

Most studies that rely on focus groups include 3 to 10 groups so that you have heard from about 30 to 100 people.

Keys to a Successful Focus Group

The keys to a successful focus group are inviting people who represent users, planning the questions to ask so they probe what you want to know, and having a skilled discussion leader who understands your goals for the session. With these in place, focus groups can help you understand what people think of your company and your product. You can find out about people's priorities, what they're looking for and willing to pay for, what they think are requirements, and what they think of as "nice to have but not necessary."

If you have a usability test laboratory, you can use the facilities for focus group sessions, too. Focus group sessions are always audiotaped and, often, also videotaped. Because the data are what people said, you may want to get the audiotape transcribed so that you can review it carefully. If you use a laboratory with a one-way mirror, you can invite developers and managers to observe and listen to the focus groups.

What You Can and Can't Learn in a Focus Group

Focus groups are excellent ways to probe users' attitudes, beliefs, and desires. They don't, however, give you information about what users would actually do with a product. The data are what people say they think or do or need. A focus group, therefore, is not a technique for verifying or assessing the usability of a product.

You can, however, combine a short performance test with a focus group. This works particularly well with documents. At the American Institutes for Research, before we revised the *Owner's Guide* for the Ford Taurus, we conducted a series of focus groups. We gave each Taurus owner who participated in the groups a copy of the *Guide* and a test booklet. Each page of the test booklet presented them with a problem for which they might need to go to the *Guide*. We asked participants to write down the words they looked for in the table of contents or index of the *Guide*, where they found the information (if they did), and what the answer was. They also wrote down the time they started looking for the information and the time they finished getting the information for that problem.

We have conducted similar focus groups with performance tests for appliance manuals and telephone bills. The performance tests give us quantitative data, such as how often people cannot find the right place in the document, how often they misunderstand what they find, and how long it takes them to find and read the information. If people have trouble with some of the tasks in the performance test, we get information on specific words or parts of the document that are difficult. The discussion that follows a performance test is also usually much richer than a typical focus group session.

Who Should Conduct Focus Groups

A skilled moderator should conduct each focus group. Other people who are interested in the discussion, such as designers and developers, should attend and observe but not lead the group.

It takes a skilled moderator to make sure that everyone participates, no one dominates, and the group stays on track with the issues that you want discussed. Designers and developers should not be running off to conduct focus groups by themselves. In many companies, the marketing department includes people with experience and training in conducting focus groups. If internal resources don't exist to conduct focus groups, you can hire external specialists.

Designers and developers should attend and observe—either behind the one-way mirror in a laboratory or unobtrusively on the side in a conference room. The information will have a greater impact and immediacy to designers and developers if they are present at the focus group than if they just receive a report about it.

(For more information about focus groups, see Calder, 1977; Goodman and MacDonald, 1987; Greenbaum, 1988; Lavidge & Payne, 1986; and Payne, 1979.)

Interviewing and Observing Users in Context

Contextual inquiry is a technique for interviewing and observing users individually at their regular places of work as they do their own work (Whiteside & Wixon, 1990; Whiteside, Bennett, & Holtzblatt, 1987; Wixon, Holtblatt, & Knox, 1990). The developers of this technique propose it as a new, nontraditional method of inquiry that can be used in the earliest predesign phase and then iteratively throughout product design and development. Contextual inquiry thus leads to a process of contextual design.

Wixon et al. argue that traditional usability methods, such as usability testing, have "fallen short of delivering timely and relevant design information" (1990, p. 329). They see contextual inquiry as a solution to that problem, summarizing their approach this way:

- Interview users about their work in the real-world environment.
- Be concrete. Talk about what the user is doing or just did, or talk in the context of a work product.

- Let the user lead the conversation. Co-interpret and co-design: Share your understanding of their work and your design ideas with users to validate and to stimulate users reflectively. Inquire about their assumptions.
- Expand and challenge the background of assumptions one brings to each interview. Probe all surprises and assumptions. Share your assumptions with users. Pick users strategically so that they are representative of the diversity of your user base.
- Summarize your understanding at the end of each session to determine whom to talk to next and what to focus on next.
- Build an understanding of users' work and of the environment to be designed.
- Based on this understanding, design and build a first cut at a user environment.
- Iterate the prototype with real users doing real work (if possible) and evaluate with contextual inquiry (Wixon et al., 1990, p. 332).

There is currently a lively debate over the value of contextual design and the validity of the criticisms its proponents have made of other usability methods. Carroll and Kellogg (1989, p. 7) criticize contextual design for having "no systematic methodology, no conceptual framework, no explicit way to abstract from particular experiences."

Indeed, the literature on contextual design does not specify how many people to interview, how you will know when to stop, how to move from an understanding of the users' work and the users' environment to a design, or how to know whether your design is usable. Contextual interviewing is very labor intensive and requires a trained, experienced contextual interviewer.

Working with users to understand what they are thinking as they do their work is certainly a useful way both to gather requirements for design and to evaluate an early prototype. We would not recommend using *only* this method throughout the process, however. Contextual inquiry supplements other techniques like usability testing, but does not substitute for them.

Conducting Usability Tests of Existing Versions

Very few products are released only once. Most designers are working on additions to and upgrades of existing hardware or software. They have a known user population and sources of knowledge about the product, but they traditionally put out new releases just as they did the old ones—in isolation from the users.

Sometimes the new functionality they are designing is in response to requests from the users, yet they've never seen whether the old functionality was easy or hard for users. Sometimes they are aware of rumblings about usability from the users, yet they have never really looked into those rumblings. They've never gone out to see users working, and they've never conducted usability tests.

The techniques we've discussed so far in this chapter, as well as those we'll discuss in the next few chapters, can help you understand users working with existing products. In addition, you can conduct a usability test on the current release of a product and learn a tremendous amount to drive the design of a new release.

Conducting Usability Tests of Competitors' Products

In many cases, the product that you are designing will be delivered to a competitive marketplace where potential users can choose between your product and others. If others already exist in that marketplace, you can use them in tests to understand their strengths and weaknesses, either by themselves or in comparison to an existing version of your product. Comparison usability tests can help you design your product to meet users' needs better than your competition does.

Comparison tests can also help you make major design decisions. A company we worked with wanted to know whether their competitor's touchscreen user interface to an engineering instrument was more effective than a more traditional interface with buttons. The answer to this question would have a major impact on the design of this company's new line of products. We conducted a usability test comparing four existing models of the instrument that used either a touchscreen or a button-based interface. This test saved the designers valuable time by allowing them to eliminate touchscreens as an alternative for their new product line.

You can also use some of the other techniques, like focus groups and contextual interviews, to gather information about competitors' products. You can hire an expert to review the interfaces to other products and suggest the strengths that you must match and the weaknesses that your product could overcome.

Setting Quantitative Usability Goals

Once you have the information from the techniques that we have discussed thus far, you have to apply them to designing your product. As we said in Chapter 1, a key component of usability engineering is setting specific, quantitative usability goals for the product. Think of it as writing usability specifications just as you write functional specifications.

Many of the usability goals come from your task analysis. A task analysis leads to a list of the tasks that users will be able to accomplish with the product. Each task in turn leads to several usability goals, which are answers to the question, "How will you know if the product is easy for people to use when doing this task?"

Some usability goals come from the company's desire to reduce costs and increase productivity. For example, you may have a goal of reducing calls to customer support by 50%.

Each goal in turn leads to design decisions that answer the question, "What are you going to do to make sure that the product meets this usability goal?"

Not setting quantitative usability goals early on leads to problems that have to be fixed up later.

Several years ago, a major computer company put a new computer on the market. The computer came with one large book that was meant to be an all-inclusive users' manual. But users could not find or use the instructions for setting up the computer. Setting up often took several hours and required that a customer service representative stay on the line with the user that entire time. After receiving numerous complaints from customers, the company set this quantitative usability goal:

> "A totally naive user will be able to take this computer out of the box and have it all connected and configured in less than half an hour without calling for support."

The company put together a team of hardware developers, software developers, and documentation specialists to figure out how to meet this goal. Part of the solution was to change the hardware and software; a major part was to create a separate, step-by-step, heavily illustrated, installation guide.

The fixes worked; naive users were able to set up the next release of the computer by themselves in less than half an hour. The fixes were after the fact, however, and therefore very costly. *Usability engineering means setting that goal before design, not after the product is out.*

Setting quantitative usability goals must be a team effort. In addition to the designers and developers, and the marketing people who may have conducted focus groups or user surveys, the team should include people who can help build usability into the product: human factors specialists, interface designers, and technical communicators.

In the next chapter, we discuss the expertise that these specialists can bring to the team and the importance of their expertise to developing usable products.

4

Basing Designs on Expertise in Human–Computer Interaction

In the last chapter, we discussed usability engineering activities that you should be using before you design. In this chapter, we describe the approach that experts take to designing usable products, the importance of using principles and guidelines from the field of human–computer interaction as you design, and how you must turn these principles and guidelines into a set of local rules for your particular product and development team.

Designing a good user interface and good documentation is a creative process, and every product brings its own challenges. However, as you design you can draw on the growing body of expertise based on research and usability testing that already exists. You may feel that your design problems are unique, but you are likely to find that others have faced and solved similar problems.

This book is not a "how-to" for designing interfaces or writing documentation. The detail in the later parts of this book is about usability testing, one method for evaluating usability. When you bring your product to usability testing, however, you want it to be the best product that you can design. Usability testing *should* be used to try out alternative designs, to fine-tune and refine products, and to find those problems that could not be anticipated or found by other evaluation methods.

When a product is designed for usability from the beginning, its designers take advantage of prior research and knowledge. The relevant areas of that prior research and knowledge are human–computer interaction (HCI) and document design. Part of usability engineering is to base your design on expertise in human–computer interaction and document design.

In this chapter, we focus on

- understanding the HCI and document design approach
- using HCI and document design principles and guidelines
- setting and using local rules

Appendix B includes lists of organizations and journals through which you can get more information about work in human–computer interaction and document design.

Understanding the HCI and Document Design Approach

The HCI approach means designing the product to ease the interactions that people have with computers, just as the document design approach means developing documentation that works for users rather than documentation that describes the system. Human–

computer interaction specialists are concerned with issues such as "What constitutes a good user interface?" and "How do I tell a good user interface from a poor one?" The answers they develop come both from setting up basic research experiments and from making sense of what happens in usability tests and other interactions with users and specific products. Document design specialists ask comparable questions about the documentation and build their knowledge base from the same two types of research and testing.

This knowledge base is distilled into general principles and guidelines. What's the difference between a principle and a guideline?

What is a Principle?

A principle is a very broad statement that is usually based on research about how people learn and work. For example, here is one principle that applies to both interface design and documentation:

Be consistent in your choice of words, formats, graphics, and procedures.

This principle is based on research that shows that people learn faster and can transfer what they learn better when what they see and do is consistent (Teitelbaum & Granda, 1983). We are all very much creatures of habit.

The principles that HCI and document design specialists have come up with are about as close to a theory of human–computer interaction and document design as we have. They state broad usability goals for all computer-related products.

What is a Guideline?

Each principle is, however, only a goal; it does not tell you how to achieve the goal. Guidelines are more specific goals that HCI and document design specialists distill from the principles for different users, different environments, and different technologies.

For example, for a menu-driven product, the principle of "being consistent" might be developed into a series of guidelines, one of which would be:

Be consistent in the way you have users leave every menu.

This guideline indicates one practice for which consistency is important (see Figure 4-1).

How Do Principles Relate to Guidelines?

One principle can lead to many guidelines, and guidelines can differ for specific combinations of users, environments, and technologies. By their nature, specific guidelines are developed only after special-

Figure 4-1. Designers need guidelines to help them be consistent.

ists gain some knowledge of each new aspect of HCI. For example, when designers first considered software windows, they could draw on the general principles of HCI and on many guidelines about consistency and other aspects of design that seemed to be relevant to using windows. However, they also had to test these guidelines in the new context and develop new guidelines by trying out alternatives with users. When designing a product using a new technology, you have to consider and transfer HCI principles and guidelines, but you must also create prototypes and conduct usability tests to come up with the guidelines that are appropriate in your new context.

HCI principles and guidelines do not substitute for usability testing, they supplement it. There is no guarantee that you will have a flawless design if you follow available guidelines. But when your design follows the HCI approach and is consistent with HCI principles and guidelines, you are more likely to find fewer serious usability problems when you bring users in for a usability test.

Using HCI and Document Design Principles and Guidelines

It is worth taking a few paragraphs to review some of the principles of HCI and document design, because they describe the characteristics of a usable product.

In a usability test, we look for instances in which a design is consistent with these principles—those are its strengths—and for instances in which it violates the principles—those are its weaknesses.

General Principles for HCI

Here are lists of general principles from three recent books on using an HCI approach in product design:

Simpson (1985)
Define the users.
Anticipate the environment in which your program will be used.
Give the operators control.
Minimize the operators' work.
Keep the program simple.
Be consistent.
Give adequate feedback.
Do not overstress working memory.
Minimize dependence on recall memory.
Help the operators remain oriented.
Code information appropriately (or not at all).
Follow prevailing design conventions.

Shneiderman (1992)
Strive for consistency.
Enable frequent users to use short cuts.
Offer informative feedback.
Design dialogs to yield closure.
Offer simple error handling.
Permit easy reversal of actions.
Support internal locus of control.
Reduce short-term memory load.

Dumas (1988)
Put the user in control.
Address the user's level of skill and knowledge.
Be consistent in wording, formats, and procedures.
Protect the user from the inner workings of the hardware and
    software that is behind the interface.
Provide online documentation to help the user to understand
    how to operate the application and recover from errors.
Minimize the burden on user's memory.
Follow principles of good graphics design in the layout of
    information on the screen.

All three of these lists have several items in common. They stress the
need for:

- giving the user control
- striving for consistency
- smoothing human–computer interactions with feedback
- supporting the user's limited memory

General Principles for Document Design

Similarly, the following are lists of general principles from recent
works on developing useful documentation:

Redish (1988) on developing useful documentation:
Ask relevant questions when planning manuals.
Learn about your audiences.
Understand how people use manuals.
Organize so that users can find information quickly.
Put the user in control by showing the structure of the manual.
Use typography to give readers clues to the structure of the
    manual.
Write so that users can picture themselves in the text.
Write so that you don't overtax users' working memory.
Use users' words.

Be consistent.
Test for usability.
Expect to revise.

Horton (1990) on online documentation:
Understand who uses the product and why.
Adapt the dialog to the user.
Make the information accessible.
Apply a consistent organizational strategy.
Make messages helpful.
Prompt for inputs.
Report status clearly.
Explain errors fully.
Fit help smoothly into the users' workflow.

Each of these principles can be developed into several guidelines. For example, the principle that you should "write so that you don't overtax users' working memory" leads to guidelines like these (from Redish, 1988):

Put the parts of each sentence into logical order.
Cross out unnecessary words.
Untangle convoluted sentences.
Use lists, tables, and step-by-step instructions.
Use parallel sentence structure whenever you can, especially in
        headings, lists, and explanations of options.

Sources for HCI and Document Design Guidelines

Brown (1988, p. 2) summarizes the objectives of guidelines when he says that they "provide a systematic approach to

1. take advantage of practical experience
2. disseminate and incorporate applicable experimental findings
3. incorporate rules of thumb
4. promote consistency among designers responsible for
    different parts of the system's user interface."

The HCI literature abounds with guidelines. Smith and Mosier (1986) have gathered most of the published guidelines into one source. They list almost 1000. Other sources of principles and guidelines on interface design are Brown (1988), Dumas (1988), Mayhew (1992), Shneiderman (1992), and Simpson (1985).

Similarly, documentation writers can gather guidelines from sources such as Brockmann (1990), Felker et al. (1981), Horton (1990), Price (1984), Redish (1988), and Redish, Battison, and Gold (1985).

Whether you are creating the user interface or the documentation, only some of the guidelines in these sources will apply to your situation. In some cases, you may find guidelines offering conflicting advice. Guidelines are not absolutes. As Dumas (1988) and Redish and Rosen (1991) explain, applying guidelines often involves tradeoffs. That's why you have to conduct usability tests even when you have followed the principles of human—computer interaction and good document design.

Setting and Using Local Rules

Even guidelines often don't go far enough to help you in your design. When several people are working on the same user interface or the set of documentation for a product, each one might implement different guidelines or implement the same guideline in a different way.

For example, consider again the HCI principle of "being consistent" and the guideline from that of "being consistent in the way you have users leave each menu." As Figure 4-1 shows, four different developers might decide to implement that guideline in four different ways.

Local Rules for an Interface—An Example

To really achieve consistency and meet both the principle and the guideline, you have to make a local rule that tells all the people who work on the user interface how you are all going to allow users to leave dialog boxes in the product you are designing. For example, you could have this local rule:

> *Provide an "Escape" option in a dialog in which users may want to leave the dialog box without making any changes or selecting any options.*

Local rules force everyone who works on the product to be consistent in their use of ways to leave menus.

Local Rules for Other Types of Products—An Example

You also may need to create local rules, because you are designing a product that is not thought of as a computer. Most of the published guidelines have come from experience designing software for use on other types of products. For example, you may create a local rule for the operation of a remote control that is used to operate menus on a display, such as "Press the 'Done' key to leave menus."

Local Rules for Documentation—An Example

Teams of writers also need to create local rules to enforce consistency and ease of use in documentation. For example, the principle that you should "use typography to give readers clues to the structure of the manual" leads to guidelines like:

Make the headings stand out from the text.
Make the hierarchy of the headings obvious.
Use a short line length for the text.
Indent lists and steps in procedures.

But each of these guidelines needs local rules. Without local rules, each writer in the company might make a different decision about how to make the headings stand out or how to make it obvious which heading is the most important. If each writer used a different strategy for the guidelines, the result would be total confusion for the users, which would defeat the purpose of the principle and guidelines.

The local rules for the guidelines about headings might look like:

First-level headings are used only for chapter titles. They are in boldface, 24-point, Helvetica, with a 2-point line (rule) underneath, flush left with the beginning of the text line. Each first-level heading starts a new page.

Second-level headings are for major sections. They are in boldface, 18-point, Helvetica, with a 2-point line (rule) over the heading. They start at the left page margin.

How Local Rules Relate to Guidelines

As Dumas (1988) explains, a major difference between guidelines and local rules is that guidelines can conflict with each other while local rules are absolutes for the context in which they are applied. That is, you might have one set of local rules for menu-driven interfaces and another for command-based ones. Division A of your company that makes industrial products might have one set of local rules, and Division B of your company that makes products for the home might have a different set. You might have one set of local rules for *Users' Guides* and another for *Technical Reference Manuals*. But for all the products for which a set of local rules is applicable, everyone working on the products must be using the same set of local rules in the same way.

Not all guidelines can be made into local rules (Redish & Rosen, 1991). For example, you cannot create a local rule that will dictate how to write *every* message for a product. You can, however, constrain messages to a specific format. For example, a local rule for confirmation messages might say:

Every confirmation message will take the form:
The [noun, < specific name > ,] has [not] been [verb].

An example of a message that follows this local rule would be:

The file, TEXT.DOC, has been stored.

Everyone on a product team who follows this rule will write similar confirmation messages.

Creating Standards, Sets of Guidelines, and Local Rules

If your organization frequently creates products, you may want to create your own set of principles, guidelines, and local rules. Many large organizations have user interface guides or standards, that is, compilations of guidelines and local rules.

Local rules take a lot of work to write and to implement, but they are a very useful way to communicate HCI practices and to ensure consistency in your products. A local design guide speaks more directly to designers than documents that are meant for a wider audience.

Using Published Standards

You may not have to create your own design guide if you are developing products in one of the Graphical User Interface (GUI) operating systems. There are published user-interface design guides for many of these:

> *Human interface guidelines: The Apple desktop interface* (Apple, 1987)
> *OSF/Motif Style Guide* (Open Software Foundation, 1991)
> *Systems application architecture: Common user access advanced interface design guide* (IBM, 1991)
> *The Windows Interface: An application design guide* (Microsoft, 1992)

The full citations for these documents are in the reference section.

These guides can save you a lot of work. They specify how to implement many of the features of the GUI user interface, such as how to create scroll bars and dialog boxes. While these guides do not specify all of the rules you will need locally to create applications, they can save you time and add consistency to many of the components of a user interface.

Recently, people have begun to study how software designers use design guides. In general, these studies show that people who are not professionals in HCI have difficulty understanding and applying guidelines (Thovtrup & Nielsen, 1991). They show that designers are very dependent on the examples that are used in these guides almost to the exclusion of other material (Tetzloff & Schwartz, 1991). There seems to be a consensus developing that the way to communicate guidelines to people who are not trained in HCI is not through a text document, but rather through software tool kits and interactive examples that can be easily applied to new situations.

How HCI and Document Design Principles Relate to Usability Testing

Understanding these principles and the guidelines and local rules that are derived from them is the basis for diagnosing the problems with products and finding solutions to those problems. Specialists in HCI or in document design view a usability test with a set of concepts that other people do not usually have. Like experts in any field, they see the world in which they work in a different way from people who are novices in that field. Their understanding of the concepts of their respective fields (HCI or document design) allows these experts to see patterns where others see only isolated events and allows them to notice things that others do not see at all.

Because the principles of HCI and good document design are the foundations of products that are usable, they are necessarily the focus of usability tests. HCI and document design principles provide a context for evaluating a product and a way to organize and communicate its strengths and weaknesses. Often, the principles become headings for chapters or sections of a report of the results of a usability test.

By understanding and using these principles as you develop the product, you will be engineering usability into the product instead of waiting for a usability test to point out weaknesses that specialists could have warned against much earlier in the design process.

If you want more information about human–computer interaction or document design, see Appendix B for lists of relevant journals and organizations.

In the next chapter, we discuss how to integrate usability into the design process.

5

Evaluating Usability Throughout Design and Development

Our focus in this book is on usability testing within the context of usability engineering. In the previous chapter, we discussed the importance of that context. In this chapter, we discuss usability testing and other methods to improve usability that you can apply during design and development.

Each of the methods we describe has strengths and weaknesses. The best approach to usability engineering is to develop a strategy that allows you to combine the strengths of several methods. We discuss the strengths and weaknesses of usability testing in this chapter and suggest other methods to make up for its weaknesses. We discuss:

- Getting experts to review the design
- Having peers or experts walk through the design
- Having users work with prototypes
- Getting user edits on early versions of documentation
- Asking users about their satisfaction
- Conducting iterative usability tests

We end the chapter by discussing some recent research comparing usability testing with other usability evaluation methods.

The evaluation methods we discuss in this chapter are not the only methods you can use, but they are commonly used and they have been evaluated in a series of research studies.

Getting Experts to Review the Design

One of the traditional methods that American companies use to get help about a special area of knowledge is to "call in an expert." Evaluating usability is one of the areas where this method is used. It is not unusual for a company developing a product to seek consultants who profess to be experts in usability. Are these experts effective? The answer to that question is not simple because it provokes other questions, such as:

- Does it work compared to what?
- Does an expert do a better evaluation of usability than the product's designers?
- Is using an expert cost effective?
- On what basis does an expert evaluate usability?
- What are the qualifications of an expert?

Recently, some research has addressed some of these questions. The primary motivation behind these studies has been to find usability evaluation methods that are cost-effective. One of the assumptions that is often mentioned in the introductions to these studies is that usability testing is an expensive method and, therefore, organizations that develop products are looking for cheaper ways to evaluate usability. For example, Desurvire, Kondziela, and Atwood (1992) open their paper on comparing usability evaluation methods by saying, "There is increasing interest in finding usability testing methods that are easier and cheaper to implement than traditional laboratory usability testing, which is frequently not performed due to the lack of funds, planning, or human factors expertise."

As we will see later in this chapter, the question of whether usability testing is expensive compared to other methods depends on a number of factors. In this section, we will focus on the effectiveness of using "experts" to evaluate usability and whether software engineers can be trained to evaluate the usability of products.

The term *heuristic evaluation* describes a method in which a small set of evaluators examine a user interface and look for problems that violate some of the general principles of good user interface design we described in Chapter 4. In one of the early heuristic evaluations, Nielsen and Molich (1990) looked at the effectiveness of training computer science students to evaluate usability. Nielsen and Molich described nine basic usability principles to the students and then had the students find violations of the principles in a user interface. The intention here was to provide these students with a set of heuristic rules, nine basic usability principles, to evaluate the usability of the product. The nine principles were:

1. Use simple and natural language.
2. Speak the user's language.
3. Minimize user memory load.
4. Be consistent.
5. Provide feedback.
6. Provide clearly maked exits.
7. Provide shortcuts.
8. Provide good error messages.
9. Prevent errors.

The motivation for this investigation was to look for a method that might be cheap to use. Giving software engineers a short tutorial on usability principles is cheaper than having designers teach usability specialists about their product and then have the specialists review the product and tell the designers where the problems are.

This first study showed that, as individuals, the student evaluators did not find many of the usability problems with the products they evaluated. The range of problems each student found was between about 20% and 50%. Nielsen and Molich then statistically aggregated the individual evaluators into groups of varing sizes and found that groups of five evaluators working separately would have found between about 50% and 75% of the usability problems. On the basis of this data, Neilsen and Molich recommended using heuristic evaluation with three to five evaluators.

Since that 1990 study, several additional studies have looked at the effectiveness of heuristic evaluation.

Jeffries et al. (1991) took a different approach to what they called heuristic evaluation. They used people with advanced degrees and experience in usability engineering as their experts. They asked these people to find the usability problems with the interface to a product without specifying any set of general principles to follow. These authors also had a group of software engineers read a report describing a set of 62 usability guidelines and evaluate the usability of the same product.

The usability experts found about three times as many problems as the software engineers and more than twice as many of the most severe problems. Since Jeffries et al. did not have an absolute measure of the number of usability problems with the product being evaluated, we cannot look at the success rate of these evaluators. Jeffries et al. recommend using software engineers to evaluate the usability of a product only when there are no experts in usability available.

It is difficult to compare the Jeffries et al. study with Nielsen and Molich because of the different definitions of heuristic evaluation. The software engineers whom Jeffries et al. had read the 62 usability guidelines are more comparable to the software engineers Nielsen and Molich used. In both studies, their success at finding usability problems was disappointing. In a related study, Desurvire et al. (1992) found that software engineers who were given a lecture on usability principles found less than half the problems that usability specialists found, but did find many specific, local problems.

The four usability experts that Jeffries had evaluate the usability of the interface have some unknown, unmeasured level of expertise in human–computer interaction. The lack of information on their expertise makes it difficult to compare their performance with other groups of "experts." The studies we describe shortly all have this weakness.

Nielsen (1992) used three groups of evaluators:

1. "Novice" evaluators, who had no training or experience in usability engineering.
2. "Regular" usability specialists, who were experts in usability engineering but with no special expertise in the usability of the type of interface they were evaluating—a telephone voice-response system.
3. "Double" usability specialists, who were experts in usability engineering and who also had experience working with telephone voice-response systems.

The novices found only 22% of the usability problems, the regular usability specialists found 41%, and the double usability specialists found 60%. Nielsen also statistically aggregated the individual evaluators into groups and found that five novice evaluators would find 50% of the usability problems, five regular usability specialists would find about 80%, and five double usability specialists would find about 98% of the problems.

These studies taken together show that software engineers are not very effective at finding usability problems. The viability of giving software designers a quick lecture or having them read a report on usability principles and be effective at finding usability problems is questionable. Some researchers are still optimistic about the potential of this concept, but the evidence produced to date is not convincing.

As you might expect, experts in usability engineering are much better at finding usability problems than software engineers and usability experts who have experience with the technology they are evaluating are best. The studies that report this finding, however, are difficult to compare, because they have no measure of what it means to be an expert.

While it is difficult to compare these studies, there is a finding that is consistent: Heuristic evaluation, when used by experts, tends to uncover many local problems. In the Jeffries et al. study, the experts using this method found 52 problems that were judged "least severe." Usability testing uncovered only two of these problems.

In the final section of this chapter, we will talk more about this finding, but it is worth noting here that conducting both a heuristic evaluation with experts and a usability test would allow you to combine the strenghts of these two methods: Usability testing would uncover most of the major, global problems, and heuristic evaluation would uncover most of the minor, local problems.

Research issue: It would be easier to compare studies using experts if we knew more about how the experts were uncovering problems. Nielsen's study (1990) suggests that just as "double" usability specialists have some knowledge they have gained from working with the technology underlying the interface, "regular" usability specialists have some knowledge they have gained about human–computer interaction. It would help us understand usability evaluation much better if we had a large number of "usability experts" talk aloud as they all evaluated the same interface. We could compare their approaches and see if there is any consistency among them.

In the final section of this chapter, "Comparing Usability Testing with Other Usability Evaluation Methods," we will look at how heuristic evaluation compares with usability testing as a cost-effective way to evaluate the usability of an interface.

Having Peers or Experts Walk Through the Design

Structured walkthroughs have become a standard method for assuring the quality of software (Yourdon, 1985). Walkthroughs are a peer-group review of a technical product. They can be used to review specifications, designs, or programming code. During a walkthrough, the team of people who are developing a product "walk through" the specifications or the programming code one step at a time looking for bugs or inconsistencies.

There is a variation of the walkthrough, called a cognitive walkthrough, designed to evaluate the usability of the user interface (Lewis & Polson, 1990). Its creators have proposed that this method is an effective way to evaluate a user interface when a full prototype is not feasible. The goal of the method is to evaluate the strengths and weaknesses of the user interface without having to create a prototype or the design itself.

The cognitive walkthrough is based on a formal model of human–computer interaction. The model assumes that people learn about an interface through a complex guessing strategy. Users make guesses about what actions to take by comparing the expected outcome of the action against their goals. They then take action and evaluate their progress toward the goals.

The walkthrough consists of answering a set of questions about each of the decisions users must make as they use an interface. The questions have to do with identifying users' goals, the ease with which users will be able to identify the consequences of a decision, and how easy it is for users to evaluate whether they are making progress toward a goal. These questions are asked for each step of each task.

After those taking part in the walkthrough answer the questions for each step, they rate the likelihood that users will have problems making the correct choice or action. Those steps at which users will be most likely to have problems need improving.

One of the advantages of this method is that it makes users' goals and expectations explicit. When a step is likely to cause problems for users, the walkthrough indicates where the problem lies, for example, in the feedback the system gives after users have taken some action.

While the walkthrough can yield useful diagnostic data, it has been tedious to perform. The designers we have worked with would not have the patience to make this method work in its paper-and-pencil form. There is a software version of the method, called the Automated Cognitive Walkthrough, that takes much of the tedium out of the process of using the walkthrough (Desurvire et al., 1992). In addition, researchers continue to simplify the cognitive walkthrough to reduce the time it takes to perform as well as the tedium of the process (Rowley & Rhodes, 1992).

Lewis and Polson (1990) propose that this method can be used by designers who do not have expertise in human–computer interaction, but we are skeptical. The validity of the method depends on an accurate and thorough understanding of who the users are and what skills and experience they have. As long as the designers have this understanding, the walkthrough may be useful. But, if the designers have an incorrect view of the users of the product, the walkthrough will be invalid.

There have been some recent research studies looking at the effectiveness of walkthroughs (Desurvire et al., 1992; Jeffries et al., 1991). Generally, walkthrough methods are less effective at finding usability problems than other evaluation methods, such as heuristic evaluations. Karat, Campbell, and Fiegel (1992) have shown that the effectiveness of walkthroughs can be enhanced by conducting the walkthrough in a group rather than with individual evaluators.

In the final section of this chapter, "Comparing Usability Testing with Other Usability Evaluation Methods," we will look at how walkthroughs compare to usability testing as a cost-effective way to evaluate the usability of an interface.

Having Users Work With Prototypes

Prototyping is not a new idea. It is a valuable tool that was first used in developing hardware. In that context, a prototype was a handmade, mechanical model of a design. It gave both designers and users a hands-on feel for the product. These hardware prototypes varied in their fidelity to the final product, from simple foamcore mock-ups to near-production models.

Until recently, designers of software user interfaces did not often use prototypes. There was no quick and easy way to simulate the look and feel of software. Creating a prototype of any complexity was just as difficult as creating the code for the final product. Consequently, designers could not conceive of creating a user interface that was separate from the rest of the software (Edmonds, 1992).

Let's look at two types of prototyes:

- Static, paper-based prototypes
- Interactive, software-based prototypes

Then we will compare the effectiveness of these two types of prototypes and look at some of the strengths and weaknesses of prototypes.

Using Static, Paper-based Prototypes

One of the ways to get users involved in design early is to show them screen images on paper of what a product will look like and ask them to try them out. These paper images are sometimes called a *screenplay.* A screenplay is a static prototype that can give you valuable information about the usability of your product.

A screenplay can be effective particularly at helping you solve problems such as developing a menu hierarchy that users can understand. Let's look at an example to see what we mean.

This is the top level menu for a hypothetical drawing program:

File	Edit	Draw	Font	Options	Window	Help

While this example of a drawing program is hypothetical, we have constructed it from some actual drawing programs we have seen.

Imagine that you have drawn a figure. You look at it and decide that you want to make the lines in your figure thicker or darker. Which menu option would you go to? Most people we have asked choose "Draw." Here is the submenu for Draw:

Draw
Palettes...
Front
Back
Group
Degroup
Grid on
Grid off
Snap to grid

People are generally bewildered by some of these choices, but decide to go back to the top level and choose another option. They often choose Edit next, but quickly decide the right choice isn't there:

Edit
Can't undo
Repeat
Cut
Copy
Paste
Select all
Select block

Next, they'll often go to Options:

Options
Preferences...
Tools...
Zoom
Unzoom
Transform...
Import
Export

From here, people usually choose Tools, but that brings up a palette for doing new work. They usually then leave this menu, flounder around in other choices for a while, go back to Draw and Edit, and after several more wrong moves, decide they can live without changing the lines. The correct choice would be Transform on the options menu. That brings up a dialogue box that permits many different changes to a drawing.

You can see how easy it is to find usability problems with menu hierarchies by making a screenplay and having users work through it. This happens to be the kind of usability problem that paper prototypes are good at revealing (Nielsen, 1990). But this was only one problem, and there may be many more. Using the static screens is slower than using an interactive software prototype, but it can work. (See the later discussion, however, in the section "Comparing Static and Interactive Prototypes" for some further limitations of paper prototypes.)

As the size of the menu hierarchy grows, a screenplay becomes more cumbersome to use, but it is useful for problems such as the effectiveness of a small menu hierarchy.

Interactive, Software-based Prototypes

Over a very short period, about five years, most of the impediments to creating useful software prototypes have disappeared. It is now possible to simulate the look and feel of a software user interface in a few hours, or a few days for a more complex product. Furthermore, prototyping tools are now available for most hardware and operating system environments.

Usability tests of prototypes of a design are becoming very common, because they allow designers to make changes before it is too late. Most software applications àre sufficiently complex that it is difficult for designers to understand how the product will work unless they create a prototype.

Ironically, software prototyping tools are also being used to display images of hardware user interfaces. For example, we have created software prototypes of a remote control for a TV and a control panel for a complex hospital bed. While these prototypes do not help users to touch or feel the product, they can present realistic views of layouts, buttons, and labels. These prototypes allow designers to get feedback on usability from users long before they create actual hardware prototypes.

The Benefits of Interactive Prototypes

In a very real sense, user-driven software design and usability testing of software would be very difficult without prototyping tools. There are four major benefits of software prototypes:

1. They make it possible to incorporate user feedback into the design early in the development process.
2. They allow designers to explore several design concepts before they settle on one.
3. They make it possible to evaluate several iterations of a design.
4. They take the fuzziness out of what the user interface is and, therefore, allow members of the design team to communicate with each other about the user interface.

This fourth benefit is worth elaborating. With an interactive prototype, a software engineer, who is involved in the details of a design, and a marketing manager, who is only peripherally involved, can use a prototype of the user interface to talk about it. The prototype reduces the likelihood that people will miscommunicate about how the user interface will look and operate.

Prototyping Less Than the Full User Interface

Prototypes are often created to explore part of the interface. For example, a design team might create three prototypes that represent different design concepts. Each prototype might mimic only a small part of the user interface. Nielsen (1989, see Figure 5-1) makes a distinction between types of prototypes that each represent only a part of the user interface:

- Horizontal prototypes reduce the size of the prototype by containing a shallow layer of the surface of the user interface. For example, the prototype might show a "desktop" screen with the names of each main menu item or icons on it. For an electronic mail horizontal prototype, users might see an opening screen with a list of messages and the main menu showing the options available. If users selected a menu option, they would receive a message indicating that further selections are not implemented or perhaps just hear an audible tone.

- Vertical prototypes fully implement a small number of paths through the interface, but do not include any part of the remaining paths. For example, all of the branches of a "Create" option of an electronic mail product might be implemented so that the user could edit, transmit, store, or print a message.

- Scenario prototypes differ from the other two types by being task oriented. A design team might decide to fully implement three important tasks that cut through the functionality of the prototype. For example, the user might be able to create a message, send it, and store it in a folder. If the user deviates from the preferred path or selects an incorrect option, that part of the prototype would not be implemented.

Nielson recommends the use of scenario prototypes as a tool for evaluating usability. The limited size of these prototypes makes it easy to change them frequently on the basis of some form of feedback from users.

There is a potential problem with partial prototypes. Because they mimic only part of the user interface, partial prototypes may lead a test team to overestimate the usability of a product. In a partial

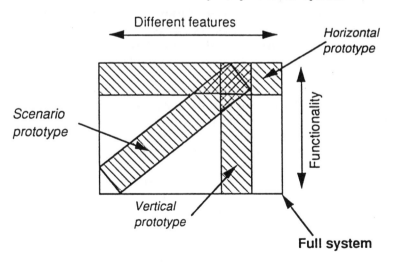

Figure 5-1.   Horizontal, vertical, and scenario prototypes (modified from Nielsen, 1989)

prototype, there are limited ways in which test participants can go astray. When a participant selects an option in a software prototype that has not been implemented, the prototype usually displays a message informing the participant that the option is not part of the prototype. In the real product, users will be able to select that option and could, by doing so, get into more trouble than they can when the option is not available. When a user interface has several global problems that cut across the user interface, the fully implemented user interface presents more ways for test participants to go wrong.

Comparing Paper Versus Interactive Prototypes

Nielsen (1990) has compared the effectiveness of using interactive prototypes with the static paper prototypes we described earlier in this chapter. He had two groups of evaluators examine either a paper version of a prototype of a user interface or an interactive software-based version created with a prototyping language.

There were 50 usability problems with each interface, 15 of which Nielsen called "major." These major problems are what we call "global." The results show that the evaluators who were using the software prototype found significantly more global problems. The one global problem that the paper prototype was effective at uncovering was a lack of consistent navigation rules in a menu hierarchy.

The results of this study suggest that when you have access to interactive prototyping tools, it is preferable to use them in place of paper prototypes.

Some Cautions About Prototypes

There is a lively debate in the human factors community about how close the prototype needs to be to the final product to be a useful tool for usability testing. The value of the new prototyping tools is that they allow designers to try out design concepts quickly (Melkus & Torres, 1988; Virzi, 1989). But they also allow designers to use the prototype to create the entire user interface and to make it look like a finished product. Used in this way, the prototype becomes a product of its own, a demanding product that requires complex debugging.

We have seen design teams who want the prototype to mimic the complete user interface and to look like a finished product. They are afraid to show users a product that looks like it is still under development because it may bias users against their design. In our view, these designers waste valuable time treating the prototype as if it were a product itself. Prototyping tools are best used to explore alternative concepts. They do not have to have high fidelity to be useful.

Another limitation of software prototyping tools is the difficulty of simulating the response time that the real product will have. With a prototyping tool, you can create a realistic looking and acting user interface, but often you cannot predict how long it will take for the final product to perform such actions as looking up information in a database or drawing a complex graphic. The prototype, which does not actually carry out these actions, may respond immediately to a command while the final product may respond more slowly. Consequently, the reactions you get from participants during a usability test of a prototype can overestimate the ease of use of the final product. If you can anticipate the length of any delays, build them into the prototype. (See Hix & Ryan, 1992, for a quantitative method for evaluating the effectiveness of prototypoing tools.)

Research issue:	Do prototypes that are low in fidelity bias users to rate them lower in usability than a prototype of higher fidelity? How much does the appearance of the prototype contribute to users' ratings of its quality or ease of use?

Getting User Edits on Early Versions of Documentation

Just as you can have users try out prototypes of the user interface, you can have them try out drafts of the documentation. The documentation might be an installation card, a quick reference card, the outline and/or sections of the users' manual, or samples of the online help.

Testing samples of draft documentation serves exactly the same purpose as testing prototypes of the interface. It allows the writers to see if they are on the right track with the content, organization, language, and layout of the documentation from a small piece of the work. Changes at an early stage save time and money, just as they do in developing the interface.

Depending on the status of the documentation and the rest of the product, getting users involved at the early stages can range from asking a few users to read and comment on parts of the documentation to including the draft documentation with the prototype of the interface in a usability test. As with any other aspect of usability engineering, a critical factor in getting users involved is making sure that the people whom you have work with the draft documentation represent real users.

Here are a few ways to involve users with draft documentation early on:

If you are concerned about whether the organization of the draft document matches the way that users will approach it, you can do a test very similar to the static prototype of the menu structure of an interface. You can give users tasks and ask them what they would look up in the manual or online help when trying to do that task. You can give them a draft table of contents to use. A draft table of contents is the outline of the manual, reflecting all the headings and subheadings that are planned for the manual.

If you are concerned about whether the content is what users need and whether the style (language) will be clear to users, you can prepare the documentation for one part of the product and see how well that works for users. With the desktop publishing resources available today, preparing draft printed documentation that looks very much like the final documentation is easy.

Getting online help into a prototype may be more difficult. If you are prototyping in the same system that will be used for the final product, Microsoft Windows®, for example, you can probably have the online help work with a prototype. If you are prototyping with a different system, and the way help works in that system is not the same way it will work in the final product, you would probably not want to put the online help into the prototype. You could still have samples of the online help available on paper.

Atlas (1981) described a *user edit* as having a user do a task, using the instructions for the product as a guide. An observer watches, listens, and takes notes. If you have the user try to follow the instructions, you can use this method to find out if that particular set of instructions is accurate, complete, and clear to the user. If the user comments on problems, or if the user hesitates, misreads, or makes mistakes, you have indications of problems in the text. To the extent that the instructions the user is trying out are similar in level of content and style to the rest of the manual, you have information that can lead to much broader changes.

As Redish and Schell (1989) point out, this type of user edit can give you very useful information about the general style and level of detail of the instructions, but it may not help you understand how well the document as a whole is organized for users. If the user edit is of a specific part of a document and the user goes through the document page by page and step by step, you are not seeing how easy or difficult it is for users to *find* the information that they need in the manual. You are, however, seeing how useful the manual is once the users have found the correct page.

Soderston (1985, p. 18) described a *usability edit* as giving a user "the task for the day, our written material, and the system." Observers watch and perhaps videotape the session. To the extent that "our written material" includes enough of the manual to make users both search for the correct information and then read (use) it, Soderston's usability edit can yield information about the organization as well as the content and language of the manual.

A major difference between Atlas's user edit and Soderston's usability edit is that, in the latter, the user is told to think out loud throughout the session. In essence, Soderston is describing a usability test of part of the product and the documentation for that part.

Having users think out loud while performing any task, from reading a text to working with a product, is also called having the user *give a verbal or think-aloud protocol.* Since the early 1980s, think-aloud protocols have been used very successfully in understanding users' problems with a wide variety of documents (Schriver, 1989, 1991). As Schriver (1991, p. 167) points out, "very often, protocols will help writers detect both problems of commission, that is, problems caused by what the text says, and problems of omission, that is, problems caused by what the text is missing."

When testing draft documentation as part of any usability test, however, keep these two caveats in mind: The first caveat is that it is very difficult to test both *whether people will* use the documentation and *how* they will use it in the same test. The second caveat is that you must make the measures that you take about the documentation match the stage of development that the documentation is at. For example, if the draft manual does not yet have either a table of contents nor an index, taking a measure of "time to find the information users need" doesn't make much sense.

Conducting Iterative Usability Tests

In Chapter 2, we discussed conducting usability tests on all parts of a product—the software and hardware user interface and the documentation—and conducting tests early and often. We are advocating an approach to product design in which designers expose a product under development to users in the form of usability tests as early as possible and continue to conduct tests a often as necessary to ensure the usability of the product.

We also advocate combining usability tests with the other evaluation methods we discussed in this chapter. In the next section, we describe which evaluation methods work best with usability testing.

Comparing Usability Testing with Other Usability Evaluation Methods

In the past two years, there have been a number of research studies comparing the effectiveness of usability testing with some of the other usability evaluation methods we have discussed in this chapter. We expect that there will soon be many more studies, and they will provide additional information about the advantages and disadvantages of each method.

We briefly discuss the recent studies here. In general, they show that usability testing compares well with other evaluation methods. There are enough differences in methodology among these studies, however, that we need additional research to give us a better understanding of the relationships between the evaluation methods.

The Jefferies et al. Study

Jeffries et al. (1991) compared the relative efffectiveness of four evaluation methods at uncovering usability problems in a software application:

1. Applying guidelines—Software engineers were given a report describing 62 guidelines of good practice in usability. The engineers studied the guidelines and then used them to evaluate the software user interface.
2. Heuristic evaluation—Four evaluators who had training and experience in human–computer interaction evaluated the software user interface. These experts were not told what basis they were to use to conduct the evaluation.
3. Cognitive walkthroughs—Software engineers working as a group were taught how to do a walkthrough of the user interface. They then conducted a group walkthrough of the product and identified usability problems.
4. Usability test—A human factors specialist conducted a usability test with six participants and identified usability problems.

There were several interesting results from this study. The heuristic evaluation found the most problems (105), compared with applying guidelines (35), the walkthrough (35), and the usability test (31). However, no single expert found more than 42 usability problems in the heuristic evaluation.

Jeffries et al. had seven usability specialists rate the severity of the problems that these methods found. Jeffries et al. then ranked the problems on the basis of the severity rating. Figure 5-2 shows the top and bottom thirds of problems ranked on severity.

As you can see, the heuristic evaluation found the most problems, although its advantage over the usability test is much smaller with the most severe problems. The experts listed a large number (52) of least severe problems. Jeffries at al. note that they are not sure that all of these problems really need to be fixed. Notice, also, how few of the least severe problems were uncovered by the usability test. This is not surprising, because tasks selected for a test are intended to sample the

Level of Severity of Problems	Guidelines	Heuristic Evaluation	Cognitive Walkthru	Usability Test
most severe	12	28	9	18
least severe	11	52	10	2

Figure 5-2. Level of severity of problems found by each evaluation method. (From Jeffries et al., 1991)

parts of the interface that are most likely to create global problems. If a local problem occurs on a screen that test participants never use, the test will not uncover the problem.

The results of this study show clearly the strengths and weaknesses of these methods.

Usability testing finds global problems very well but is poor at uncovering local problems. Heuristic evaluation, on the other hand, finds many specific, local problems. It would appear, therefore, that heuristic evaluation and usability testing nicely complement each other.

Jeffries et al. computed a cost-benefit analysis of the four methods. Again, heuristic evaluation yields the highest payoff. The four experts took a total of 20 hours to do their evaluation; the usability test took nearly 200 hours.

This study shows the value of having more than one expert review the usability of a design. Clearly, if you have four experienced usability specialists available to you, asking them to independently evaluate the interface is the most cost-effective evaluation method. If you do not have usability experts available, the only other method that uncovers a substantial number of severe usability problems is usability testing.

An interesting question that arises from this study is whether the usability test uncovers problems that the other methods do not find. Jeffries et al. did not conduct this analysis, but they report, as an anecdote, that a severe problem that resulted in users being unable to log into the system after deleting a directory was uncovered by one of the participants in the usability test. This problem was not uncovered by any of the other methods.

Usability testing finds global problems very well but is poor at uncovering local problems.

The Bailey et al. Study

While using both heuristic evaluation and usability testing may prove complementary, Bailey, Allan, and Raiello (1992) have shown that changing many of the local problems that are uncovered with heuristic evaluation did not improve the usability of a software user interface. They had experts list the usability problems with a user interface. The experts uncovered 43 usability problems with the product. Bailey et al. also conducted a usability test with the product. They fixed the single most serious problem with the product and retested it. They then fixed the single most serious usability problem with the product and retested it. They continued with this procedure of fixing a usability problem and then retesting two more times. The results showed that there was no statistically significant improvement in preformance after the two most serious problems were fixed.

This study suggests that many of the specific problems that are uncovered in a heuristic evaluation do not influence the performance of users. We do not know whether these small problems would influence users' perception of the ease of use of a product.

The Karat et al. Study

Karat et al. (1992) conducted a study comparing usability testing to walkthroughs. In this study, two different products were evaluated to assess the reliability of the methods. In addition to having six individual evaluators conduct a walkthrough, they also had six pairs of evaluators conduct a walkthrough together to see if walkthroughs are made more effective when there is group interaction. The usability tests had six test participants using the products.

The results show that the usability tests uncovered about twice as many problems as the group walkthroughs and three times as many as the individual walkthroughs. The usability tests also uncovered significantly more severe problems than the walkthroughs.

Figure 5-3 shows the number of *unique* usability problems found by each method, that is, finding a problem that none of the other methods found. As you can see, the usability test uncovered many more unique problems than the other methods. About two-thirds of these problems were severe.

Karat et al. also conducted a cost-benefit analysis of the methods. As you might expect, the usability tests required the most time to conduct, but required less time-per-usability problem than the other methods.

	Usability Tests	Team Walkthru	Individual Walkthru
System 1	13	1	0
System 2	8	0	2

Figure 5-3. Unique usability problems uncovered by each method. (From Karat et al. 1992)

The Desurvire et al. study

Desurvire et al. (1992) compared usability testing with heuristic evaluation and cognitive walkthroughs. In addition, they had three different types of evaluators: usability experts, software engineers and nonexperts.

One of the unique features of this study was that the software engineers had designed the product they were evaluating. One might think that software developers who understand the internal workings of a product will be able to find more usability problems than software designers who are evaluating a product they did not design.

Consistent with Karat et al., the usability test in the Desurvire et al. uncovered the most problems, and the usability experts found more problems than the nonexperts or the software engineers. Figure 5-4 shows the number of problems that were uncovered by each of the conditions.

As you can see, the usability test found more than twice as many problems as the heuristic evaluation, which, in turn, found more problems than the cognitive walkthrough. The usability experts found about twice as many problems as the software engineers, who, in turn, found about twice as many problems as the nonexperts.

Comparing the Studies with Each Other

The one major inconsistency among these studies is the effectiveness of the performance of experts using heuristic evaluation. Jeffries et al. found that the experts uncovered more problems than the usability test did, while other studies found that the experts uncovered less than half of the problems uncovered by a usability test. It is difficult to compare these studies on these factors, because they each used

	# of Problems	% of Problems
Usability test	25	100%
Heuristic Evaluation		
Experts	11	44%
Software Engineers	4	16%
Non-Experts	2	8%
Cognitive Walkthrough		
Experts	7	28%
Software Engineers	4	16%
Non-Experts	2	8%

Figure 5-4. **Number and percent of usability problems uncovered by each method (From Desurvire et al. 1992)**

different experts and did not measure the expertise or experience of the experts in any systematic way.

One of the consistent findings of these studies, however, is that heuristic evaluation when conducted by experts uncovers many more local problems that other methods. Usability testing does just the opposite, that is, it uncovers the global problems.

Taken together, these studies suggest these conclusions:

- Usability testing uncovers more usability problems than other evaluation methods.
- Usability testing finds more global problems than other evaluation methods.
- Usability testing finds more unique problems than other methods.
- Usability testing uncovers fewer local problems than other evaluation methods.
- Usability testing takes more hours to conduct than other methods, but is cost effective when considered on a cost-per-problem-uncovered basis.
- Heuristic evaluation, conducted by usability specialists, is better at uncovering usability problems than walkthroughs.
- Heuristic evaluation gains in power when there are several usability experts working independently.
- Heuristic evaluation uncovers more minor problems than other methods, but changing these minor problems may not improve performance.
- Cognitive walkthroughs are less effective than heuristic evaluation and usability testing at uncovering usability problems.
- Software engineers are not very good at uncovering usability problems, even when they are given a short lecture or report on principles of human–computer interaction.

Our recommendation, at this time, from the available evidence is to conduct both usability tests and heuristic evaluations to take advantage of each method's strengths. As Jeffries and Desurvire (1992) note, "the best evaluation of a user interface comes from applying multiple evaluation techniques." Usability tests will uncover the global problems and will also uncover more problems that the other methods miss. If you only conduct usability tests, however, you run the risk of having many undetected local problems in your product. While any one of these problems is probably not serious enough to keep users from completing tasks or frustrating them, the combined effect of having many local problems is likely to make the user feel that the designers were sloppy in their development effort.

In the next chapter, we discuss how to integrate usability testing into an organization that develops computer-based products.

6

Establishing a Usability Program in Your Organization

Throughout this first part of the book, we have emphasized the importance of considering usability throughout the design and development process. We have placed usability testing in a context of usability engineering as one among a flexible set of methods to apply throughout the process.

We end this part with a discussion of the importance of a team approach to establishing a usability engineering and a usability testing program. We see a parallel between the history of software quality assurance testing and the history of usability testing.

In its early days, software testing was viewed very narrowly as a way to find "bugs" near the end of development. The software quality assurance movement changed that view to one in which a variety of increasingly sophisticated techniques are integrated into development (Beizer, 1984).

As with quality assurance programs, a usability engineering program tests early and often. As with many creative processes, such as writing and designing usable products, you can't expect to get it right the first time. The best writers and usability engineers know that. They produce the best products by continually evaluating as they create.

To make such a dynamic approach to usability work, you need to focus on getting people with the right skills together at the right time during development. Your usability testing program needs to be integrated into the development process rather than standing to one side of the process.

In this chapter, we discuss

- understanding the barriers to focusing on usability
- using usability testing to stimulate interest in usability
- fitting usability testing into your organization
- building a usability lab in your organization

Understanding the Barriers to Focusing on Usability

Although you may prefer to concentrate on specific, practical techniques for making products easy to use, you must consider the organizational context in which testing occurs. Organizational and managerial structures and processes are critical. They will, in the end, determine whether you get to use what you know about making interfaces and documentation usable, whether you get to assess the usability of your prototypes and drafts, and whether you get to influence product design.

In many well-established companies, history and organizational structures impede bringing users and usability into the development process.

Tradition: The Assembly Line Model

The traditional development process is what we might call the "assembly line model" (Redish, 1989). (See Figure 6-1.)

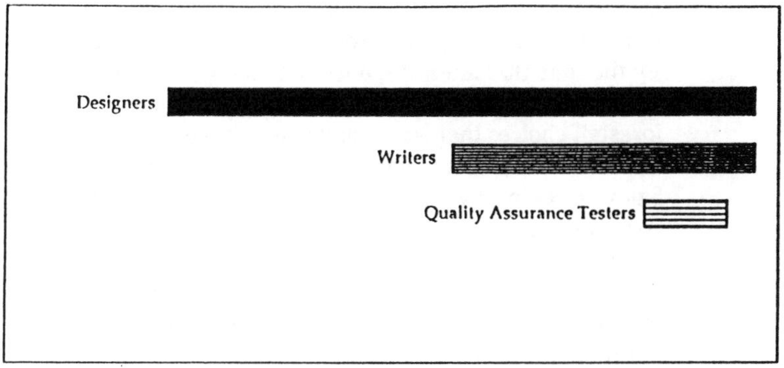

Figure 6-1. The assembly line model of the development process.

In the assembly line model, each department has its separate responsibilities. In the traditional development process, each developer and each writer has his or her own responsibilities and is left to independently create a portion of the total product.

Traditionally, the assembly line for a product focuses first on functionality. The developers work for a long time to create a product that is driven by the possibilities of the technology or, in a company developing products for its own use, by a user department. User-interface reviews and documentation are an afterthought, given to either the programmer as a secondary job or to a writer brought in late in the project.

In the traditional model, users enter the process only in a field test (often called a "beta test") or, more recently, in a late-stage usability test; but because of the timing and the organizational separation, information from the users has little effect on the product.

Despite counterexamples, this model is still the prevalent one in many major American and Canadian companies. It does not foster a focus on users and usability. Redish and Selzer (1985) pointed out that getting companies to conduct even modest usability tests was a management problem. As they said,

> The problem in most businesses and bureaucracies is that the two sets of costs (test it now or fix it later) do not come from the same budget. The manager who must get the manual to the printer on a certain schedule and within a certain cost is not responsible for whatever havoc the manual might cause later on. (p. 51)

Why does this model make it difficult to achieve quality (usability) in documents and other parts of products? Separating the budget for development from the budget for caring for users after the product has been released is one reason. Here are six more reasons.[1]

1. *Development occurs in successive, separate stages.* The product is defined by one group; developed by another. By the time that interface, documentation, or usability specialists are involved, decisions have been made that forestall choices that would have been better for users.

2. *Departments have turf battles over who can talk to users.* Sales representatives or the marketing department may consider the users to be *their* customers. They may be leery of letting developers, writers, or anyone else "from the back room" meet the users. Information received through intermediaries, however, seldom has the same impact as information received directly.

   As we said earlier, one of the greatest benefits of usability testing is that it is an eye-opening experience to many developers and writers who may be seeing actual users, their predictions, and their problems for the first time. After an initial refusal to believe that the users in the test really do represent the people for whom the product (document) is meant, many observers "from the back room" become instant converts to the importance of usability.

3. *Feedback doesn't get to the people who need it.* Help-desk staff, trainers, and sales representatives may hear about users' problems, but the feedback seldom gets to the developers and writers. The people who need to change do not even know that their work has caused problems for users. They have no basis for doing anything different on their next project. The lack of feedback gives developers the myopic view that their product is usable, that they are already in touch with users, and that, therefore, usability testing will only add time and expense to the development process.

4. *Internal competition fosters a lack of mutual respect.* The assembly line model fosters a narrow focus on one's own part of the project. As departments compete for scarce resources, they bolster themselves at the expense of others.

---

[1] Grudin (1991) covers some of the same points in his excellent elaboration of the ways in which the organizational structures of large product development organizations hinder bringing users and usability into the process. He also discusses problems like reluctance on the part of users to get involved, difficulties in identifying the right users to involve, and all the competing and conflicting goals that the people involved in development are dealing with at the same time.

If they have different needs, goals, and languages, they may find it hard to understand and respect each other. A lack of respect for the value and professionalism of others within the company, for example, between development and marketing or between development and documentation spills over to a lack of respect for the user, who may be represented by one of these groups.

5. *Managers are forced to focus on head count rather than on overall budget.* A false sense of economy prevails in many companies where managers live by "head count" or "slots" rather than by overall budget. They must assign programmers to write online help or even print documentation rather than hiring technical writers. Their developers and writers are given minimal training and expected to conduct usability tests, because slots do not exist to hire a trained usability testing staff.

   Managers may not fight the head count problem in part because they do not appreciate the professional status of documentation writers, interface designers, and usability specialists. If "anyone can do that," why worry about more slots to accomplish these tasks? This attitude does not help the user, nor does it help developers who must accept tasks for which they have no training. In a team-based process, multiple roles work, because expertise can be shared within the group.

6. *Usability and documentation are low priorities.* In comparison to other problems that companies have with the development process, the factors that we think of as critical are often forgotten. Companies have major problems meeting schedules, budgets, and functional specifications. They fail to see that even if they achieve the goal of producing a working product on time and within budget, the product will be worthless if people cannot use it effectively and efficiently to accomplish real tasks.

   For example, the United States Department of Defense (DoD) funds the Software Engineering Institute (SEI) at Carnegie-Mellon University in Pittsburgh. One group within the SEI is tasked with solving DoD's problem that few companies developing large-scale software have a well-defined, well-managed process for assuring successful development. This group has developed a very detailed model of how companies need to progress through a series of stages to put management and development discipline and practices in place that will improve the chances of successful software development.

   However, the SEI model defines successful development

only as adhering to schedules, meeting budgets, and producing software that functions according to specifications (Humphrey, 1989). Neither the model nor any of the materials about it even addresses issues of usability or producing useful manuals and online help.

Needed: A Cyclical, Team Model

Is there any hope? Yes. Small and new companies, not burdened by bureaucracy and tradition, are showing the way to focus on usability. For example, Intuit Company of Palo Alto, makers of *Quicken*, one of the best-selling software products on the market, has infused a focus on usability throughout their development process.

According to an article in the April 1991 issue of *Inc.* magazine, everyone in the company takes on multiple roles. Even the President spends a few hours a month answering customer-support calls. A product development manager goes out on "follow me home" assignments, observing new customers in their homes as they install and begin to work with the product. The results are impressive. Intuit has a sales force of just two people; satisfied customers sell the product for them by word of mouth (Case, 1991).

Other isolated examples exist within major American and Canadian companies. Gould and his colleagues were able to apply their four principles in developing an electronic messaging system for the 1984 Olympics (Gould et al., 1987). They were working in a research environment, however, not in a purely development mode. Thus, they were spared the organizational problems we have just outlined and others that Grudin (1991) discusses. For example, they were able to reduce the available functionality of the product as they learned through iterative usability testing that simpler functionality would make the product easier to use.

Even some of the older, larger companies, realizing that the assembly line model does not foster development of usable products, have moved towards some version of a model that has teams working together through iterative cycles as shown in Figure 6-2.[2]

This model is a braid to indicate the interwoven, team approach in which developers, writers, usability specialists, and users work together throughout the process (Redish, 1989). The spiral in Figure 6-2 gives a better picture of the process, because it also shows its cyclical, iterative nature. Although the movement is primarily forward, what the team learns as they assess usability makes them back up and revise throughout the process.

---

[2] In large companies with many corporate sites and business units, change is likely to be uneven. While some products are being developed with some features of usability engineering and a team approach, others are still being developed on the assembly line model.

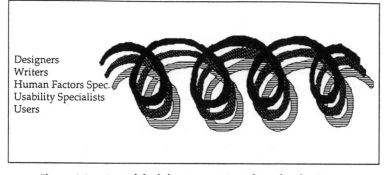

Designers
Writers
Human Factors Spec.
Usability Specialists
Users

Figure 6-2.   A model of the team approach to development.

Using Usability Testing to Stimulate Interest in Usability

Over the past few years, we have worked with many organizations that have been looking for a way to initiate a more systematic approach to usability. Typically, the perception of the need for a focus on usability is uneven within these organizations. A few people are enthusiastic about having a user-driven approach to design, but many more are indifferent or openly skeptical about the value of usability for them.

Any data that are available on either the usability of these organizations' products or the perceptions of usability by users of those products is usually ambiguous. Frequently, there are as many anecdotes about how usability is irrelevant to users as there are about how usability is the key element in decisions to use or buy a product.

When the people who are advocates for usability in such organizations come to us for advice, they want to know how to initiate a usability program. Our advise is that usability testing is the one activity that is most likely to push the organization out of its inertia about designing for users.

Conducting a usability test is often a successful way to stimulate interest in usability within an organization.

People who have been developing complex products but have never systematically watched users set up, learn, or use those products find watching a usability test fascinating, shocking, sometimes humiliating and painful, but invariably eye-opening. They see just how unusable parts of their products are. The experience of attending a test and seeing the quantitative results from a test is often enough to stimulate both a demand for more testing and a discussion about how to improve usability.

What happens after an initial test is run and an organization becomes enthusiastic about improving usability? To get the full benefit of the results of testing, the testing has to fit into the normal product development cycle of the organization. How you do that depends on what your organization is like.

Fitting Usability Testing Into Your Organization

Every organization has a personality. To take two extremes, some organizations are quite formal and hierarchical in their approach to management, while others are quite informal and democratic. While it is always somewhat misleading to generalize, many of the small organizations who are new to creating computer-based products view themselves as more informal and democratic than what they perceive the more established, larger organizations to be.

Every organization falls somewhere on this continuum of management structure. To establish a viable usability testing program in your organization, you need to have a sense for where it falls in this continuum and design an approach to testing that matches the personality of the organization.

We have seen a number of different approaches to integrating usability testing into product development.

There is no single right way to integrate usability and usability testing into product design.

In the cases we have seen, the approach an organization takes to integration mirrors its management style. In addition, the way usability testing *gets started* in an organization is also a function of management style as well as size.

To illustrate the different approaches, we will describe two very different programs that exemplify the extremes of how usability and usability testing fits into product design.

Usability Testing at Ajax Industries

Ajax Industries is a large product development organization that believes in having an organizational structure with clear lines of authority and a design process that is controlled through conformance to specifications. One of this organization's strongest beliefs is that all testing functions must be organizationally separate from design functions.

At Ajax, usability testing is performed by trained, experienced usability specialists. The product managers are required to submit their products to the Usability Lab for testing before the product can be released to beta sites.

The testing specialists take the product from the designers and conduct an independent usability test. While the testing specialists consult with the designers to become familiar with the product and to develop a list of usability concerns, no members of the design team are allowed to become part of the test team. When the test is conducted, the designers are encouraged to attend, but they must watch from a separate room and not interfere with the test team.

After the test is finished, the test team prepares a written report and submits "bug" sheets describing the usability problems with the product. These bug sheets are the same sheets that the people doing the function testing use when they find problems with the program or other deficiencies in meeting the functional specifications. The sheets are submitted to a separate quality assurance group that makes sure that each "bug" is dealt with by the design team. Ajax Industries is proud of its products and its systematic approach to usability testing.

Usability testing started at Ajax as a slow evolutionary process. Jane, one of the people who works in marketing for Ajax, learned about testing from a professional colleague. She became excited about testing and convinced her boss to let her run a small test with one camera and five test participants. She worked on the test while still doing her regular job. The results of the test opened a few developers eyes to just how much their products missed the mark on usability. Jane received approval for a larger test with a more important product. After two years of effort, Jane received approval from upper management to build a lab and recruit a small staff to run tests. The testing program gained momentum and eventually, after many meetings and much coordination, became a formal part of Ajax's development process.

Usability Testing at Omega Industries

Omega Industries is also a large organization that believes that its people are its most important asset. Its management style and structure are very informal. It encourages its people to dress casually and to participate actively in decisions.

Omega Industries uses a process of consensus to make most decisions about technical matters. While the testing specialists are placed in their own group, they reside under the manager of R&D just as the product engineers do. Product managers are encouraged to submit their products for usability testing, but they are not required to do so.

The testing group is small. It does not have enough people to fully staff testing teams. Instead, the testing group uses only one if its specialists per test.

The approach at Omega is that the design team "owns" the product and the test. They decide with the help of one testing specialist what they want to test. They participate as members of the test team, usually taking on the roles of data recorder and camera operator, while the testing specialist serves as test administrator and briefer. (See Chapter 16, "Preparing the Test Team," for more on these roles.)

The design team also "owns" the data from the test and can decide for itself whether it will make changes to the product as a result of the findings from the test. Often, the design team decides that it does not want to spend the time writing a formal test report. With the help of the testing specialist, they document the test results in an informal technical memorandum. Omega Industries is proud of its products and believes that it maintains the loyalty of its people through its democratic management style.

Usability testing was started at Omega at an informal staff meeting on a Friday afternoon. John had heard about usability testing at a professional conference. He mentioned it to Jim, a Senior Vice President. Jim was interested and had John set up a visit to a lab in another company. Two weeks later, Jim approved a small budget for John to start testing and buy some equipment for a lab. Consistent with the style at Omega, the informal lines of communication allowed testing to get started faster, but it never became a formal part of software develoment.

As you work to establish usability testing in your organization, consider how it will fit within the management style of your organization.

Building a Usability Laboratory

As an organization moves into a usability engineering program and conducts some tests, the issue of whether to build a usability laboratory arises. Let's discuss this issue by looking at three questions:

1. Why build a usability lab?
2. When is the right time to build a lab?
3. How do you build a lab, and what does it cost?

Why Build a Usability Lab?

In Chapter 2, we make the point that you do not need a lab to conduct a usability test. We do recommend, however, that you build a lab if you are going to conduct tests on a regular basis. It is much easier to conduct a test and record quantitative data in a lab because

- you can simulate more easily the situation in which users will be using the product alone
- you can mix two or more camera views of the test, allowing whoever is watching the test or a videotape of the test to see more of what is happening
- you can record events with a computer-aided data logger without disturbing the participant
- the members of the test team and visitors can talk about their observations without disturbing the test participant

In addition to the benefits to the test itself, there are additional benefits to having a lab:

- A lab gives a usability program visibility. A lab can be an indicator that your organization is actively committed to improving usability. When people within the organization see the lab being built and used, they recognize that the organization is paying more than lip service to the importance of usability.
- Managers and technical professionals will enjoy tours of the lab, increasing the awareness of usability in the organization. Lab tours are also a good way to make managers more knowledgeable about usability and usability testing. People almost always like to look at equipment and see demos of how the lab works. Managers also can invite their counterparts in other companies to tour the lab and see how committed your organization is to usability.
- The lab can be used for other, related activities. Often space is a scarce resource, so it helps when the space for a lab can be used as much as possible. The nature of testing and of product development is such that there will be gaps between tests. At those times, you can use the space for other activities.
- If the test room is big enough to fit a conference table, you can conduct focus groups in the lab.
- Managers can sit in the lab and use new products or prototypes while they make comments about how using a product feels to them. Staff working on the product can watch in the observation room or view a videotape of the managers' comments and insights.[3]

When Is the Right Time to Build a Lab?

The short answer to this question is that there never is a perfect time to build a lab. There are always many reasons why the space, funds, and time available can be used for other purposes. Product managers, who control product budgets, are often reluctant to spend their project funds for a facility they view as a corporate resource. Consequently, the push to build a lab often comes from outside the R&D segment of an organization, from marketing or senior management.

In the competition for scarce resources, however, there are some times that are better than others for getting approval for funds for a lab . Sometimes a lab is built because there is an important product under development or because products are moving to a new

---

[3] Mary Beth Butler of Lotus Development Corporation told us about this technique.

operating system environment or because there are year-end funds available. The labs we are familiar with have been built for these reasons and many more.

One of the factors that is common among organizations that build labs is that they feel that they have a continuing need to test products. Usually, these organizations have enough products under development that a lab would be overbooked if they tested every product. Building a lab is more questionable when your organization only produces one or two products. There are, however, independent organizations that conduct tests and you may be able to borrow or rent some time in labs that are near you.

How Do You Build a Lab and What Does It Cost?

We have built three labs in our own organization, helped many organizations build labs, and watched as some of our colleagues built theirs. There are almost as many variations in how labs are configured and equipped as there are labs. Consequently, rather than trying to create a set of rules about building a lab that probably would not apply to your organization anyway, we have described, in Appendix A, a sample of labs that are representative of the variety of existing labs. The labs we describe range from low-budget university facilities to facilities that have a suite of more than 10 rooms. For each facility, we show a floor plan and a list of equipment. We also give you an address for each lab so you can contact someone to ask additional questions.

Estimating the total cost of building a lab is difficult, because it depends on factors that vary from organization to organization. Among the factors that influence costs are

- how much space is available—Is there empty space that is not being used or will the space for the lab created by squeezing it from existing facilities?
- the configuration of the space and whether it needs modification
- the status of electric power, air conditioning, sound proofing in the space
- whether the organization has a department that can do or manage the construction
- how your organization depreciates capital investments

Chances are you will have construction costs for relocating walls and for the installation of additional power, air conditioning, and sound proofing.

The audiovisual equipment for a typical lab is the easiest item to estimate. Table 6-1 shows a list of equipment for a lab that has been adapted from Wiklund (1993). You can see that for a modest cost of about $20,000, you can purchase the audio and video equipment for a lab. Because most organizations depreciate capital equipment, the cost of the equipment is usually spread out over a 5-year period.

For most organizations, the largest cost for building a lab is not for construction and equipment but for hiring and training a staff to conduct tests. While the number of people with experience in testing is growing, there is a shortage of people who have the training and experience to conduct a valid test.

Many new labs are started by people who push hard to get their organization moving toward an active usability program. These people may be in documentation, marketing, or engineering groups. They are highly motivated, energetic people, but they typically do not have training in empirical data collection and analysis.

This situation worries us. We hope that university departments that teach behavioral science-based empirical methods will include usability testing in their programs. Usability testing and empirical research are not the same. We question the assumption often made by our university colleagues, that if they teach their students how to conduct laboratory research, the students will, without additional training, be able to conduct usability tests. As we show in Chapter 2, the two methods are only superficially related. The best testers have special training in usability testing to supplement their other skills.

We have completed our discussion on usability and the context of usability testing. We now move on to Part II, in which we discuss the details of how to plan and prepare for a usability test.

Table 6-1.   Audio-visual Equipment Costs for a Typical Usability Lab

Qty	Item	Unit cost	Total
3	13 in. monitor	300	900
1	25 in. monitor		540
4	SVHS editing VCR	1,134	4,536
1	Edit controller		386
1	A/V mixer		2,070
1	Character generator		504
3	Video camera	1,284	3,852
4	AC adaptor	192	68
2	Pan & tilt mechanism	582	1,164
3	8 X lens	486	1,458
2	Camera mount	41	82
1	Camera body (for tripod mount)	342	342
1	AC adaptor (tripod mount camera)		90
1	Tripod		336
1	Editing console		664
1	Assorted cabling		1,316
	Installation and training		700
			$19,708

Part II

Planning and Preparing for a Usability Test

In this part, we describe how to plan and prepare for a usability test. We take you from the initial planning steps for a test to the point at which you are ready to conduct it. It is no accident that this part of the book has the most chapters. Conducting a useful usability test takes planning and attention to detail.

Chapter 7, "Planing a Usability Test," discusses the need for planning and introduces the topics that become the chapters that make up the rest of Part II. We describe how long it takes testing teams with different levels of experience to conduct different types of usability tests.

Chapter 8, "Defining Your Goals and Concerns," discusses the need to make the goals for a usability test explicit. We describe the importance of listing usability concerns for a product or document before you move on to the other steps in planning a test.

Chapter 9, "Deciding Who Should Be Test Participants," stresses the importance of audience analysis. We describe developing user profiles, determining how many groups of participants to test, and deciding how many participants to test.

Chapter 10, "Recruiting Test Participants," discusses the procedures for finding test participants and ensuring that they show up for the test. We describe turning user profiles into qualifying questions, the advantages and disadvantages of the various sources of test participants, and minimizing "no shows."

Chapter 11, "Selecting and Organizing Tasks to Test," discusses selecting tasks that probe the parts of the product you want to test. We describe creating a list of tasks, determining the resources you need for each task, and eliminating tasks when there are too many to test.

Chapter 12, "Creating Task Scenarios," discusses how to transform task lists into the scenarios that the test participants will understand. We describe the importance of describing tasks at the correct level of complexity and including all of the information that the participant will need to attempt the task.

Chapter 13, "Measuring Usability," discusses the range of possible measures and the place of measurement in usability testing. We describe how to understand what you can measure, the options you have to establish quantitative usability criteria, and how to match measures with your usability concerns and test objectives.

Chapter 14, "Preparing Test Materials," discusses the written materials that are used in usability testing. We describe and present examples of the forms, questionnaires, checklists, and product documentation used in usability tests.

Chapter 15, "Preparing the Testing Environment," discusses the preparation of the test and observation areas. We describe preparing the product being tested, arranging equipment and props, and using recording equipment and materials.

Chapter 16, "Preparing the Test Team," discusses the roles that test team members can play during a test. We describe what the roles are and the options there are for mapping people onto roles.

Chapter 17, "Conducting a Pilot Test," discusses the importance of a pilot test and the consequence of not doing one. We describe when and how to conduct an effective pilot test.

In Part III, we describe how to conduct and ensure that improvements are made to the usability of what you test.

7

Planning a Usability Test

In this chapter, we introduce the process of usability testing. We begin by discussing the common question, "How long does usability testing take?" Then we look at the importance of planning, the steps you need to take in planning, and some general principles for planning.

How Long Does Usability Testing Take?

The first question that most clients and managers ask about usability testing is, "How long is all this going to take?"

It is a legitimate question. Time for testing has implications for budgets and schedules. To have iterative testing, each test should take as little time as possible—*while still yielding useful information and without unduly burdening the test team.*

A usability test can take from a few days to a few months.

Clients and managers must also realize that development doesn't stop while testing occurs. Planning, for example, can take place at the same time as development of the prototype or part of the product to be tested. Moreover, companies that follow a usability engineering approach build testing into the budget and schedule so that testing is neither a surprise nor disruptive to the development process.

What Influences The Time It Takes?

The time you'll need will depend on factors like

- how much usability engineering has already gone into the product—how much has already been done to set objectives, analyze users, and analyze users' tasks
- how complex the product is
- how much of the product you are going to test
- how much setting up you need to do—whether you have to arrange for facilities, special equipment, or information for participants to work with
- whether you have a preselected pool of participants to choose from
- how many participants you need to get the information that you want; how much time you need from each participant
- how much training and prior experience the test team has both with the product and with usability testing
- how much experience all the people involved have working together
- how much education, negotiation, and review there needs to be between developers and testers at each stage of the testing process
- how many other tasks the test team and development team are doing at the same time

- how formal a report is required—whether you will prepare a technical memorandum of findings and recommendations or a complete, polished report or just meet with the developers and take minutes of the agreements that are made

How do these factors work together? Let's look at several examples of usability testing from different companies in different situations.

Testing in Many Companies – 8 to 12 weeks

Companies that follow the formal test process often allot 8 weeks or more for a usability test. (Remember that the rest of the project doesn't stop during this time. Product development and test planning go on at the same time.)

At Microsoft, for example, test specialists spend time working with product teams defining the goals and concerns that each test will cover. Test specialists find that these "problem definition meetings" are also educational sessions for the product developers. The test specialists may be raising issues that developers have not yet considered. Thus, it may take a few meetings to reach consensus on the focus of the usability test (Simpson, 1992, personal communication).

Microsoft test specialists also write a formal report and produce an edited, highlight tape for developers. One advantage of producing formal reports is that other test specialists and product developers can have access to the information from previous tests. Reading about previous tests can help developers avoid similar problems in their own products as well as helping test specialists plan and analyze new tests (Dieli, 1992, personal communication).

At Microsoft, test specialists have found that developers are most easily convinced when the testers "talk from data." Taking the time to do careful data analysis is thus an important part of their procedure (Dye, 1992, personal communication).

The Microsoft usability team also does rapid iterative testing of prototypes, helping to find the best implementation of design decisions, on a much shorter time scale. These tests usually focus on just a few features and include about six to eight participants who come for about an hour each. Two usability specialists conduct these tests in about a week (McClintock, 1992, personal communication).

As you increase the number of test participants, the time you need for recruiting and for analyzing data also increases. Hewlett-Packard asked our group at the American Institutes for Research (AIR) to test the documentation for the new version of an operating system. They wanted the test to cover several different manuals and several different groups of users. They were willing to spend the time and effort to have 10 people representing each group and to have a complete report with a highlight tape and a presentation to managers. The test took more than 8 weeks.

Shortening the Test Time – 4 to 6 Weeks

Completing a usability test in less time requires strong collaboration between professional usability specialists and the development team, but refusing to conduct a test because the developers have only a month or 6 weeks to fit the test into their schedule will not make the product easier for its users. Here's how AIR and General Electric Information Services (GEIS) worked together on a 6-week test of a new software product:

Week 1: The testers and designers spent about 3 days working together to determine who participants should be, how many participants to have, what criteria to use in recruiting, what tasks to have them do, and what special arrangements needed to be made.

Rest of week 1 and week 2: While appropriate participants were being recruited, the test administrator became familiar with the product and created the scenarios and questionnaires for the test. One way to reduce the time for testing is for the client to provide lists of appropriate participants or to do the recruiting.

End of week 2: The test team conducted a pilot test. Because the regular testing started at the beginning of the next week, the test team had to make the necessary changes over the weekend. Fortunately, few were needed.

Weeks 3 and 4: Conducting the test took about two weeks. Twelve people participated. Six were potential users of the software. Six were system administrators who set up and configure this type of software. The people in the second group were customers of GEIS. GEIS recruited these customers and made travel arrangements for them.

GEIS also had two members of the development team attend all of the test sessions. They were responsible for handling technical problems that might arise, such as software crashes. (If you do usability testing early, as you should, the software is still being developed; crashes happen.) Having technical people from the development team at the test saved time that we would have spent on the phone with them getting the software working again. They also got to observe the test, which is always good for developers to do.

End of week 4: During the test, the test administrator kept a running list of the problems, always focusing on how specific instances were indicators of more general, global problems. Every day or so, he talked with developers to keep them informed about the major (global) problems that the test team was seeing over and over.

Shortly after the last participant left, the test team met with the development team to go over the list of problems and agreed on ones that the developers could begin to fix right away. If the problems aren't obvious at the end of the testing—and they often aren't—you can still shorten the time by concentrating on getting out a memo of findings and recommendations within two weeks of the test and then writing the more complete formal report later.

Week 5: The test team analyzed the data to confirm the problems they had seen and to see if there were problems that had not been obvious during the test. One team member began the report. You can write the sections on background and methods even before the data analysis is ready.

Week 6: The test team finished the report and made a tape of test highlights.

Many people that we know are starting testing by doing a small-scale, rush job, sometimes taking even less than 4 weeks, and often fitting it in with their other responsibilities. You *can* have a valuable test with real users and real tasks in a couple of weeks. It may mean lots of overtime; it may mean skimping on how many participants, how many tasks, and how much analysis you do. It probably means not writing a full report. But if it convinces managers that usability testing is worthwhile, it may mean that you will get the resources you need to do more in the future.

Testing Small Pieces with Well-established Procedures – About 1 Week for a Test

Some companies have developed procedures for turning around test results very quickly. At WordPerfect, the standard usability test now takes about one week (Young, 1992, personal communication). WordPerfect usability specialists can test that quickly because of this combination of factors:

- In-house usability specialists conduct the tests. They know the procedures and the facilities well; they can quickly understand the implications of what they see users do in a test.
- The specialists are also very familiar with the products that they evaluate.
- Each test covers only one or a few features of a product.
- Specialists know in advance about the features they will be evaluating.
- An experienced recruiter selects participants from a pool of people who have already filled out questionnaires about their backgrounds.
- Participants can do relevant tasks with each feature in a short time. Each participant comes for only about 1 hour.
- The specialists generally write only a short report; they seldom create a highlight tape. The specialist and the developers meet to go over the findings in the short report and agree on what needs to be done.

- Developers have bought in to the importance of usability and accept the findings of the usability evaluations.

This procedure has evolved at WordPerfect over time. They weren't able to do it this way when they first started out; nor is this the only procedure that they use. This procedure focuses only on small additions or changes to existing products. It would be difficult to use such a rapid procedure if you were concerned about larger issues, wanted to test many aspects of the same product, or wanted to see how several features work together. WordPerfect specialists also run longer evaluations when the situation warrants them.

"Just in Time" Testing – 1½ Days
Can you do testing in even less time? Yes, but . . .

We know of one case in which a test was completed in 1½ days. This test was done by an experienced team of five people who worked long hours to test a product at Silicon Graphics Company. An administrative assistant recruited and scheduled participants. A documentation specialist met each participant and conducted the pretest briefings and posttest interviews. A human factors specialist and a documentation specialist conducted the sessions (one each in different laboratory suites). A human factors specialist put the raw data into the computer and ran the analyses.

Dr. Anna Wichansky, who managed the test, notes in her description of it that only someone with extensive experience in usability testing and intense dedication should even attempt to conduct a test in such a short time (Dumas, 1991). From Dr. Wichansky's notes here are some of the factors that made doing the extremely short test possible:

- The team knew ahead of time the problems that engineering and manufacturing were worried about. They could concentrate on those problems when collecting data.
- Everyone on the team had done what they were doing before. Nobody was on a learning curve.
- The Silicon Graphics facilities can accommodate 12 participants per day, 2 at a time for 2 hours each.
- The lab at Silicon Graphics is maintained so that it is working 99.9% of the time. Dr. Wichansky makes everyone, including herself, responsible for making sure the lab is always ready.
- Six of the 12 participants were recruited from a pool of appropriate internal people. Six were recruited by an outside agency that was alerted the day before and that typically finds appropriate participants in 4 hours or less.
- An experienced human factors professional (Dr. Wichansky) was doing dry runs on the data as soon as she coded it into

the computer to make sure that she could get analyses immediately after the last test session.

- The team did not write a formal report. Dr. Wichansky prepared slides showing the results and recommendations (Wichansky, 1991).

Educating Developers and Managers About Time for Testing

It is ironic and unfortunate that when a company first begins to think about usability testing, developers and managers are likely to apply the greatest pressure for fast results and yet none of the features that reduce the time for testing are likely to be in place. Developers and managers may have no appreciation of the time and effort that usability testing takes. The company probably has no usability specialists nor procedures for usability testing. If the product has been developed without a focus on usability, part of the time for testing has to be spent determining who the users are, what tasks they will do, how to recruit them, and how to measure how well the product is doing. A formal report and a highlight tape may be needed to convince the developers and managers of the need to make the changes. The test may uncover an overwhelming number of problems.

Whenever we have to compromise on time because our clients have not started to even plan the usability test until very late in the development process, we take the opportunity to educate them. We point out that if they had an established usability engineering program, they would not have left usability testing until it was almost too late. If they had an established usability engineering program, they would have already worked through many of the planning steps in the testing process. If they had an established usability engineering program, they would have worked on the usability of the product throughout development and would be less likely to find numerous, serious problems in the usability test.

Planning is Critical to a Successful Test

Bringing in "just a few people" to "see how they work with the product" will be a waste of time unless you have thought about

- what aspects of the product might not be as usable as they should be
- how well the "few people" represent the actual users of the product
- what tasks you will have the people do in the short time that they have with the product

Good planning is absolutely necessary for a smooth and useful test. If you skimp on the planning, you will regret it during and after the test.

- what information you are going to collect as you observe these people work with the product
- how you are going to analyze the information that you collect
- what you are going to do with the information once it is analyzed

Planning Involves a Series of Specific Steps

Planning a usability test involves these activities:

- defining the goals and concerns that are driving the test
- deciding who should be participants
- recruiting participants
- selecting and organizing tasks to test
- creating task scenarios
- deciding how to measure usability
- preparing other materials for the test
- preparing the testing environment
- preparing the test team—assigning specific roles, training team members, and practicing before the test starts
- conducting a pilot test and making changes as needed

You can use this as a checklist of steps in planning a usability test. The list is also a table of contents to the next 10 chapters of this book.

Planning Requires Team Work

The planning should be led by a testing professional, but he or she must work closely with others on the team. There are many decisions to be made in planning a test, and the more that all the groups involved on the product team come together in planning the test, the more likely you are to have a useful test.

These people	May Bring This Perspective to Planning a Usability Test
Usability specialists (human factors specialists)	knowing what can be accomplished in a usability test and how to plan one; understanding the interface and potential problems users may have

Designers and developers	understanding the product and the tasks users can accomplish with the product
Technical communicators	knowing which aspects of the documentation should be tried out in a test; understanding potential problems in the ways that the product communicates with users
Trainers	understanding the problems that users are likely to have
Marketing	knowing who the users should be
Help desk or customer assistance	knowing about problems users have with earlier versions or similar products

Planning Must be Managed and Tracked Carefully

Planning a usability test, just like any other part of a development project, needs to be well managed with a quality control system that allows you to schedule activities, assign responsibilities, track progress, and document decisions.

You should at least keep a written log of the decisions that the planning team makes for each of the planning activities. You'll find it useful both for conducting the test and for reporting on the test later.

Writing an actual test plan is also a good idea. Writing the plan forces you to articulate the planning decisions. Sharing the test plan with all the groups who are involved in the project and getting agreement on it helps avoid problems later and builds commitment from the product's owners. The table of contents of Part II of this book could also serve as an outline for a test plan.

The first item in our planning list is "Defining goals and concerns." That's the topic of the next chapter.

8
Defining Goals and Concerns

Most products are far too complex for you to test every group of users and all your concerns at the same time. Even with a simple product, so much happens so quickly in a usability test that if you have not thought about what to focus on, you may miss important events. For each usability test, therefore, you have to start by considering what you want to learn—that is, by defining specific goals and concerns.

Defining goals and concerns makes the rest of planning much easier. All the other decisions—who should participate, what tasks they should try, what data or equipment you will have to set up, what you will measure—flow from understanding what you want to learn.

In this chapter, we discuss

- making choices among goals and concerns
- moving from general concerns to specific ones
- understanding sources of goals and concerns

We also introduce an example that we will use throughout the rest of the book: testing an electronic mail program.

You can begin the planning with goals or concerns or a combination of both.

A goal is usually stated as a declarative sentence, for example, "Users will be able to select the correct icon in less than 30 seconds with no more than one mistake." If the product is being developed in a usability engineering approach, you may have many quantitative usability goals like this one. The point of planning is to decide which are of primary interest for this particular usability test.

A concern is usually stated as a question, for example, "Will users be able to select the correct icon quickly and accurately?" If no one has set quantitative usability goals for the product, you will probably raise questions (concerns) as you plan the usability test. (We'll urge you to define "quickly" and "accurately" before you test. See Chapter 13, "Deciding How to Measure Usability.")

Making Choices Among Goals and Concerns

In planning a usability test, you almost always have to make choices. Here are just two examples:

Is your main concern whether people will use the manual at all, or whether people will find the manual easy when they do use it? It is very difficult to get an answer to both of those questions at the same time. You'll set up the test differently depending on which concern you want to resolve. (See the section on "Testing Different Aspects of the Documentation," in Chapter 2.)

Is your main concern whether new users will be able to get up and running to do basic tasks quickly, or whether users who have had the product for 6 months can figure out more advanced functions? You may be concerned about both, but you'll have to plan two different tests to learn about both.

Moving From General Concerns to Specific Ones

Only by moving from general concerns to specific ones will you be able to actually plan the test. Saying "we want to learn whether the product is easy for users" is a good start, but much too vague. What aspects of the product worry you? Which groups of users are you particularly worried about? What tasks will let you know if those worries are valid? What measures will let you know if the users are in fact having trouble with those tasks?

> Are you worried that new and casual users will have trouble selecting the right icon in your drawing program, for example, the icon for grouping objects? Then you must have users who are new to the program or who use it infrequently as your participants in the test. You must have a task that includes grouping objects—and you may want to instruct participants to do the tasks with the icons and not with the menus. You'll also want to count "wrong icon choices."

Stating general concerns often helps you decide who to have as participants in the test. Making the general concerns more specific helps you decide what tasks to have them do, how to set up the test, and what to measure.

Consider this example from Kay Chalupnik of IDS Financial Services, Inc., an American Express Company in Minneapolis (Chalupnik, 1992):

> The usability testing group that Chalupnik heads was asked to provide data to answer this question: Which of two laptops should the company buy for its sales representatives?
>
> General concern:
>   comparative ease of use of two laptops for sales representatives
>
> In order to know what to test, however, Chalupnik's group had to delineate more specific concerns, which they found by talking with sales representatives. Here are just two of the many specific concerns in this test:
>
> 1. Which laptop makes it easier to learn quickly how to call up and change a client's files?

(Sales representatives don't want to look incompetent in front of clients. Both sales representatives and clients are busy people. For this specific concern, Chalupnik planned tasks to call up a client's file and change it in specific ways. She measured time and errors.)

2. Which laptop is easier to use under typical lighting conditions in the field?
   (The laptops would be used in restaurant offices and even while standing on a street corner. Because she could not simulate the lighting problem in the lab, Chalupnik took the cameras out of the lab and ran the test in actual field sites and street corners.)

Understanding Sources of Goals and Concerns

Both your general and specific goals and concerns can come from several sources, such as:

- task analysis and quantitative usability goals
- timely issues
- a heuristic analysis or an expert review
- previous tests of this or other products

Concerns From Task Analysis and Quantitative Usability Goals

The goals and concerns for a specific usability test should come, at least in part, from the usability engineering techniques that you have already used to plan the product. In that sense, usability testing is a progress report on part of the product—seeing how well you are doing in moving towards a subset of your quantitative usability goals.

Here is an example:

A general goal for the product:	Menus should be easy to navigate through.
Quantitative usability goals for the product:	Users will be able to find the menu choice they want in less than two minutes with no more than two wrong choices the first time they need it. They will remember it correctly (no errors) after the first time and select it in less than one minute.
General concern for this test:	Can users who are transferring to this product from another word processor find the correct menu choices as they need them?

Specific concerns for this test:	Can transfer users add a header to a document? (A later task will have them change the header to test the quantitative goal for selecting the same menu choice again.) Can transfer users adjust the size of a picture in their document? (A later task will have them put a border around the picture to test the quantitative goal for selecting the same menu choice again.)

Concerns From Timely Issues

The issues that worry you and lead you to a usability test are likely to be different, depending on where you are in the process of designing and developing the product. Consider these examples:

- Your company is developing a new product. Members of the development group differ strongly on which of two design philosophies to incorporate into the interface. Resolving the issue with a usability test is far better than spending months arguing about it. The test at this point would be limited to the specific concerns that examined the differences between the two philosophies.
- You did early usability evaluations and user edits of the manual, but it didn't have an index during the earlier tests. The index is now ready and you want to focus in this test on whether users can find what they need in the index. The general concern is whether users can find what they need in the manual by using the index. (Note that you would have to tell users to find the appropriate instructions in the manual by looking in the index before attempting the task. You would also have to be careful about the way that you word the task scenarios. See Chapter 12 on writing scenarios.)

Concerns From a Heuristic Analysis or Expert Review

Most of the specific concerns for a usability test come from thinking about different groups of users and their tasks. Some, however, come from thinking about the product itself.

Any problems that have been predicted by a heuristic analysis or an expert review should be candidate concerns for a usability test. Any problems that the designers themselves are worried about or that others—such as planners, other designers or developers, human factors specialists, or technical communicators—have raised should be candidate concerns for a usability test. Even if there haven't been any earlier analyses or reviews, concerns like these may arise when usability specialists get involved in planning the test.

> Suppose that in looking over the documentation for a new machine that you were going to test, you notice that the part names seem rather technical. The instructions for cleaning and maintaining the machine don't include any pictures. The developers don't think that's a problem. They tell you: "The users all know the parts and these names. It won't take them more than 5 minutes to clean it at the end of each day."
>
> One of the company's general goals, however, is to keep calls for technical support and maintenance to a minimum. If users call because they can't figure out what to clean or because they give up on trying to clean the machine and that makes it need maintenance sooner, that general goal will not be met.
>
> Based on that goal, you might express a strong concern about the assumption that users won't have problems cleaning the machine. That concern would in turn lead to including a task that has participants "do the required end-of-day cleaning" and to measures such as time for the task, calls for assistance, and errors in selecting the right part to clean.

Concerns From Previous Tests

If you are working in a usability engineering approach with iterative testing, your primary concerns may come from earlier tests. If you are doing rapid prototyping, you may be conducting several tests in a row that address the same set of concerns.

Even later in the process when you do more formal, larger scale usability testing, one test may raise concerns that suggest another test. As we will discuss in Chapter 21, "Recommending Changes," even when a usability test has helped you to identify problems, the solutions aren't always obvious. Change is not always an improvement; sometimes you need to retest.

A test may raise concerns that you hadn't realized were important and don't feel that you got enough information about.

> Let's say you've just tested some of the features of a new time management software package. One of the participants expressed much more frustration and took much longer to do the tasks than the others. That participant was the only executive in the group. Your company wants to market this product to executives as well as to managers and support staff, but you don't know if this person was typical of executives. You might plan a second test with five executives, focusing on tasks they are likely to do with the product.

Even in your first test of a product, some concerns may come from tests of other products.

Let's say you are developing a version of your product for a multitasking, multiwindow environment and want your current users to migrate to it. You've heard from other people that in situations like yours, users have been frustrated even trying to start working because they have trouble manipulating the windows. You would probably want to include tasks that have participants work with the windows to see if this is a problem for your users. If you've built solutions into your product to help users overcome the learning curve for working in the new environment, you would be concerned about how well your solutions work for your users.

Introducing Our Ongoing Example: Testing an Electronic Mail Program

Throughout this book you will find examples from a wide range of products. We provide the variety on purpose; we know our readers work in many different fields.

Variety is valuable; so, however, is continuity and consistency. To provide an ongoing thread throughout the book, one of the examples we will use will be of the same product—an electronic mail program.

We chose electronic mail because it is meant for a general user population. It does not require knowledge of any particular technical domain. Furthermore, electronic mail is becoming ubiquitous both in business and at universities. Many of you use it regularly. Many others are at least familiar with the concept.

(If you aren't, think of it as a way to send and receive letters, memos, and other documents through the computer. You don't have to weigh the envelope and buy stamps; you don't even have to worry about envelopes. You can usually send files that you've created outside the electronic mail program along with your messages. You can often send the same message to many people at the same time and type it only once. You do have to somehow be connected to the people with whom you can correspond through a computer network that you can reach by hardwire or by modem.)

The specific product that we discuss here does not actually exist. Our example is an amalgam of many different electronic mail programs we have worked with. The product has a menu-based interface and is used on personal computers that are linked through networks to other personal computers in the same company.

Unfortunately, we have been asked to conduct a usability test of this product at a rather late stage in its development, and very little usability engineering has gone into creating the version we are testing. Here are just some of the general and specific concerns we might list as we begin to plan this usability test:

General concern: Will new users (people who have not seen this particular program before) be able to become productive quickly?

(Although we are also concerned about how easily users will be able to work with some of the more advanced features after they've had the product for some time, we think we should concentrate in this test on making sure that users will be able to do basic tasks quickly. If people don't have success with the product when it is first introduced into a company, they won't continue to use it.)

(As we will discuss in the next chapter on "Deciding Who Should Be Participants," we are concerned both about people who have never used electronic mail and those who have used another program and will be told by the company to switch to this one.)

General concern: Will new users be able to navigate through the menus quickly and easily?

(This concern comes from the general plans for the product as well as from the usability specialist's review. The developers want users to be able to select the appropriate menu items correctly and quickly. The usability specialist predicts that users may have problems because the names on the menus do not appear to be in users' terms.)

Specific concerns about navigation for new users: Will new users be able to find the right menu path to:
   read a message?
   write and send a message?
   respond to a message?
   forward a message?
   save messages and delete them from the list?
   retrieve a message that they have saved and then reply to it?
   set up a distribution list?

Ways to measure concerns about navigation:
   wrong menu choices
   time to complete tasks

General concern: Will new users be able to select items from lists on the screen quickly and easily?

(This is not a concern that the developers originally had. These functions exist in the product. A quick expert review by the usability specialist, however, has raised the concern that the way this functionality works is not the way that most users will expect it to work. Just by asking 10 potential users how they would do this task, even without any prototype, the usability specialist has found that 10 out of 10 gave the same sequence of steps that they would expect to take. That sequence will not work in this product. It will give users a different message from the one they want. It will create a distribution list consisting only of the first name that users select.)

Specific concerns about selecting from lists:
Will new users be able to read a specific piece of mail and skip over mail they don't want to read at this moment?
Will new users be able to select more than one name from a list of

names and addresses when they want to send the same mail to multiple people or when they want to create a distribution list?

Ways to measure concern about selecting from lists:
  selection errors
  time to complete tasks

The actual test might have many concerns, each with several more specific concerns leading to specific tasks and measures. We will return to this list of concerns and add to it as we discuss other planning issues such as "Selecting and Organizing Tasks to Test" (Chapter 11), "Creating Task Scenarios" (Chapter 12), and "Deciding How to Measure Usability" (Chapter 13).

Before we get further into tasks and measures, however, let us return to the issue that is usually addressed in the most general concern: *Who* are you most concerned about? *Who* are you going to have come in to participate in the usability test? *What characteristics* should you use to select participants who will help you to accurately predict the problems that other *real* users will have when they try to use the product? That's what we cover in the next chapter.

9

Deciding Who Should Be Participants

One of the cardinal rules of usability testing is that the people who work with the product in the usability test must be like the people who will actually use the product.

The participants must represent the people who will use the product.

If the product is for office workers, software engineers are not appropriate participants. If the product is meant for experienced oscilloscope operators, students who are just learning oscilloscopes are not appropriate.

As you decide who to have as participants, you'll go through these steps, which we cover in the rest of this chapter:

- developing user profiles
- selecting subgroups for a test
- defining and quantifying characteristics for each subgroup
- deciding how many people to include in a test

Developing User Profiles

Ideally, of course, you or others will have developed a profile of the actual and potential users of the product, long before the time for a usability test. If it hasn't been done, however, you have to do it as one of the first steps in planning the test.

To get useful results from a usability test, you must know the users—and potential users—of the product.

Developing a good profile of users should be a joint effort of the marketing department, usability specialists, and product designers. If this is a new product, the user profile should be based on general market research, on an analysis of the customers of competitors' products, on focus group sessions, and on observing and interviewing prospective users. If you will be testing enhancements to an existing product, the user profile should be based on surveys, focus group sessions, contextual interviews, and usability tests of the current version of the product. These are some of the techniques that we discussed in Chapter 3 in the first part of the book.

Unfortunately, products are sometimes still being designed without a clear understanding of the needs and skills of the people who will use them. In that case, you may have to prepare profiles of the users as you plan the usability test.

Thinking About Relevant Characteristics

In developing a profile of users, you want to capture two types of characteristics:

- those that all users will share
- those that might make a difference among the users

Consider the electronic mail program we are using as our ongoing example. This product is aimed at the corporate, rather than the home, market. The software company that is developing this product has decided that the market they want to aim for is mid- to large-size corporations. When we look for participants for the usability test, therefore, we will want to look for people who work in mid- to large-size corporations and who have reason to communicate often with others in the company.

Some of the companies that are potential customers will be introducing electronic mail to their employees for the first time. Others will be switching employees from another electronic mail product to this one. Therefore, in the usability test, we will want to include some participants who are new to electronic mail and some who have experience with other electronic mail programs.

Other key decisions we have to make about this test are

- whether to include participants who have no experience with computers at all
- whether to include participants who have used only stand-alone personal computers and who have never logged into a network
- whether to include participants who have used terminals connected to a mainframe, but who have never used a menu-driven, personal computer application like this one

The appropriate decisions depend, of course, on the market for the product. We would have to ask for more information about the market.

> In organizations that will be buying this as their first electronic mail product, will many users also be getting on computers for the first time? Will many users be experienced at personal computer applications but be new to the networking environment? Will many users already be adept at other menu-driven products?

When you probe for information like this, don't be surprised if you get fuzzy answers like "It depends" or "All of the above." Keep pressing to find the people who know the market and then to find out the answers to your questions. If, as indeed may be the case, the market includes people in all of these categories, the team has to decide which of these users are your primary concern for this usability test. If this is your first usability test for the product, you may want to focus on "typical" users—those who represent the largest part of the market. If you have already tested with "typical" users, you may have a particular concern for users who represent a smaller part of the market.

Deciding Which Factors Matter Most

In our work, we have found that specific, relevant experience and motivation matter more for understanding differences in how people interact with products than do demographic factors like education, income level, and age. Most products that we test are designed for people with average physical and mental abilities. Of course, if the product is meant for a population with special characteristics, such as an educational program for children, a service for the elderly, or a teletype machine for hearing-impaired people, you would make the relevant demographic characteristics an important part of the user profile.

Here are some of the factors to consider in developing a profile of a product's potential users:

- work experience, such as:
  - job description
  - length of experience on the job
  - length of experience with the particular tasks that the product handles
- general computer experience, such as:
  - length of experience working with a computer
  - types of applications used
  - length of time using each application
  - frequency of using each application
- specific computer experience, such as:
  - length of experience with specific, relevant hardware (mouse, function keys, pen-based, etc.)
  - frequency of experience with that hardware
  - length of experience with the relevant operating system (UNIX, Windows, Macintosh, etc.)
- experience with this product, such as:
  - length and frequency of using basic features
  - length and frequency of using advanced features
- experience with similar products, such as:
  - length and frequency of using basic features
  - length and frequency of using advanced features

Thinking Broadly About Users

As you develop profiles of the users, we urge you to *think broadly*. Here are four examples of what we mean by thinking broadly about users:

1. Don't just consider people who are now doing this job. Think about job turnover and new hires. In most companies, although a job description remains the same for many years, the people who actually do that job change frequently. What's the rate of turnover in the job that this product is meant to handle?
2. Don't limit yourself to the current market. Growth for most companies means getting more people to accept and use the

product. Who are these new people, in terms of the characteristics that you have said might make a difference in how
easy the product is to use or learn?

3. If you are developing an internal product, don't necessarily
limit yourself to the group for which the product is being
developed. Think about future expansion. What other
groups in the company might be using this product a year
from now? Would it ever become an external product, and,
if so, who would be the market for it?

4. Think about differences within a category. For example,
experienced workers and novice workers may have very
different reactions to a new product.

On the one hand, if the product is structured by the tasks of
the job or is similar to something they have used before,
experienced workers may find the product easy to use,
while novice workers may find it difficult.

On the other hand, if the product is introducing a new
interface or is changing the way that the job has been done,
experienced workers may have a more difficult time with it
than novices. If the novice workers are also younger, they
may have more experience with computers in general and
less fear or reluctance to try new methods.

As you plan the usability test, plan to include participants from both
ends of the range of each category that you choose to include.

At the end of this chapter, you'll find a form called "Developing a
user profile." You'll also find two filled-out examples of the form with
explanations.

When you understand who the users are and have thought about
which characteristics might make a difference in the usability test
results, you have to decide how to group people for the test and
which subgroups of users to include in the test. That's the topic of the
next section.

Selecting Subgroups for a Test

A subgroup is composed of the people who share specific characteristics that are important in the user profile. For our electronic
mail example, one subgroup might be people who have previous
experience using electronic mail.

Dividing Users into Subgroups

As you add and combine characteristics, the number of subgroups
that you have grows very quickly. To understand how this works,
let's consider a different example.

Suppose the product you are going to test is a billing system for law offices. The billing system will be used by both lawyers and their secretaries, and you believe they may have different reactions to the product. At this point, you have two subgroups:

1. lawyers
2. legal secretaries

You believe the product's acceptance and ease of use is going to depend on how comfortable the person already is with computers. Adding that characteristic at two levels of experience gives you four subgroups:

1. lawyers with "a lot of" computer experience
2. lawyers with "very little" computer experience
3. legal secretaries with "a lot of" computer experience
4. legal secretaries with "very little" computer experience

You will have to define what you mean by "a lot of" computer experience and what you mean by "very little" computer experience. We'll come back in a moment to the problem of defining levels within a particular characteristic.

Adding Another Characteristic
Let's continue thinking about the relationship between different characteristics and the number of subgroups. Suppose that you also decide that previous experience doing billing might make a difference in the product's acceptance and ease of use. If you were to add that characteristic to the usability test, you would have eight subgroups to test:

Lawyers with:
1. a lot of computer experience and also experience in billing
2. a lot of computer experience but no experience in billing
3. very little computer experience but with experience in billing
4. very little computer experience and no experience in billing

Legal secretaries with:
5. a lot of computer experience and also experience in billing
6. a lot of computer experience but no experience in billing
7. very little computer experience but with experience in billing
8. very little computer experience and no experience in billing

You can see that the number of subgroups increases exponentially as you add each new characteristic. Adding a fourth characteristic with two levels would give you 16 subgroups.

Selecting the Most Critical Characteristics

You are likely to have the time and money to include only two to four subgroups in a test. You usually have to select the one or two characteristics that are most relevant to your goals and concerns.

Some subgroups may be less critical to your goals and concerns than others. For the new billing system, you might be most concerned about lawyers who are new to computers. If budget or time constraints forced you to have fewer subgroups than you would like, you might decide to make a painful tradeoff and not include experienced computer users in your test, even though you realize that usability problems that affect only experienced computer users may not show up in the test. Having a usability expert review the product from the experienced computer user's point of view might make the tradeoff less painful.

Gathering Other Information

You can—and should—gather information about the other characteristics. If you find anomalies in the test data, you can look back at your information on each test participant and see if one of the other characteristics helps to explain the anomalies.

Let's say that you decide to run the usability test of the legal billing software with groups divided by job description and computer experience. When you analyze the results, you find that one of the computer-experienced lawyers found the product much easier to use than the others in that subgroup. You look back at the information you gathered on each test participant and find that the other lawyers had never done their own billing, but this lawyer had been billing her clients herself for many years. That experience in billing might explain the differences in the behavior that you observed.

You'll have that other information about each participant if you ask for it either on a survey form that you use as you recruit or on a pretest questionnaire that you give each participant when he or she arrives for the usability test. (You'll find an example of a survey form for recruiting in the next chapter on "Recruiting Participants." You'll find an example of a pretest questionnaire in Chapter 14 on "Preparing Test Materials.")

Defining and Quantifying Characteristics of Each Subgroup

To decide who fits into your subgroups, you have to define and quantify each characteristic for each subgroup. In our example of the billing system, you have to decide what to count as "very little computer experience" and as "a lot of computer experience."

You might define *computer experience* to mean "uses a personal computer with business software" and "very little" as "none to three months worth" and "a lot of" as "at least 1 year." This distinction would be based on your belief from interviews and observations that someone who has used a computer for only up to three months is still learning about using it, while someone who has been using a computer for a year or more understands most of the keyboard and screen conventions. You could also define computer experience by the number of different applications used or by frequency of use rather than by time, if either of those criteria is a better indicator of experience for users of your product.

Leaving Out "Intermediate" Users

Note that these definitions of "very little" and "a lot of" leave out a middle group. People who have used the computer regularly for more than 3 months but less than 1 year would not fit into either category. You would not select them as participants in this test.

For many categories, you could set three or more levels of experience. For "length of time using a computer," you could say that relevant subgroups would be:

novice	0 to 3 months
intermediate	more than 3 months, less than 1 year
experienced	more than 1 year

Selecting participants from the extremes of the range for a particular characteristic will often give you more useful information than selecting from the middle.

If you cannot include 3 to 5 people from each of these subgroups in your test, however, we suggest that you drop the middle group.

If you find that participants from both the novice and experienced subgroups have the same problem, you will feel comfortable generalizing that intermediate users are also likely to have that problem.

Selecting a Range of Participants Within Each Subgroup

Even within each subgroup, you will find a range of potential participants. If you set a requirement of at least 1 year of personal computer experience, you may well find participants who have much more experience than that. Try to get a range of people within the subgroup. If all of your participants have close to 1 year of experience, you may be missing what will happen when the product gets to people who have 5 years of experience.

Setting a Minimum and Maximum for a Subgroup

For some tests, you may want to exclude people at the extreme of a subgroup. You might want to set both a minimum and a maximum requirement for a particular subgroup.

Let's say that your concern is how easily the Windows version of a spreadsheet will be for people who have been using that program in a DOS environment. You are particularly concerned about "typical," "average" users, not about "hackers" or "power" users. One of your subgroups might be people who have used the program at least 3 times a week for 6 months or more in a DOS environment. That would be your minimum requirement. To define and separate the "typical" or "average" user from the "hacker" or "power" user, you might say that you will exclude participants who have *created*, not just used, macros in this spreadsheet program.

Deciding How Many People to Include in a Test

The issue of how many participants you need in a usability test is one of intense interest and discussion in the usability community. Remember that a usability test is not a research study. The purpose of a usability test is to uncover the most serious problems that users are likely to have with a product.

Nielsen and Molich (1990) found that not quite half of all major usability problems were detected with three participants. Virzi (1992) found that 80% of the usability problems in a product were detected with between 4 and 5 participants and 90% were detected with 10 participants. In addition, all of the *global* problems in the product he tested were detected with 10 participants. Additional participants were less and less likely to reveal new information.

The number of people to include as participants in a test depends on

- how many subgroups you need to satisfy your goals and concerns
- how much time and money you can get for the test
- how important it is for you to be able to compute statistical significance for your results

Most of the time, you will not want to use inferential statistics, that is to measure results to a particular level of confidence and range of error in a statistical test. However, if an entire product line hinges on what you are testing, or if the product represents a particularly large investment, the company may want to include enough participants for you to use statistical tests of significance. (See Chapter 20, "Tabulating and Analyzing Data," for more on the place of inferential statistics in usability testing.)

A Typical Test Includes 6 to 12 Participants

A typical usability test now includes 6 to 12 participants in two to three subgroups. As you can see from Nielsen and Molich's and Virzi's results, you need 3 to 5 participants in each subgroup to feel comfortable that you are seeing the problems. Three participants for each subgroup is probably an absolute minimum. With fewer people in a subgroup, you won't know if you are seeing idiosyncratic behavior or something that is likely to generalize across the subgroup. Even if you are testing an early prototype, you should still plan on at least 3 people representing each type of user.

You See the Same Problem Many Times

With 3 to 5 people in each subgroup, you are likely to see enough to feel comfortable with the conclusions that you reach. After you've seen several people make the same mistake, you don't need to see it a 10th or 20th or 50th time. You'll know that you've uncovered a problem. Moreover, when an interface has global problems, you will see the same problem many times with each participant.

> If a menu hierarchy is poorly structured, you are likely to see each participant fail several times to find the correct option. Although the option the participant is looking for may differ from task to task, the problem will be the same—the user's assumption about where to find the option does not match the hierarchy that the designers built.

You may see some problems that are common to and confined to one of your subgroups. After all, you divide users into these subgroups for testing *because* you are concerned that they will have different problems or that one subgroup will have a problem where another does not. However, you are likely to also see many problems that cut across your subgroups. In many situations, your quantitative data will show that all or almost all the participants, regardless of their background, had the same problem.

You Have to Balance Time, Money, and Information Gained

Time and money, unfortunately, most often determine the number of participants in a usability test. Because most usability tests are conducted 1 participant at a time, and a typical test session lasts half a day, a test with 10 participants takes a week of lab time. More participants obviously means more time in the lab. Having more participants may also increase the time you need for recruiting and the time you need to analyze the results.

Some teams do shorter tests, particularly when they are testing prototypes. They have 3 to 6 people a day, for 1 to 2 hours each. That way, they can complete the observing and recording part of the test in a shorter time or watch more people working with the product. Be careful, however, not to overwhelm the test team, particularly if they are new to usability testing. Being in the laboratory with the participants is very intensive, often very tiring, work.

The determining factors in how many people to include in a usability test should be not only time and money, but also the number of subgroups that you need in order to cover all the important characteristics that differentiate groups of potential buyers and users.

Deciding how many participants to include is always a balancing act. On the one hand, you want results quickly and at minimal cost. On the other hand, you want to be sure that what you are seeing is typical of what will happen to the product when it is released. To make the most of the limited number of participants in a typical usability test, you must

- decide carefully which characteristics are the most important so that you define subgroups that will be most useful
- collect other relevant information to help you account for other differences that show up in the results
- select people for each subgroup who are representative of the full range of qualifications for that subgroup

In this chapter, we've looked in detail at the first two of these items. We'll cover more about the last item in the next chapter on "Recruiting Participants."

Examples of Forms to Help in Developing User Profiles

The following pages contain examples of:

- a blank form for developing a user profile for a usability test (Figure 9-1)
- two filled out examples of the form (Figures 9-2 and 9-3)
- an explanation of each example

Developing a user profile for a usability test

1. Product name: _____

2. General characterization of the user population:

   _____

   _____

3. Characteristics of the users that are relevant to the test:

   _____

   _____

   _____

   _____

4. Which of the characteristics that you listed in 3. should all
   users in the test have in common and how will you define them?

   _____

   _____

   _____

5. Which of the characteristics that you listed in 3. will vary
   in the test and how will you define them?

   _____

   _____

   _____

Figure 9-1. Sample form for user profiles for a usability test

Developing a user profile

1. Product name: `New billing software`

2. General characterization of the user population:

> `lawyers and`
>
> `their secretaries or office managers`

3. Characteristics of the users that are relevant to the test:

> `computer experience`
> `job experience`
> `billing experience`
> `other database experience`

4. Which of the characteristics that you listed in 3. should all users in the test have in common and how will you define them?

> `lawyer in private practice for at`
> `least one year`
>
> `legal secretary or office manager for`
> `at least one year for lawyers in`
> `private practice`

5. Which of the characteristics that you listed in 3. will vary in the test and how will you define them?

> `computer experience`
>
> `"very little" = 0 to 3 months`
>
> `"a lot of" = 12 months or more`

Figure 9-2.   A user profile for a test of Legal Sofware's billing system

Explanation of the Example in Figure 9-2

Legal Software is developing a new billing system for law offices. They come to The Testing Laboratory (TTL) to find out how usable their new product is. Working with the designers from Legal Software, usability test specialists from TTL identify the market for Legal Billing as all lawyers who bill clients and their legal secretaries or office managers (Question 2).

Thinking about the way that people will use Legal Billing, TTL specialists and the client decide that acceptance and ease of use of the product may depend on factors like other computer experience, whether they already use a billing system, experience with other software of the same genre (databases), and how much experience they have at their jobs (Question 3).

Because Legal Software is particularly concerned about whether the product will be better accepted and used by lawyers or their secretaries/office managers, the team decides to include a group of each and then defines the characteristics that will put a person in one or the other of those groups (Question 4).

Legal Software wants their product to be useful even to people who may buy a computer just to use this product. Therefore, they are very much concerned about how much prior computer experience is needed to make these users comfortable with the product. The test team decides to form subgroups based on computer experience (Question 5).

Legal Software is also concerned about whether people who don't now handle their own billing will find their product so easy to learn and use that they will switch to it. However, they cannot afford to have more subgroups, so TTL agrees to ask questions about experience in billing in a pretest questionnaire. They'll also ask questions about the other factors that they identified in Question 3.

Explanation of the Example in Figure 9-3

You are developing our example electronic mail software. You are especially concerned about introducing this software in mid- to large-size companies and being sure that decision makers who have to communicate will find it easy to use. You want to capture both the market of users who are new to electronic mail and those whom you can convince to switch from another product to yours (Question 2).

You decide that the characteristics of users that are relevant to this usability test are

- size of the company (number of employees)
- job level of participants (managers or not)
- experience using electronic mail software
- computer experience
- experience using applications in a networking environment (Question 3)

To focus on decision makers in the companies that are your primary market, you will include only people who work in organizations of at least 50 people and who manage at least 2 other people (Question 4).

The resources that you have for the test will only cover 10 participants. You can only have two subgroups of 5 participants each. You will have a group of "novices" defined as "managers who have

---

Developing a user profile

1. Product name: E-mail

2. General characterization of the user population:

   employees in mid- to large-size
   companies with local area networks

3. Characteristics of the users that are relevant to the test:

   size of company
   role in company (managers)
   experience with electronic mail
   experience with computers
   experience with networks

4. Which of the characteristics that you listed in 3. should all
   users in the test have in common and how will you define them?

   size of company: 50 or more people

   role: manager of at least two people

5. Which of the characteristics that you listed in 3. will vary
   in the test and how will you define them?

   electronic mail experience
        "novice" = none
        "experienced" = used 6 months or
        more

   networking experience
        "novice" = none
        "experienced" = used 6 months or
        more

Figure 9-3.   A user profile for a test of our electronic mail example

never used an electronic mail program and who have no experience
using a computer in a networking environment." You will have a
group of "experienced users" defined as "managers who have used a
different electronic mail program in a networking environment for at
least 6 months" (Question 5).

10

Recruiting Participants

Once you have decided which groups of users to include in the test, you have to find users from each of those groups and convince them to come. In this chapter, we discuss:

- finding appropriate participants—including the pros and cons of using company employees for usability tests
- building a database of qualified participants
- reaching and screening potential participants
- deciding who should recruit participants
- planning how many calls it will take to find a participant
- knowing when to recruit
- knowing what to say when you are recruiting
- arranging for payment or other incentives
- making sure that participants show up
- having a back-up—but not double booking

Finding Appropriate Participants

Testing with the wrong participants can lead to two types of problems:

The more closely participants represent actual users, the more useful your test will be.

- If the participants are more experienced than the actual users will be, you may be lulled into a false sense of security. Novice computer users working with a product at home may have much lower tolerances for vague messages or difficult-to-use screens than your fellow employees who have worked with computers for a long time.

- If the participants don't have as much experience as your users will, you may see more problems than you actually need to deal with. If you are developing accounting software and have accounting terms in your menus, but you test with the general public, you may see more wrong menu choices than you would with the correct audience.

The first of these two situations is much more common. We find that companies often test with people who are more experienced than actual users. They still see many problems, but they don't see all the problems that are going to plague the actual users.

Where Should You Go To Find Participants?

Sometimes the product leads you to very specific sources:

For this type of product	*Look to this source*
travel reservation system	travel agencies
bank teller system	banks
new version of existing operating system	customer lists
medical office software	phone lists of local doctors' offices

In each of these cases, the source is the appropriate place to go for people with at least some experience. If you also want to test with people who have very little experience, you will have to ask for new people in these jobs or go to another, outside source such as a temporary agency. If you want to sell the new version of an existing operating system only to old customers, customer lists are the best source to use. If you also want to sell the new version to people who have been using a different system, you won't find those people on the company's list of customers.

Going to the places where people now do the jobs that your product handles will provide you with appropriate participants. These people are likely to be familiar with the tasks that you'll be asking them to do. They're also likely to be excited about your new product and eager to try it out.

The only down side to using people from actual job sites is that it may be difficult to schedule them for the test time. You need to help them convince their supervisors that letting them participate in the test will bring benefits to their company. Be prepared to tell the people you are recruiting about benefits like getting an early view of a new product, being able to give feedback to the developers about a product that they will be using, and having a special relationship between their company and yours.

Should You Use Company Employees?

If your product is strictly for internal use, company employees are the users—and, therefore, the right participants. Even in that case, you might also consider how much turnover there is in the jobs affected by the new product. If you want to stay inside the company for an internal product, you might work with the Personnel Office to get new employees as participants. If you can go outside, consider having both employees and outsiders who represent potential new employees, with the outsiders coming from a temporary agency.

If your product is not for internal use, company employees are usually not the best participants. Here are some of the reasons people often cite for using company employees and some thoughts about those reasons:

- tighter security for an unreleased product
BUT:
> You can have outsiders sign a confidentiality agreement. People who come to you through a temporary agency will be checked out by the agency, although you may have to emphasize the confidentiality issue when you set up the recruiting with the agency.
- lower costs
BUT:

The costs may actually be higher. Consider the cost to the company of the time the person spends in the lab rather than at his or her regular job. And you often must still provide some incentive to employees. This may be additional money, or a gift certificate, or bonus points, if your company has a bonus system.

- recruiting is easier

BUT:

You will have to work with managers to get released time for the participants. It may be more difficult to recruit through union rules or the company's hierarchy than to go outside.

The most serious reason for not using company employees, however, is still that employees may not represent the actual users. Even if the employees are new to the particular product, they may know too much about similar products. You may unwittingly be using company jargon in the product, and employees, even from other departments, may be perfectly comfortable with that jargon. You won't find out whether the product's language is going to baffle the outside users whom you want as customers.

Research issue: Are employees more or less likely to be critical of a product than participants from outside the company? Several testers who use company employees as participants believe employees are more willing to be critical than people from outside the company. Employees understand that everyone has a stake in making the product usable before it goes on the market. (We should mention that these testers generally work for large companies. They recruit participants who are not part of the product team and who qualify as users in all other respects.)

We are divided in our own perceptions on this question. We have seen both insiders and outsiders be unduly kind to products. We have seen both insiders and outsiders give products high ratings even when they have struggled and verbalized their frustrations. Telling them that we are not the product developers but a neutral third party and are honestly seeking their criticisms doesn't seem to make a difference.

In any case, the real issue with using employees should not be comments but behavior. If employees have an easier time with the product than the external user will, the usability test won't tell you what you need to know.

Where Else Can You Go to Find Participants?

Four methods you can use to find participants are

- working with temporary agencies
- advertising
- networking
- working with professional associations

Working with Temporary Agencies

You can recruit many groups of people through agencies by finding an agency that places the type of people you need. Working with different temporary agencies, we have successfully recruited

accountants	legal secretaries
bookkeepers	nurses
computer network managers	office workers
engineers	paralegals
lawyers	programmers

Working with a temporary agency has several advantages:

- They do the screening, which saves you a great deal of time.
- They find people for your different subgroups. You tell the agency the specific qualifications that you need, and their job is to find people with those qualifications.
- You pay the agency, so you aren't dealing with paying several individuals.
- If someone doesn't show up, the agency has an obligation to find a replacement immediately.
- People who work through temporary agencies are used to doing different jobs on different days. An assignment for half a day won't bother them. For many, coming to the lab is an exciting opportunity and a welcome break from their normal routine.

When you work with an agency, you pay for the participant's time just as you would if you used the agency to hire the person to do a regular job. If you need skilled programmers to be your participants, you pay for a half day of each programmer's time just as you would if you had the person come in to do programming.

Although it may seem expensive, the cost of paying an agency to recruit for you is usually a bargain. Most agencies charge about 33% above the cost of the participant's time. That means you pay $133 when the participant gets $100. This added cost is minor compared to the cost you would have incurred recruiting qualified participants.

You often have two ways to pay an agency: a fixed price for each participant, or a fee over what it cost to pay the participants. It is generally better to use the cost-plus-fee method, because you get a wider range of qualified people. With fixed price, the agency has an incentive to find you people who are just barely qualified, so they can maximize the amount they make on each participant. If you are concerned about controlling the cost of what you will pay, you may agree on an upper limit.

You must be careful in dealing with agencies, however. In our experience, they tend to be overly optimistic about the number and quality of the people they can recruit for you. They do, generally, have many contacts, but some will already be busy and others won't qualify. If they tell you they can find you 10 people, the actual number will be closer to 5.

Moreover, some agencies specialize in placing people for long periods of time. They do not want to spend time recruiting people for half a day. You must have a cooperative agency. Scout around until you find one that wants the job.

You must give the agency a list of the qualifications the participants must have. Give it to the agency *in writing* and make it clear to them that you will not accept participants who show up, but who are not qualified.

The most important issue you will have to deal with in working with an agency is not cost; it is ensuring that you get qualified participants.

In one study in which we were testing a manual for C language programmers, we informed the agency that the participants had to have at least one year of C programming. One day the agency sent a participant who turned out to be a writer who had prepared manuals for applications written in C, but who was not a programmer. We refused to accept this person for our test and told the agency we would not pay for her time. Because we had made our requirements clear to the agency, we had no problem resolving this misunderstanding.

Another possible problem in working with an agency is the issue of confidentiality. If the product is confidential, emphasize this in your discussion with the agency before they start to recruit. Show them the form that you will have people sign. Emphasize that they must tell people that they will have to sign this form and will have to agree not to talk about the product to anyone.

You must also make sure that the agency tells the participants that they will be coming to participate in testing a product, not to do more traditional work. You do not want participants to be surprised when they arrive for the test.

Advertising

You can use ads in local papers, on university, supermarket, or electronic bulletin boards, or in newsletters of specific groups to attract participants. This may be an effective way to reach a wide range of people at minimal cost.

One group we know was testing a product that will be offered through an online dial-up service. They arranged with the service to put a notice about their test on the service's bulletin board. Interested people could send the company back a note through the online service.

Advertising may have several disadvantages:

- It's slow. It may take 2 to 4 weeks to get the number of people that you need through an advertisement.
- The security is looser than with other methods because you are spreading word of your product more widely.
- You may have to do more to make sure that people show up than you would with other methods.

Networking
An inexpensive way to get participants, especially for a product meant for the general public, is to use your personal networks. But again, be wary of skewing the results by getting people who know company jargon because they hear their spouses use it, who won't be critical even when something goes wrong because they know you and don't want to hurt your feelings, or who don't really represent the range of users that you should be involving in the test.

Working with Professional Associations
If your product is for a particular profession, working with the local chapter of the relevant professional association may be your best source of participants. They may be willing to share their membership list, announce your need at a meeting, or put information about your usability test in their newsletter.

Building a Database of Qualified Participants

Whichever route you take to find participants, consider building a database of people who might be appropriate for the types of usability tests that you do. You can collect relevant information about potential participants when you are not as rushed as you will invariably be during each usability test. Then, you can select appropriate people from your database to recruit for each test.

Reaching and Screening Potential Participants

Once you've decided where to find a pool of appropriate participants, either for a particular test or to set up a database of people for many tests, you have to have a way to reach those people and screen individuals to be sure that they fit the profile of users you want as participants. If your test plan includes subgroups, your screening also has to let you put each person into the appropriate subgroup. Typically, you create a questionnaire for this screening. The questionnaire can be filled out by a potential participant or be used by a recruiter over the phone.

Four Ways to Reach and Screen Participants

You can combine reaching, screening, and recruiting potential participants in at least four ways:

1. If you have a large pool of potential participants, especially if you have lead time and will be doing several tests, you may want to send out letters and questionnaires as the first step in recruiting.

   > A group that develops and tests software for the travel industry contacts many travel agencies in a certain geographic area as the first step in recruiting. When they get back filled-out questionnaires, they follow up with phone calls to people who seem to be appropriate participants.

   This is a relatively inexpensive way to gather names of many potential participants. People who aren't appropriate for this test might be for a future test and could be contacted later. This method assures that participants are interested volunteers and saves the time of making many calls to people who aren't interested or whose employers won't let them participate.

2. A variation on that theme is to separate the questionnaire from the initial letter in which you try to interest potential participants. If an electronic mail system is an appropriate way to reach potential participants, you might want to first get the names and e-mail addresses of people who are interested and who meet some very general requirements. You would then send the questionnaire only to those who express interest.

3. You may not have the time or the need to gather names of a pool of potential participants before you start to screen. If you are working with a temporary employment agency, the pool of participants are the people who are signed up with that agency. The agency does the screening, usually by telephone, but you have to give the agency detailed requirements or a screening questionnaire and instructions for using it.

If you already have names of potential participants, for example, from your database, or from a client's customer list, or from the membership list of the local chapter of a professional association, the people on that list make up your pool of potential participants. The person on the test team who is going to recruit the participants needs the screening questionnaire and instructions. The screening is done by telephone.

4. Another variation on the theme is to get out a message that has interested people contact you, as in situation #2. Instead of sending the questionnaire, however, you screen and recruit them by telephone, as in situation #3.

What to Put in an Introductory Letter
The main purpose of an introductory letter or message, whether it goes with the questionnaire or precedes it, is to get people interested in the test. In your introductory letter, tell people about

- the type of product—so they can see why they would be relevant participants in your test
- the environment—that it is a lab with video cameras and that you'll ask them to think out loud as they work
  You want to make this point to avoid surprises when the participants see the facility and to avoid recruiting people who are just too shy to become comfortable in the lab setting.
- how long the test will last
- the incentive—how much you will pay them or what you will give them for participating

At the end of the chapter, you'll find a sample introductory letter.

What to Ask on a Screening Questionnaire
Whichever technique you use, you should write out a questionnaire that will help screen participants to see if they match the user profiles you've set for the usability test. The questionnaire that you construct will differ depending on whether potential participants fill it out themselves and send it in or someone uses it to screen and recruit participants over the phone. In the former case, you usually send the same, entire questionnaire to everyone. In the latter case, you usually develop the questionnaire so that the screener/recruiter follows branches depending on the potential participant's answers. At the end of the chapter, we give you examples of both types of questionnaires.

In either case, your two primary goals for the questionnaire are to

- find out quickly if an individual is an appropriate test participant
- put the individual into the appropriate subgroup

You may have as a third goal to get information about the items on the user profile that you thought might be important, but that you did not use as the conditions for forming your subgroups. However, you can also wait and collect this information on a pretest questionnaire when the participants come to the usability test laboratory. See Chapter 14, "Preparing Test Materials."

Keep the screening questionnaire as short as possible to save time for both you and the people you are trying to recruit. The following are some guidelines for a screening questionnaire:

1. Ask only what you need to know.
2. Ask specific questions. If you set up subgroups for your test based on the amount of experience that a person has had with a particular situation, ask about that situation with choices that match your criteria for subgroups.
3. In a screening questionnaire to be used over the telephone, ask questions in an order that allows the recruiter to stop when the person's answers indicate that he or she is not an appropriate participant for your test.

If you are sending out questionnaires that have to be returned to you, expect a return rate of 10 to 25%. And remember that only some of the people who return the questionnaires will actually meet your criteria.

Deciding Who Should Recruit Participants

The recruiter should be someone who

*   understands usability testing
*   is enthusiastic about the test

If you are working with a temporary agency, meet with the agency recruiter and get that person knowledgeable and excited about the test. Invite the recruiter to see the lab at the same time that you go over the screening questions together. If the team that is planning the usability test is also doing the recruiting, choose someone on the team who likes to talk with people.

Planning How Many Calls It Will Take to Find a Participant

If you are doing the recruiting yourself, consider how many calls you'll need to make. Here are some of the factors that influence that number:

1. The more specialized skills and experience you need, the more calls you should expect to make. An engineer who manages a local area network is going to be more difficult to find than someone who has used an answering machine with a home telephone.
2. When you specify more criteria or more stringent criteria, you'll need to make more calls. An engineer who has managed a local area network with a token ring configuration for at least six months is going to be more difficult to find than someone with any background who has worked with any kind of local area network for any length of time.
3. If you do not have help in limiting the search, you'll need to make more calls. If the participants should be people who already use a particular software package, having a list of customers would make the search much more efficient, and, therefore, less time-consuming and less expensive than calling people without such a list. If you are recruiting from questionnaires that potential participants have returned or from your own database of prequalified participants, you should be able to recruit with a minimal number of calls.

These factors can act together. If you have to find nurses with at least six months experience in an intensive care unit, you might have to make 10 to 15 calls to find each one. However, if the client already has a list with the names of nursing supervisors at intensive care units in the local hospitals, you might be able to reduce the number of calls to find each participant to only 4 to 6.

We have found that it takes between 4 and 15 calls to find each qualified participant for most tests. For very difficult recruiting situations, in which we have stringent criteria for highly skilled people and no help in getting to the right people, we have sometimes had to make as many as 20 or 30 calls to get each qualified participant.

Knowing When to Recruit and Schedule Participants

How far in advance should you recruit and schedule the participants? Some testers who work with a database of prequalified participants can recruit people on just one or two day's notice. Some temporary agencies can also recruit on short notice. As with the number of phone calls, the more stringent your criteria, the more difficult it will be to recruit at short notice.

Our best answer is a few weeks before the test. If you wait too long, obviously, people may have a hard time fitting the test into their schedules. If you recruit too far in advance of the test, you may have two problems: First, many people do not know what their work schedule will be more than a month in advance. This is particularly true of people who work on rotating schedules as many people from airline pilots to computer network operators to nurses do. Secondly, people are more likely to forget the test if you recruit too early.

You can, however, qualify them a month or more in advance and then call them back later to schedule the exact time and renew their enthusiasm about coming.

Knowing What to Say When You are Recruiting

If your recruiting phone call is the first contact that anyone has had with potential participants, you have to start the recruiting with all the points that would have been in an introductory letter. Plan it as a script for the recruiter. (See the section earlier in this chapter on "What to say in an introductory letter" and the sample letter at the end of the chapter.) If people did get an introductory letter, you still want to go over the major points of it with them as a reminder. These points are

- You are looking for people to help you find out how easy a [type of product] is.
- They will be helping you by evaluating the product.
- They'll be coming to your lab. They'll be videotaped. You'll ask them to think out loud as they work so you can hear how the product works for them and what they think of it.
- You will pay them [amount] or you'll give them [whatever the incentive is].

If you already have filled-out questionnaires from potential participants, go over the questionnaire in the recruiting phone call to verify the information. People sometimes misunderstand questions; sometimes they stretch the truth. You may need to probe for details about some of the experiences to be clear about the answers you are getting. Keep notes of the phone call; they may help you later to understand which group of users this person represents.

If you do not have filled-out questionnaires from the people you are calling, one critical purpose of your call is to find out quickly if the person is an appropriate participant and which subgroup he or she represents.

In any case, you want your phone call to get people interested and excited so that they will agree to come and will remember to come. Your enthusiasm about the value of usability testing and your ability to make people feel comfortable about the experience are the key elements, along with the incentive you are offering, in getting people to agree to participate.

If people ask about the product they'll be using or the tasks they'll be doing, give general answers. Don't go into detail. They probably don't want it, and you don't want to give different levels of information to different people before they come to the test.

Usually, you will be recruiting and scheduling people in the same phone call. That means that you must have your test schedule with you so that you can work out with the participant when he or she will come. Don't assume, however, that just because people agree to the schedule, they will show up without reminders. (See the section later in this chapter on "Making sure that participants show up.")

Arranging for Payment or Other Incentives

You may be testing a product that people are so interested in that they will come with no extra payment or incentive. That is likely, however, to be the exception rather than the rule.

- If you are testing a new version of an existing product and the people you want as participants are all users of the existing product, you may get people who are willing to participate just to see the new product before it is released and to be involved in creating it.
- If you are developing a product for internal use, you may have ready access to users without any extra payment. They'll be doing the test instead of their job. What you need in that case is the enthusiastic cooperation of their managers so that users know the test is important and so that they don't get stuck having to make up work on their own time.

In most cases, however, you will have to budget for payment or other incentives for the participants. If you are working with a temporary agency, the agency will charge you for each participant just as if you had hired the person to use his or her skills for nontest tasks. You don't pay the participant anything in addition to what you pay the agency.

If you are recruiting on your own and taking people away from their jobs, you'll have to decide what the appropriate incentive is. Are they being paid by their employer for the time they spend in your lab? Are they taking time off and doing this on their own? Are they losing salary or business in the time they spend with you? Will they have to make up the work they miss because of the time they spend at the test?

Even when you do need an incentive, it doesn't always have to be money. Depending on the cost to you and the perceived value to the potential participants, you might use gift certificates, travel to the test site, samples of the product, or samples of other products as incentives. Some companies have systems in which employees get points for a variety of extra activities, including participating in usability tests. Employees accumulate these points and can use them for bonuses, extra privileges, or discounts on company products.

How much should you expect to pay participants? There is no simple answer to this question. The successful incentive is the one that motivates people to come.

For half-day tests, we have paid participants as little as $50. Generally, for professional people who come during the work day, our incentives start at $100. We have successfully recruited anesthesiologists with MD degrees for that amount, although we did have to test at night to accommodate their schedules, and we had to make a strong appeal to their interest in helping to design new technology.

For a test that required many programmers, we started out at $100, but went up to $150 to get a higher response rate. One difficult challenge we had was to recruit people who manage local area computer networks. These people are hard to find, extremely busy, and dedicated to keeping their network "up." We had to offer these people $200 to get any response at all. Even then we had trouble getting them to agree to come, and we had many last minute cancellations.

Research issue: Are participants more or less likely to rate the product highly when they are being paid to participate? People are reluctant to give poor ratings to products even when their behavior shows that the product was difficult for them to use. They blame themselves for their difficulties. They make comments that indicate they want to be nice to us, even when we tell them we want their honest opinions and that it is not our product. We do not know if being paid influences their reluctance to give low ratings.

Making Sure That Participants Show Up

In a usability test, you are observing one or two participants at a time. You need the participants to come when you expect them.

A 10% "no show" rate is common. Some people just forget. The best you can do is reschedule them. Others will call to cancel at the very last minute, sometimes for reasons that are truly unavoidable. We know of no way to eliminate all no-shows, but following the suggestions on the next few pages should help you keep the percentage down.

We have not collected systematic data on the types of people who are more or less likely to show up. Our sense is that participants who are more educated and who have more responsible jobs are more likely to come, despite their busy schedules.

When our qualifications for participants are stringent, for example, an MD anesthesiologist with at least six months experience in an operating room, we seem to have less trouble with no-shows than when our qualifications for participants are easy to meet, for example, anyone who has used a personal computer for at least six months. Perhaps we impress the more-difficult-to-find participants with the importance of their role as a specialist. Perhaps, the more-difficult-to-find participants get more excited about the possibility of an early view of a new product that is relevant to their jobs.

If your participants represent a broad, general audience, you may have to take special care to confirm the appointment both in writing and by phone.

What can you do to make sure the participants come? Two keys are

- to make the usability test sound interesting and nonthreatening
- to confirm the appointment immediately and again a day or two before the scheduled time.

If you scheduled the appointment more than two weeks before the test, you should make two follow-up calls: one a week before the test, and one a day or two before.

Make the Usability Test Sound Interesting and Nonthreatening

Your tone of voice and attitude about the experience will influence the people you want as participants. When you recruit the participants, explain the purpose of the test positively and enthusiastically. Answer questions willingly, but don't be too specific.

You might say something like this: "We've been asked to find out if a new portable telephone is easy to use. If you've ever thought about buying a portable telephone, you might be interested in trying this one out. Your help would make telephones like these easier for people like yourself."

Confirm the Appointment

Confirm at least twice—by mail immediately after you've recruited the participant and by phone a day or two before the scheduled time.

Send a confirmation letter immediately. People are more likely to come if they have a piece of paper from you with the information on it than if they have written it down themselves from a phone call.

Your confirmation letter should include the following information:

- thanks for agreeing to participate
- the date and time you expect them to be there
- where to come, including a map and directions
- how long to expect to be with you
- the purpose of the test
- reminders about the video cameras and thinking out loud
- any other instructions the participants need (for example, if they need to bring anything)
- the payment or other incentive you'll be giving them
- a person's name and a phone number to call if they have questions or need to reschedule

The phone number should be one at which there is always a person or at least a recorder. Most people will let you know when they have to cancel. Having a phone at which they can always reach someone, or at least leave a message, will turn some no-shows into people whom you can reschedule.

You can use the sample confirmation letter at the end of the chapter as a model.

Telephoning the participants a day or two before the actual test time is another critical step in ensuring that participants show up. A pleasant call not only reminds participants that you are expecting them. It allows them to ask questions or get over any qualms they may have. You can check that they have the directions and know how to get to the usability lab. It's also your way of letting them know how much you appreciate their participation and that you'll be giving them whatever the payment or incentive is for participating.

Having a Back-up – But Not Double Booking

Should you book two people for each test time to be sure that someone will show up? We recommend against double booking. It's expensive. You have to pay both people, even if only one participates in the test. It may cause negative feelings about the company and product. If both participants show up, you'll have to choose one and disappoint the other. It increases your recruiting effort. You have to find twice as many people in each category as you actually need.

Instead of double booking, put more effort into making sure that the people you have recruited are going to come. And have a contingency plan for a time when you have a no-show. Two useful contingency plans are to have a back-up and to allow extra testing time.

As you schedule participants, you may find someone who could come at any time and on short notice. Make that person your back-up for that group and arrange a way to reach the person quickly if you have a no-show. If you have subgroups in the test, for example, novices and experienced users or lawyers and paralegals, you'll want to have a back-up for each subgroup.

If you can, plan to have the lab available to you for an extra day or two to make up for no-shows. If you get a morning or afternoon without a test participant in the middle of a solid week of testing, you'll find you have plenty to do. Use the time to make sure that all your paperwork and tapes are organized, to work on the list of the problems you are seeing, or to think about the global implications of what you are seeing and begin to develop recommendations.

Now that you have planned how to get appropriate users to come to the test, you need to think about the tasks that you will have them do. In the next two chapters, we discuss choosing the tasks to test and turning the tasks into scenarios that you give to the participants.

Examples of Forms to Help You Recruit Participants

On the next few pages, you'll find a sample

- introductory letter to raise interest in a usability test
- screening questionnaire for potential participants to fill out
- screening questionnaire to be used over the telephone
- confirmation letter

All of these are for the electronic mail example. We start with a reminder of the types of users we are recruiting and with plans for recruiting them.

What Types of Users Are We Recruiting?

Let's assume that we have set the following criteria for the usability test of an electronic mail program:

- The participants will all work in companies that have at least 50 employees. This is because the product is aimed at the corporate market of at least medium-sized companies.
- They will all be managers with at least two people reporting to them. We decided to focus on managers for three reasons: Managers are likely to be major users of electronic mail; they generally send and receive lots of messages. Managers are "gatekeepers"; their views of the program are likely to influence its acceptance in the company. Managers may be less skilled at the computer than their technical or support staff, and we are concerned that the product be easy to use even for people with only minimal skill at the computer.
- Because we are testing a new product, we do not have to worry about eliminating users of earlier versions of this product.
- Half will have no experience with an electronic mail program and no experience in a networking environment. This will be the "Novice" group.
- Half will have had experience using another electronic mail program over a network for at least six months. This will be the "Experienced" group.
- We are also interested in knowing about people's personal computer experience and which electronic mail programs they have used, even though we are not basing recruiting decisions on those factors.

How Are We Going to Recruit Them?

Our main recruiting effort will be through personal networks. For financial reasons, all our participants will come from the geographic area that is convenient to the usability test laboratory. We will recruit people whom we know personally and who meet our criteria. We will also use our personal networks to be introduced to likely participants whom we do not know personally.

In some cases, we may get permission to send a short note to a list of appropriate people in a company. For those situations, we will use the introductory letter in Figure 10-1 along with the questionnaire that is Figure 10-2. To recruit the experienced participants who are already using another electronic mail program, we might work with someone in their company to send something like the short introductory letter as a recruiting notice over their electronic mail, asking them to call us. Then we would use a questionnaire to screen participants during a telephone call.

If you are not experienced at screening and recruiting participants over the telephone, you might want to write out all the branches and exact words in the questionnaire as we have done in Figure 10-3. Experienced recruiters may be able to use the same questionnaire that you would send out to potential participants and have all the branches in their heads. They know by experience when to recruit and when to end the conversation.

Because our prospective participants are managers, we will offer $75 for the 3-hour test. That is probably much lower than their salary, but we believe that the incentive to try out the software will add to the money to attract them to come to the test.

Figure 10-4 shows a sample confirmation letter you can mail to each participant you recruit.

```
┌─────────────────────────────────────────────────────────────────────────┐
│                          Company Letterhead                               │
│                                                                           │
│  April 22, 1993                                                           │
│                                                                           │
│  Ms. Jane Smith                                                           │
│  Ajax Industries                                                          │
│  Anycity, State, Zip                                                      │
│                                                                           │
│  Dear Ms. Smith:                                                          │
│                                                                           │
│                                                                           │
│        RE:  Participating in evaluating the usability of software         │
│                                                                           │
│  We are contacting people who are interested in improving the ease of use of │
│  electronic mail software.  We are committed to making computer software serve │
│  the people who use it.  Among the tools that we use to make software products │
│  easier to learn and use is usability testing.  In a usability test, people such as │
│  yourself come to our laboratory to use products that are being developed.  The │
│  feedback from users that we get during these tests helps us to find where the │
│  products work well and where they need improvement.                      │
│                                                                           │
│  Would you be interested in participating in such a test?  If so, please fill out the │
│  attached form and send it back to us.  We pay the people who come to our lab $75 │
│  for a test that lasts about three hours.  We videotape these sessions so that we can │
│  conduct detailed analyses of how the product performs.  When you send us the │
│  form, we will put your name into our user data base.  We are planning a series of │
│  tests for May and June.                                                  │
│                                                                           │
│  We look forward to receiving your form.  Thank you for your time.  If you have │
│  any questions, please call me at 617-275-0800.                           │
│                                                                           │
│  Sincerely,                                                               │
│                                                                           │
│  John Doe                                                                 │
│  Usability Lab Director                                                   │
└─────────────────────────────────────────────────────────────────────────┘
```

Figure 10-1.   Sample introductory letter to raise interest in a usability test

154

Your name: _____

Your phone number: _____

1. How many employees does your company have? _____

2. How many people do you supervise or manage? _____

3. Do you use a personal computer for tasks such as word processing or spreadsheets?

   ____ yes   ____ no

4. If you answered "yes," how lor.g have you been using a personal computer?

   ____ less than 6 months

   ____ 6 months to 2 years

   ____ more than 2 years

5. Do you use or have you used an electronic mail program?

   ____ yes   Which one(s)? _____

   ____ no

6. If you answered "yes," how long have you used electronic mail?

   ____ less than 6 months

   ____ 6 months to 2 years

   ____ more than 2 years

7. Do you work on a network in which you have to "log in" with a user ID and a password or do you work strictly on a stand-alone personal computer?

   ____ network

   ____ stand-alone personal computer

Thank you for taking the time to fill out this form. Please mail it to us in the accompanying envelope. We will put your name in our database.

Figure 10-2. **Sample screening questionnaire for potential participants to fill out**

Questionnaire for _____ test

Person's name: _____

Phone number: _____

Thank you for your interest. I'd like to ask a few questions to see if you meet the profile
of the people we are including in this particular test.

1.　　Do you work in a company that has 50 or more employees?

　　　____ Yes　　*Go to Question 2.*

　　　____ No　　*Say:* "Thank you for your interest, but we're focusing on companies with
　　　　　　　　　　50 or more people. May I keep your name and phone number for
　　　　　　　　　　future tests?" If person says, "Yes," write "keep" on form. Thank
　　　　　　　　　　again and end the conversation."

2.　　How many employees does your company have?

　　　____　　　　*Go to Question 3.*

3.　　Do you supervise or manage at least two people?

　　　____ Yes　　*Go to Question 4.*

　　　____ No　　*Say:* "Thank you for your interest, but we're focusing on managers in this
　　　　　　　　　　particular test. May I keep your name and phone number for future
　　　　　　　　　　tests?" If person says, "Yes," write "keep" on form. Thank again
　　　　　　　　　　and end the conversation."

4.　　How many people do you supervise or manage?

　　　____　　　　*Go to Question 5.*

5.　　Do you use a personal computer for tasks such as word processing or
　　　spreadsheets?

　　　____ Yes　　*Go to Question 6.*

　　　____ No　　*Go to Question 7.*

6.　　How long have you been using a personal computer?

　　　____ less than 6 months　　*Go to Question 7.*

　　　____ 6 months to 2 years　　*Go to Question 7.*

　　　____ more than 2 years　　*Go to Question 7.*

7　　Do you use or have you used an electronic mail program?

　　　____ Yes　　*Go to Question 8.*

　　　____ No　　*Go to Question 10.*

8.　　Which electronic mail program or programs have you used?

　　　(1)_____

　　　(2)_____

　　　Go to Question 9.

156

9. How long have you been using electronic mail?

    _____ Less than 6 months   *Go to "Thanks anyway" at bottom of page.*

    _____ 6 months to 2 years   **RECRUIT (Experienced)**

    _____ More than 2 years   **RECRUIT (Experienced)**

10. Do you work on a network in which you have to "log in" with a user ID and a password or do you work strictly on a stand-alone personal computer?

    _____ network   *Go to "Thanks anyway" at bottom of page.*

    _____ stand-alone personal computer   **RECRUIT (Novice)**

Thanks anyway:

If person has no e-mail experience, but does have network experience, say:

    "Thank you for your interest, but we're focusing on new users who have not worked on networks yet. May I keep your name and phone number for future tests?" If person says, "Yes," write "keep" on form. Thank again and end the conversation.

If person has e-mail experience, but less than six months, say:

    "Thank you for your interest, but we're focusing on people with more experience using e-mail. May I keep your name and phone number for future tests?" If person says, "Yes," write "keep" on form. Thank again and end the conversation.

Figure 10-3. Sample questionnaire for screening by telephone

June 2, 1993

Ms. Jane Smith
Ajax Industries
Anycity, State

Dear Ms. Smith:

RE: Confirming your schedule to evaluate an electronic mail program

Thank you for agreeing to help us evaluate a new electronic mail program. We expect you at this time and place:

DATE:	Wednesday, June 16, 1993
TIME:	9 AM
PLACE:	American Institutes for Research
	45 North Road, Bedford

You can reach us easily from Route 95. Take the Exit marked "Route 4, Bedford" and continue down Route 4 for three miles. I have also enclosed a map.

Expect to spend about three hours with us. We'll ask you to use the product to do just the types of tasks you might do in your work. Our client wants to find out how to improve this product and is eager to get feedback from people like yourself who would typically use a product like this.

As I explained, we'll videotape the session. We'll only use the tapes to help us evaluate the product; and we won't use your name. We'll also ask you to think out loud as you work with the product. That way, you can tell us how the product is working for you.

We have only one person at a time come to work with the product, so we are counting on you to come. If you will be unable to come, please call me at least two days in advance so we can reschedule. You can leave a message on our phone any time of the day or night. We look forward to seeing you. **You will receive $75 for helping us.**

Sincerely yours,

John Doe
Usability Specialist
PHONE: 617 - 275 - 0800

Figure 10-4.   Sample confirmation letter

11

Selecting and Organizing Tasks to Test

One of the essential requirements of every usability test is that the test participants attempt tasks that users of the product will want to do with it. When you test a product of even modest complexity, however, there are more tasks than there is time available to test them. As you plan, you need to decide which tasks are the most important to include in the test. In this chapter, we describe how to:

- select tasks to test
- determine the resources you need for each task
- set priorities and order tasks

Selecting Tasks

Usability testing is a sampling process. You cannot test every possible task users can do with a product. What tasks, then, should you sample?

- Tasks that probe potential usability problems
- Tasks suggested from your concerns and experience
- Tasks derived from other criteria
- Tasks that users will do with the product

Tasks That Probe Potential Usability Problems

The first and most important criterion for selecting tasks is to use tasks that probe the potential usability problems with the product.

A good task to select is one that has the potential to uncover a usability problem.

As with any testing procedure, the more problems you find in the limited time available, the more successful your test will be (Myers, 1979). The designers of the product may be surprised at this goal. They may view usability testing as a way to verify the usability of the product, that is, how easy it is to learn and use. You may need to remind them that the goal of quality assurance testing of software is to find the "bugs" before the product is released. The quality assurance process *assumes* that any complex software program has bugs in it. A good software testing procedure finds more bugs than a poor one. The goal of a usability test is similar: develop a procedure that will find the serious usability problems. Consequently, you look for tasks that will probe areas of potential usability problems.

Tasks Suggested From Concerns and Experience

Another source to use to identify tasks is the list of usability concerns you develop with designers. We have discussed this list in Chapter 8, "Defining Your Goals and Objectives." The people who develop a product always have some ideas about where there are potential problems. They know what parts of the product were difficult to design and where they disagreed about the best approach.

Designers are often correct in knowing the kinds of *major* problems the test should probe. For example, if they made a major decision to select an interaction style such as touch, they may want you to look at the types of problems that users frequently have with touch-sensitive devices, such as touching outside of the touch pad.

> For our electronic mail example, there are several potential usability problems we identified as concerns. For example, we suspect that users would have difficulty selecting a new mail message to read. When you have more than one new message to read, the software always displays the newest message first. If you do not want to read that one, you must select the one you want by using the arrow keys to move a highlight bar down the list of messages and pressing the space bar to mark it with an arrow symbol. Because the space bar is an arbitrary mapping here, we expect users to have trouble marking a message.

> We also suspect that users will have problems creating folders, because the procedure for creating your first folder is different from the procedure you use to create additional folders. When you have no folders and you try to save a message, the software asks you to create a folder. All of the messages you save will go into that folder until you create others. The procedure to create the additional folders requires a different process with a different menu. It seems likely that users will have trouble with this task.

While designers have useful ideas about where users will have problems, they often ignore the more basic problems users might have with the product. They may anticipate that users will have difficulty configuring software, but not that users will have difficulty starting a system and putting in a diskette.

There is a famous videotape made during a usability test at Digital Equipment Corporation. The tape shows how two naive users do not understand what a floppy diskette is and how to insert it into a disk drive. The designers had not anticipated that users would not know how to work with diskettes. This finding made it possible for designers to improve the design of the hardware so that users who have no experience with diskettes are less likely to have problems starting to install the product.

> For our electronic mail example, there are not enough status messages to tell users that they have accomplished an action. For example, when you send mail, the software displays a message indicating that the mail was sent or forwarded or replied to. The message, however, flashes so quickly on the screen that we expect users will miss it. We were concerned that some users will send mail several times when they are not sure it has been sent.

Besides probing problems that designers identify and the basic problems users often have with complex interfaces, there may be other potential problems. Your experience as a tester is invaluable here. In a very short time, you will see the common problems in the products you test. For example, if you know that users frequently have problems manipulating windows in applications that sit within a multitasking user interface, you will want to include some tasks that require participants to open, close, move, and resize windows.

Your list of potential problems may grow longer than you could possibly test. Do not worry about the length of the list at this point. You will shorten it later.

Once you have at least a preliminary list of problems, you need to begin to create tasks that will probe each problem. For example:

- As we described above, we expect users of our electronic mail system to have difficulty identifying a new message to read. We, therefore, want to include a task that requires users to select a new mail message to read that is not the oldest message in the list of new messages.
- The designers of the interface to a new patient monitor for a critical care unit in a hospital used a dedicated key allowing users, here doctors and nurses, to temporarily silence all alarms. When users press this key, a message appears in a message area near the top of the screen that says "Alarms silenced." It is very important that nurses and doctors see this message, even when they themselves did not silence the alarms. The designers are not confident that the highlighting, size, and positioning of this message will allow users to notice it. To probe this question, you would need a task that requires participants to silence the alarms and you would need to find out if they could verify that the alarms were silenced. You also might want a second task in which the alarms have been silenced by someone else, and you ask the participant to describe the state of the alarms.
- The writer of a manual for an update to an operating system is concerned about the commands that were modified from the earlier version of the operating system. These commands change the way that computer operators will perform some of their most frequent tasks, such as system configuration. The writer wants to know whether participants can find the appropriate sections in the manual quickly and whether they can then follow the new procedures. To probe this question, you would need to include tasks that ask participants to do the tasks that require using the new commands.

Tasks Derived From Other Criteria

In addition to selecting tasks because they relate to usability problems and concerns and goals, you can use other criteria for selecting tasks for a usability test. Good choices are tasks that are difficult to recover from if done wrong.

Tasks That Users Will Do With the Product

All of the tasks you have selected thus far will be tasks that users will do with the product you are testing. There are other tasks that users can do with a product over and above those that relate to usability problems, concerns, or goals. For example:

- new or modified
- critical to the operation of the product
- frequently done
- done under pressure

If the development team has conducted a task analysis, you can extract the tasks from it. Otherwise, it is best to have a meeting with the developers, and with users as well, to create a list of the tasks.

Here is a list of tasks to test from our electronic mail example:

Set a password for the mail account
Create a personal mailing list
Move messages between folders
Sort items in folder
Read any new mail message
Read a selected mail message
Create and send a mail message
Edit a message
File a mail message
Create a folder
Forward a message
Delete a mail message
Delete a folder
Find a mail message
Send a CC ("Carbon Copy") of a message
Reply to a mail message
Attach a file to a message
Create a distribution list
Set the useful life of messages
Archive a message/folder
Set priorities on messages
Create a folder that several people can share
Sort the messages in a folder by date

As you can see, this list is too long for a half-day usability test. We will need to pare it down, but before we do that, let's look at the resources we need to test each task.

Determining the Resources You Need for Each Task

Before you can start eliminating tasks from the list, you need to get some additional information about each task:

- how long it will take to do the task
- what hardware, software, procedures, and other resources will you need to run the task

You do not have to create this information in minute detail at this point. But, you will need to have a general idea about time and resources to make decisions about eliminating tasks. You also will be using this information to create checklists to help you keep track of all of the resources you will need to conduct the test (see Chapter 16, "Preparing the Test Team").

Estimating Task Times

There are two types of task times that you need to estimate as you prepare for a test:

1. The time it will take to run the task during the test.
2. The time that users will feel is acceptable for completing a task.

In this chapter, we are concerned about the first time, that is, how long it is likely to take for a test participant to complete a task. We need to estimate this time so we can plan how long each test session will take.

The second time is important for setting quantitative criteria for a task. As we discuss in Chapter 13, "Deciding How to Measure Usability," you want to estimate how acceptable a task time is to *users* so that you can set criteria for measuring the usability of the task.

It is important that you understand the difference between these two times. The fact that you estimate that it might take a test participant 20 minutes to complete a task does not mean that users will find 20 minutes acceptable.

Use a time estimate for the participants who are most naive and who are likely to take the longest time.

As you try to decide *how long each task will take during the test*, consider the characteristics of the participants who will be in the test.

Your estimate will only be an educated guess, but you need to make it anyway. As you develop these estimates consider

- the time it would take an experienced person to complete the task—this will provide a baseline
- the problems that a typical participant might have and the time it will take to recover from them

- any additional time it might take to set up the task or to get ready for the next task

Your estimate may take the form of a range rather than a single value. Here is an example.

> You are testing the user interface and the documentation for an upgrade to an operating system for a minicomputer. A task you want to test is to do a partial weekly backup, that is, you will ask the participants, who will be computer operators, to backup all the files that have been created over the past 7 days. How long is it likely to take to complete this task? Clearly, the minimum time is the time it would take an expert operator who knew the commands to type them, load a blank tape, wait for the files to be copied, and then rewind and remove the tape.
>
> The major unknown variable here is the number of files there are to back up. You have control over this variable, because you have to make the files for the test. If you want to test the condition in which more than one tape is used for the backup, you will need enough files to fill more than one tape. Suppose that you decide that you will have enough files to make a 10 minute backup. It will take an expert 30 seconds to type the commands, 2 minutes to select and load a tape, about 10 minutes for the files to be copied, and 2 minutes to rewind, remove, and label the tape. Thus, the minimum time to do this task is about 15 minutes.

In our experience, estimates for task times become more unreliable as the number of usability problems with the product increases. If you see that there may be many usability problems with the product, plan to test fewer tasks. You may want to wait until the pilot test before you decide how many tasks you can test.

If you have set an upper time limit for a task, you should plan to allow the test participants to work on the task for at least that amount of time.

Listing the Resources You Need for Tasks

Once you have generated an estimate for the time it takes for tasks, list all the resources you will need to test the task. This list is also critical to your planning for the test. It will provide you with the material for your testing checklist to keep the test team organized. You need to create this list now to make decisions about whether to include tasks in the test. As you develop this list, consider:

The hardware you will need. Include not only the hardware the participant will need to attempt the task, such as a personal computer with a printer, but also the hardware you will need to set up and run the task. For. example, for a test of the user interface to

- electronic mail software, you will need a computer or terminal connected to at least one other computer or terminal to send and receive mail. If you are testing a remote service you also may need a modem and a dedicated telephone line into the test room
- a workstation in a network, you will need at least one other workstation or printer to serve as a remote node, as well as cables and connectors
- a digital oscilloscope, you will need signal generators, cables, and connectors to simulate the electrical signals you will need to have for participants to measure
- a business telephone, you will need at least one phone for the participants and one phone for the observation room for sending and receiving calls. These phones may need to be connected through the same switching unit.

The software and data files you will need.   Again, include both the software and data the participant will use and the software and data you use to conduct the test. For example, for a test of the user interface to

- electronic mail software, you may need
  - a mail account, with appropriate privileges, set up for the test participants
  - additional mail accounts for the people participants will send messages to and receive messages from
  - messages in the participants' mail account that the participants will sort, retrieve, attach other messages to, etc.
  - mail folders to place messages in
  - group distribution lists
  - a backup copy of all messages to use after each participant completes the test
- database management software, you may need
  - a relational database with sort keys
  - tables and other views of the data
  - histograms, pie charts, and other graphics to edit
  - a backup copy of the database and files to use after each participant completes the test
- business telephone system, you may need
  - an intercom number for the participants' phone and any other phones they will call or receive calls from
  - a list of waiting messages
  - a list of other users of the phone system
  - phone messages that have been archived
  - a backup copy of waiting messages for use after each participant completes the test

Instructions and procedures you will need. To attempt the tasks in a test, users need such information as names for messages and names of people to send the messages to. In addition, you will need procedures and tools to help you set the product up the same way for each participant. For example, for a test of the user interface to

- an electronic mail system, you might need
  - a user name and password for participants to get into their mail account
  - a message for participants to type
  - a reply for participants to type
  - a procedure for you to use to put the hardware, software, and data files back to their initial state after each participant completes the tasks
- a business telephone system, you might need
  - intercom extension numbers and outside telephone numbers for participants to call
  - names of fictitious office mates and other people participants will talk with
  - scripts for test team members to use when they interact with participants
  - a procedure for you to use to put the hardware, software, and data files back to their initial state after each participant completes the tasks

Creating the Final List of Tasks to Test

To summarize what you have created thus far, here is what a list of resources might look like for a task to send a reply to a message in a test of our electronic mail example:

Time	3–12 minutes
Hardware	Two PCs connected to network
Software and data files	Electronic mail software Mail account for participants Incoming mail message to reply to Existing account to send reply to
Instructions and procedures	Text of reply (or information to create text) Procedure for restoring account to initial condition

Once you have completed your list of tasks and resources, you will usually need to eliminate some tasks, because participants will not have time to complete all of them. For most tests it takes about 1 hour to

- start the test
- give the prebriefing
- give the participant a break halfway through the test
- have the participant fill out the posttest questionnaire
- give the debriefing

To complete the tasks, therefore, participants will have about one hour less than the total time they will be in the test. For example, if you plan to have participants available for half a day or about 3½ hours, they will only have about 2–2½ hours to work on tasks.

Scheduling participants for half a day is a common practice. For products that are even moderately complex, you need to give participants at least 2 to 3 hours to explore the product. If you are testing a prototype or only part of the product, you may be able to spend less time with each participant.

Scheduling participants for more than half a day will cause you some logistic problems. You must take participants to lunch or arrange for them to get lunch. You also have to be concerned about fatigue. As we discuss in Chapter 18, "Caring for Test Participants," usability testing is an emotional experience for participants. Many of them will be tense; they will need frequent breaks to retain their concentration if they have to perform for more than a few hours.

As you look for ways to eliminate tasks so that participants can complete the test on time, consider

- the objective of each task and whether you can achieve more than one objective with it. For example, an objective such as having participants navigate three levels down a menu hierarchy can usually be combined with an objective for performing some function that is on the third level of the hierarchy.
- whether a task that uses expensive resources is worth testing. For example, if you need an extra signal generator to simulate a complex signal to an oscilloscope, consider if the objective of that task is critical to the evaluation of the product
- whether time-consuming tasks are more important than the two or three tasks you could include instead

Putting the Tasks in Order

The final step in creating the list of tasks is putting them in the order you will have the participants attempt them. There are two important points to consider here:

1. The tasks should flow in the natural order in which users
    will do them. For example, users will create a mail message
    before they edit and send it.
2. Tasks that are important to the evaluation of the usability of
    the product should come early in the test rather than near
    the end. It is likely that some participants will not finish all
    the tasks. So, if you leave important tasks until late in the
    test, you will collect less data on them.

From the long list of tasks we generated for our electronic mail
example, we selected the most important tasks and arranged them
into an order that seemed to make sense from a user's perspective:

>   Read a selected new mail message
>   Create a mail message
>   Edit a message
>   Send a message
>   Create a folder
>   Store a message in a folder
>   Forward a message
>   Find a message
>   Delete a message
>   Reply to a message
>   Attach a file to a message
>   Create a distribution list
>   Set the useful life of a message
>   Archive a message
>   Make a shared folder
>   Set special priorities on a message

As you can see, the tasks near the beginning of the list are the ones
that we suspect users will want to do most often, while the tasks at
the end of the list are infrequently used. If test participants are not
able to finish all of these tasks, they will have tried the most
important ones.

 In the next chapter, we will discuss turning tasks into scenarios.

12

Creating Task Scenarios

Once you have the list of tasks for the test, you have to decide how to present those tasks to the participants. One way that works well is to give the participants "scenarios"—situations in which the task is embedded in a reasonable and very short story. In this chapter, we look at the art of creating interesting and informative scenarios. We discuss these questions:

- What is a scenario?
- What makes a good scenario?
- Do you always give participants written scenarios?
- How do you divide up the tasks and scenarios for participants?
- How do you make participants stop between tasks?

What Is a Scenario?

You use scenarios to tell participants what you want them to do during the test. Scenarios describe the tasks in a way that takes some of the artificiality out of the test.

Here are two examples of scenarios:

Scenario 1:
You've just bought a new combination telephone and answering machine. The box is on the table. Take the product out of the box and set it up so that you can make and receive calls.

Scenario 2:
You can save numbers in the telephone's memory and then call those numbers without dialing all the digits each time. Your best friend's number is 212-555-1234. Put your friend's number in the telephone's memory.

Here's an example of a scenario for our usability test of the electronic mail program:

Scenario 1:
You have just arrived at your desk after a short vacation. Check to see how many mail messages you have waiting for you. If there are any messages from Mr. Green, a Vice President of your company, read them.

As you can see, a scenario makes the task more realistic. In a scenario, you give the goal and whatever information a user would actually have when coming to do this task. You do not give the steps. The point of the test is to see if a typical user can figure out the steps that this product requires.

What Makes a Good Scenario?

A good scenario is:

- short
- in the user's words, not the product's
- unambiguous—so all participants will understand it

A good scenario:

- gives participants enough information to do the task
- is directly linked to your tasks and concerns

Short

Time is precious in a test. You do not want participants to spend more time than necessary reading the scenarios.

People also read at different rates. Because you are timing the task, you do not want these different reading speeds to unduly influence the task times. The way to keep that difference small is to write short scenarios.

Depending on the software or other means you are using to time the tasks, you may or may not be able to separate the time participants spend reading the scenario from the time they spend doing the task. See Chapter 15 on "Preparing the Test Environment" for more information on measuring time.

Most scenarios can be kept very short. If you set up the entire test so that the participant has a consistent and plausible "role," you can write each scenario to fit into that role.

Here are a few more examples of scenarios:

Scenario:
There have been some staff changes in your office.
Set up a new account for E. Dickenson.

Scenario:
You have successfully completed installing the compiler.
Test it with the program DEMO.FTN

Scenario:
You need to make a presentation to your manager about the month's sales figures.
Copy the spreadsheet SALES1.WKS into the SALES table.

In the User's Words, Not the Product's

The whole point of usability testing is to predict what will happen when people use the product on their own — without a developer or usability specialist looking over their shoulders or answering their questions.

If you are testing a menu-driven product, one of the concerns you are probably testing is whether users will choose the right menu option. If you are testing a graphical user interface with icons, one of your concerns is likely to be whether users will select the right icon. If you are testing a device with labeled buttons, you are likely to be concerned about whether users will know which button does what.

Don't give that information away in your scenarios. If you do, the product may do well in testing and still fail in the marketplace.

> Suppose you are testing a product that lets users save their mail in "logs." The menu choice for this is "log." If you write a scenario that says, "Now log the mail that you just read," the participants may successfully do the task without even understanding what task they are doing. When other users get the product in their offices, they may never store their mail because they make no connections between the task as they say it to themselves and the menu choice "log."

> To test this task realistically, you must write a scenario that describes the task the way users will say it to themselves. That might be: "Now store the mail you just read." Or it might be: "You don't want that message to sit in your list of mail forever, but you may want to read it again later. Save it so that you could get it back to look at later." Now you have a realistic test of whether users recognize the product's word "log" as the right one for the task they represent to themselves as "storing" or "saving."

Scenarios that are worded too closely to the product may lead to a false positive test. That is, the product may fare well in the usability lab and still fail in the marketplace.

This issue of making sure the scenarios are worded well is very important. However, don't go overboard. If you have done a lot of previous usability work to be certain that you are using plain English, users' terms, don't make up new, unusual terms for the scenarios.

Developers may have a hard time seeing this problem because the words in the product are so familiar to them that they cannot imagine users not understanding the terms. A usability specialist should either write the scenarios or review them carefully, looking for words and phrases that are product words and might not be the ones users would look for.

Unambiguous — So All Participants Will Understand It

You're trying to see how easy the product is to use. You don't want misunderstandings about the scenarios to interfere with learning as much as you can about the product.

When writing scenarios, watch out for these common pitfalls:

- not being clear about when the task is over
- not giving the information people need to do the task

In this scenario, for example, where are you supposed to stop?

Ambiguous scenario:
You have a message from Jane Jones about the Fourth Quarter Budget. Read it and write a response in which you answer her question.

Should you send the reply or just compose it and wait for further instructions?

If any of the scenarios are ambiguous, you are likely to see the problem in pilot testing. This is one reason for conducting a pilot test, as we explain in Chapter 17.

Enough Information to Do the Task

In addition to telling participants the general task or goal that you want them to accomplish, you may need to give users some data to work with. If, in a real situation, they would have information about a specific case when they come to do the task, you have to supply the information for such a case.

Suppose you are testing a new touchscreen product for retailers. You've set up a general scenario for your participants so they are in the role of a salesperson in the linen department. One of the tasks you are concerned about is whether they can handle a sale that includes multiple items. You have to give them a situation in which that task will occur.

If you are giving the scenarios in writing, you might create one like this:

Scenario:
A customer comes up to your station with several items.
She wants to buy them on her store charge card.
She gives you her store charge card (Account #9-80-786-5).
And she gives you the items, which are
- two twin-bed-size sheets. Each sheet is item #347689.
- a package of pillow cases. The package is item #346988.
- two pillows. Each pillow is item #456897.
Ring up the purchase for her.

Note: For this test, a better way to deliver the scenarios might be to have team members pretend to be customers. For this scenario, someone would walk up to the participant/salesperson with the items and a store credit card. See the section, "Do You Always Give Participants Written Scenarios?" later in this chapter. You still have to plan all this information and make sure that the database you are using for the test has that customer and those items in it. Otherwise what you are really testing is how users deal with the messages they'll get when they try to enter a nonexistent account number or incorrect item numbers.

Note that you haven't told the participants *how* to do the task. You've only given them the same information that they would have if they were doing such a task in real life. That's the key to a useful scenario: the participants should feel as if the scenario matches what they would have to do and what they would know when they are doing that task in their actual jobs.

You have to give the participants enough data to be able to do the task. Don't give them extra data unless they are likely to actually have that data when doing the task and you are specifically testing a concern about whether they will know which data to use in the task.

You don't always have to spell out all the data. For example, if you are testing an editing program and you want the participants to write a note, you don't have to give them the exact wording of the note, but you should give them some information to write about.

We find that if you give nonspecific instructions, such as "Write a note to Brett Jones at Headquarters," some people will spend a great deal of time deciding what to write about. That throws off your comparison of time for the task you are testing. We also find that if you give participants all the words to type, however, the task is boring. What works best is to tell them something like this: "You need to let Brett Jones at Headquarters know about the staff meeting next Friday at 2 p.m. in the main conference room." With this much information, you will get to observe how each participant goes about addressing and composing a note—which you want to know—and yet not find large disparities in the time they spend deciding what to say—which you do not want to know.

Directly Linked to Your Tasks and Concerns

You should be able to name the task or tasks that go with each scenario.

Each scenario tests one or more of the tasks on the list that you decided to include in the test. Each of those tasks, in turn, is directly linked to one or more of your goals or concerns.

You don't give these task names to the participants. They get only the scenarios. But the team should know exactly what each scenario is testing. Sometimes the task–scenario link is obvious from the wording of the scenario, but sometimes it is not.

The following is an example in which the link is obvious:

Concern:	Can users figure out how to use the remote control to turn off the television set?

Test setup: Participants have been told to use the remote control for all tasks.

Task description: Turning off the TV.

Scenario: You've finished watching the TV for now. Turn it off.

In this second example, the link between the task and the scenario is not obvious from the wording of the scenario:

Concern: Will users understand the messages on the small one-line screen of the photocopier?

Test setup: The photocopier has only two sheets of paper in the bin that will be used in this task. Packages of different size paper are available on a supply table nearby, but the participant has not been told that they will be needed.

Task description: Figuring out what is wrong; adding paper correctly.

Scenario: Please make one copy of this five-page paper.

Do You Always Give Participants Written Scenarios?

No, you don't always give the scenarios in writing. You want to make the test as realistic as possible, and another mode of delivering the scenarios may be more realistic than having the participants read them. It might be appropriate to

- have test team members pretend to be "customers," "supervisors," or "colleagues" and walk into the test room to deliver the scenarios in person
- use the product to deliver the scenarios
- For example, in testing telephones, the scenarios would

probably include telephone calls to the participant as well as calls the participant makes.
- mix the modes; give participants scenarios in writing, but then interrupt with calls or visits

Whatever mode you use to present the scenarios, however, you must write them out as part of your test plan. Even if the participant never sees the written scenario, you must be sure that each participant gets the same scenario delivered in the same way. Therefore, if test team members are play-acting scenarios over the phone or in person, they have to use the exact same scenarios with each participant. That may mean memorizing the situation and words as if this were theater.

The following are some examples of test situations that have lent themselves to different modes for delivering the scenarios:

- To test a new part of the airlines reservation and check-in system, the test team at American Airlines set up a ticket counter in the usability laboratory. The participants were representative gate agents. They stood behind the counter as they do on their jobs. The scenarios were delivered by test team members acting as travelers.
- To test a new multifunction telephone, the test team at AIR set up the usability laboratory to look like an office. The participants were representative office workers. They were each given a set of written scenarios, but the test team knew that not all the scenarios were included in the participant's package. The test team's version of the package included some scenarios that the test participant did not see, such as: "Call the participant on the phone and say: . . . ."
- To test an objective that users be able to easily suspend what they are doing and turn to a different task, the team testing an electronic mail package decided to interrupt participants in the middle of writing a memo. The participants started what they thought from the written scenario was a task to send a memo on a particular topic to a particular person. A person on the test team had instructions to interrupt over the intercom after the participant had addressed the memo and typed about two lines of the message. The prescripted interruption gave the participants a plausible reason to want to stop working on the memo they were writing and instead immediately send a different message to a different person.
- AIR conducted a test of a monitor that nurses would use at a central nursing station on a hospital floor. One of the concerns was whether nurses would know what to do when two alarms about patients went off at the same time. The nurses got a scenario that told them to monitor their patients'

status. While they were doing that, two alarms went off. Preparing for that scenario required writing software to make the alarms sound during that task.

Match the mode of presentation to the situations in which the product you are testing will be used.

How Do You Divide Up the Tasks and Scenarios for Participants?

If you have a list of 15 tasks that you want to test, you may have exactly 15 task scenarios for the participants, but you may have more or less. You do not have to have a one-to-one correspondence between tasks on your list and your scenarios.

You may have more scenarios than tasks if you want to test the same task more than once. One of your concerns may be how quickly users will learn to do a particular task. You may hypothesize that users will make a few wrong icon choices the first time they try something, but then, after that, they'll know which icon to select and won't make any errors the second time they need to use that icon. In that case, you might have two or three scenarios for the same task in your test.

You may have fewer scenarios than tasks if you combine two or three tasks and have participants do them together.

In deciding how to match up scenarios and tasks, the major issue you have to consider is whether you want separate measurements of time, errors, or other codes for particular tasks. If the software program that you are using to measure the participants' performance can automatically give you time only between the code for "start task" and the code for "stop task," you have to give each task for which you want a separate time as a separate scenario. An example may help to explain this point more clearly:

> Let's say you are testing a project management program. You are concerned that it will be accepted by the company's managers only if it is faster to use than keeping their manual records. You know that speed in doing the tasks is dependent not only on the system's response time, but also on how quickly managers find the right menu choices and the right fields to fill in or change. Time is one appropriate measure of the ease of use of this product.
>
> Your task list for this test includes these three tasks that project managers have to do:
> - get a project's file
> - make changes to the schedule
> - add a new person to the project team

You could write a scenario that had your project manager participants do all three of these at once. In that case, you would automatically know only the total time, total errors, and total frustrations for the combined set of three tasks.

However, you might want to know how much time it takes the participants to do each part, how many errors they make doing each part, and whether one of these tasks is more frustrating than the others. In that case, you would create three scenarios. Participants would stop at the end of each one. The data-lo gging software would give you the time, error count, and frustration count for each task, that is for each scenario, separately.

In the first case, the one in which you have the participants do all three tasks as part of one scenario, you would give the participants a page that might look like Figure 12-1.

Task 1

You are the project manager for the BOOK project. You've just found out that there's been a change in schedule and staffing for the project and you have to make the computer files reflect those changes.

- Get the BOOK project on your screen so that you can change it.

- Deliverable #3 is going to be two weeks late. Change the file to reflect that.

- To make even that new deadline, your boss has authorized you to add another designer, Jed Brown, full time for two weeks starting tomorrow. Jed earns the same salary as Betsy Moore. Add Jed to the project staff.

Figure 12-1.   Three tasks as one scenario, timed together

In the second case, in which you want to know separate times and other counts for each task, you would give the participants the same instructions, but you would separate them into three tasks, giving each task as a separate scenario on a separate page. It might look like Figure 12-2.

Task 1

You are the project manager for the BOOK project. You've just found out that there's been a change in schedule and staffing for the project and you have to make the computer files reflect those changes.

Get the BOOK project on your screen so that you can change it.

Task 2

Deliverable #3 is going to be two weeks late.

Change the file to reflect that.

Task 3

To make even that new deadline, your boss has authorized you to add another designer, Jed Brown, full time for two weeks starting tomorrow.

Jed earns the same salary as Betsy Moore.

Add Jed to the project staff.

Figure 12-2. The same three tasks as separate scenarios, timed separately

How Do You Make Participants Stop Between Tasks?

If you want to time the tasks separately, you have to get the participants to stop between each task. In some organizations, the usability testers give participants the tasks one at a time. That way, they always know when the participant has finished one task and when the participant begins the next task. If you run your test that way, you can also ask questions about the task, conducting a mini-interview after each one.

However, if your test consists of many short tasks, going in to the participant between each one may be disruptive. In a typical test in the AIR lab, we give the participants a booklet of the scenarios that we want them to do during the test. Each scenario that we want to time separately is on a separate page. Because "task" is an easier and clearer word for participants than "scenario," we label the pages as "Task 1.," "Task 2.," and so on.

To remind participants to stop at the end of each task, each page includes two sentences near the bottom:

Please tell us when you have finished this task.
Please wait for us to tell you to turn the page.

At the beginning of the test, the person who interacts with the participant, the "briefer," also reminds the participant:

- to wait for the briefer to say when to begin the first task
- to say out loud when the task is done
- to wait again between each task until the briefer says to go ahead

Putting the scenario for each task that you want to time separately on a separate page is one way to get participants to stop between each task. The entire test team will appreciate having a few moments between each of the participant's tasks to finish their own work and be ready to observe again.

When we want to get participants' reactions to each task, we include a short posttask questionnaire in the booklet after each task. You can see an example of a posttask questionnaire in Chapter 14 on "Preparing Test Materials." A posttask questionnaire, like the mini-interview that some teams do between tasks, allows you to get the participant's immediate reaction to each task. Answering a few questions after each task also gives the participant something to do while the test team finishes logging their own comments.

Now that you have turned your task list into the specific scenarios that you'll give to the participants, we'll turn to the question of what you want to observe and measure while participants are working with the product.

13

Deciding How to Measure Usability

In this chapter, we consider how to plan the observations and measurements for a usability test. We begin with a brief discussion of the purposes of taking quantitative measures of what participants do in a usability test. Then we talk about

- understanding what you can measure
- matching measures to your goals and concerns
- matching measures to the product's stage of development
- setting quantitative criteria for each measure and each task

In the first part of the book, we urged you to set quantitative usability goals as you plan a product. Setting quantitative usability goals lets you define just what you mean by "ease of learning" or "ease of use" for a particular product. These goals can also help you plan the observations and measurements for each usability test. If you set quantitative usability goals before you design the product, you have a rational basis for a usability test: You are testing to see how well the product is meeting those predesign goals.

There are two main reasons for planning your observations and for measuring participants' performance with the product. The first is that, in a typical test, a great deal is happening very fast. If you don't think about what you want to focus on, if you just go into the test "to see how the product is doing," you may miss critical information that you need to understand how to fix the problems that people are having.

The second reason for planning is that you need accurate counts of relevant measures to know how serious participants' problems with the product are. You may need the numbers to convince managers and developers that the problems are real, serious, and need to be fixed.

Understanding What You Can Measure

In a usability test, you are collecting both

- performance measures: that is, counts of actions and behaviors that you can see
- subjective measures: that is, people's perceptions, opinions, and judgments

Performance measures

Performance measures are quantitative. You can count how much time people take, how many errors they make, how many times they repeat the same error.

Most performance measures require careful observation, but not judgmental decision, to know if the behavior being counted did or did not take place. If only one icon accomplishes what the task requires, when the participant chooses an icon, the choice is either right or wrong.

For a few observable behaviors, there is an element of the observer's judgment in deciding what to count as the behavior. An obvious example is deciding when a participant is "showing or expressing frustration." To avoid the problem of differences among participants being due to different observers' judgments, we strongly recommend that the same person be in charge of counting the performance measures throughout a usability test.

The list that follows gives examples of performance measures for testing the usability of products, including the interface, online help, and print documentation. You would not use all of these in one test. You would pick the ones that are relevant to your product and your concerns. The list is not exhaustive. You may well want to measure something else for your particular situation.

Examples of Performance Measures in Typical Usability Tests

time to finish a task
time spent navigating menus
time spent in the online help
time to find information in the manual
time spent reading in the manual
time spent recovering from errors

number of wrong menu choices
number of incorrect choices in dialogue boxes
number of wrong icon choices
number of wrong function keys chosen
number of other errors
number of repeated errors (the same error more than once)

number of calls to the "help desk" or for "aid"
number of screens of online help looked at
number of repeated looks at same help screen

number of times turned to the manual
number of times turned to quick reference card
number of pages looked at in each visit to the manual
number of searches in the index in each visit to the manual
number of searches in the table of contents in each visit to the manual

observations of frustration
observations of confusion
expressions of satisfaction

What About Counting Keystrokes?

One of the most talked about but unused measures of performance is capturing keystroke data. Software tools are available that will take each key press and mouse action and put them into a file in which you can tabulate their occurrences and analyze their sequences.

Keystroke data can be very informative. When the application you are testing uses function keys, you can count how often participants use them. You can also tabulate how often the functions in an application are used.

> Imagine, for example, that you have designed an application like the MS-DOS version of Lotus 1-2-3 and you want to know how often participants access each of the items in the Worksheet menu hierarchy. You could count the times that participants press the / key that displays the menu and each of the letter codes that follow the /. For example, the occurrences of /P tell you how often participants use the Print option in the menu and the occurrences of /PP tell you how often participants print directly to a printer.

In our experience, however, when we are diagnosing the usability problems with a product, we rarely wish that we had keystroke data. We are able to see enough with our cameras to capture the errors that users make and to record those errors in our data-logging software.

> If participants choose /PP when they should have chosen something else, it is obvious to us, because the software tries to print to the printer rather than showing on the screen the result of what the participants should have chosen. Our human data recorder codes the wrong menu choices in the data-logg ing software, capturing not only what the participant chose but also indicating what he or she should have chosen.

If you are considering purchasing or creating a keystroke-capture program, keep these three points in mind:

- You must have keystroke-capture software that is compatible with the hardware you are using for the product you are testing.
  If you are testing software that runs on a 386-personal computer, you can use a keystroke-capture program that was designed for that hardware. But, if you then want to test software that runs on a workstation, you may not be able to use the same keystroke-capture program.
- It takes time to tabulate and analyze keystroke data. Keystroke-capture programs generate a tremendous amount of data. Typically, you will be interested in a minute fraction

of that data. Finding and checking each of the occurrences you are looking for can take a great deal of time and effort. This effort may not be worthwhile unless the usability problem you are documenting is a high-priority issue.

- Identifying the data you want may not be easy.
  In many situations, participants have more than one way to accomplish the same task. For example, in the Windows version of Lotus 1-2-3, participants can accomplish the same goal, namely printing a worksheet on a printer, by pressing /PP or by clicking with a mouse on a printer icon and on an OK option in a dialogue box. You would need to identify both of these sequences to count the occurrences of printing. In addition, you will probably be interested in the *wrong* keystrokes that people made as they tried to do a task. You would not find those by looking for the correct sequences. You would only find those by studying the record to see where the correct sequence should show up and then reviewing the participants' actual sequence of keystrokes.

In general, it is much easier to focus on the wrong keystrokes only and to code those in your data log of the usability test where you can write a comment with each occurrence that you record.

While there certainly are occasions when keystroke data would be useful to have, we urge you to consider carefully whether it is worth the effort to sift through keystroke data to document a usability problem. In our experience conducting workshops and speaking to audiences about usability testing, we find that many people ask about capturing keystrokes without understanding how time-consuming it is to analyze the data and how easy it often is to document usability problems in other ways.

Subjective measures

Subjective measures may be either quantitative or qualitative. For example, you can give people a 5-point or 7-point scale and ask them to rate how easy or difficult a product is to use. The judgment is subjective, but you get a quantitative response. You can talk about the participants' average rating of the product.

You can also collect participants' spontaneous comments about the product by asking them to think out loud as they are working with it. Their comments are both subjective and qualitative. You can, however, report frequencies—that is, how many people made comments about a particular problem.

In a typical usability test, you might collect subjective measures such as these listed below.

Examples of Subjective Measures in Typical Usability Tests

Ratings of:	
	• ease of learning the product
	• ease of using the product
	• ease of doing a particular task
	• ease of installing the product
	• helpfulness of the online help
	• ease of finding information in the manual
	• ease of understanding the information
	• usefulness of the examples in the help

Preferences and reasons for the preferences:	
	• over a previous version
	• over a competitor's product
	• over the way they are doing the tasks now

Predictions of behavior and reasons for the predicted behavior:	
	• Would you buy this product?
	• Would you pay extra for the manual?
	• How much would you pay for this product?

Spontaneous comments:	
	• "I'm totally lost here."
	• "That was easy."
	• "At this point, I'd call tech support."
	• "I don't understand this message."

To get spontaneous comments from the participants in a usability test, you must encourage them to think out loud as they are working. As they think out loud, you can capture their spontaneous comments on the videotape, in the data-log ging software, or in your notes.

For all the subjective measures except the spontaneous comments, we use questionnaires that participants fill out after each task or at the end of the test. You'll find hints on developing posttask and posttest questionnaires, as well as sample questionnaires, in the next chapter, on "Preparing Test Materials."

In the rest of this chapter, we focus on performance measures: how to select the ones you want and how to set expectations for them for a particular product, task, and test.

Matching Measures to Your Goals and Concerns

The performance measures that you choose should be directly related to the quantitative usability goals that you set and to the concerns that are driving this particular usability test.

Each goal and concern should lead you directly to one or more performance measures. Here are just a few examples:

Collect only what you need to measure your goals and concerns.

Remember that you cannot cover everything in one usability test.

- If you are concerned about users choosing the right menu option, count "wrong menu choices."
- If you are concerned about how easily users can find what they need in the manual, collect time data. If you can measure specific times within a task, measure "time to find information." If you can only measure total task time, count "references to the documentation" and "time for the task."
- If you are concerned about ease of learning the icons, count "wrong icon choices" and "repeated errors."
- If you have a goal of reducing calls to the help desk, count "calls to the help desk."

Research issue:	Is counting calls to the "help desk" in a test a good way to estimate the calls that the released product will generate? Do participants act differently towards the help desk during a test than they would in their homes or offices? Are they more or less likely to call the help desk during a test?

How Do You Collect Performance Data?

Many usability test laboratories use software programs for collecting ("logging") data on participants' performance. Some labs develop their own data-logging software; others use a commercially available product[1].

---

[1] A commercially available data-logging product is TestLogr from Usability Sciences Corporation, 5525 MacArthur Blvd., Suite 340, Irving, TX 75038, 214-550-1599.

The commercially available product and most privately developed, proprietary programs allow you to set codes for whatever behaviors interest you. For example, if you are collecting data on number of wrong menu choices, you can set a code, perhaps W, for "wrong menu choice." In most of these programs, you can set as many as 20 different codes, although you do not want to have to watch for more than 6 or 7 in a particular test. In most, setting and changing the codes is very easy.

One of the members of the test team sits at the computer and enters the relevant code each time the participant does something that the test team is coding. We use the term *logging data* for this role and call the person the *data recorder*. Figure 13-1 shows the main screen of AIR's logging program during a particular test.

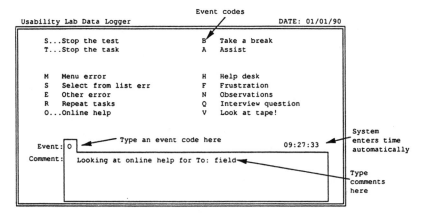

Figure 13-1.   The main screen of AIR's logging program, during a test

The logging programs keep track of time and, therefore, can give you time for a task. Some only give you time for an entire task. Others allow you to analyze time between specific codes within a task.

Most of the data that you collect with the logging program are performance measures, codes that you want counted up. For example, if you specify the code I for "wrong icon choice," the programs will tell you how many times the data recorder on your team typed I as the event code for each participant in each task.

You can also use the log for notes. You can specify a code for the participants' spontaneous comments and another for team members' observations. The programs allow the data recorder to type comments or observations right into the log with each coded entry. You don't have to analyze the frequency of these, but you can print them out. They're more accessible from the log than from the videotape.

What Should You Consider in Building or Buying a Data-logging Program?

Philips and Dumas (1990) provide guidelines on what makes a data-logging program effective and easy to use. You can use these guidelines to set functional requirements whether you are looking for software to purchase or are planning to develop your own.

A data-logging program should have these features (Philips & Dumas, 1990):

- Include preset codes for events that happen in every test. For example, the software should already have codes for starting and stopping the test. That way the test team only has to add codes that are relevant to the specific measures for their test.
- Allow the test team to add codes easily for events that are specific to their test. Codes should be a single letter or number or a function key, for example, O for references to the online help.
- Allow a short description with the code, perhaps up to 20 characters including spaces. The software should show the codes and descriptions on the screen when the data recorder is working. (See Figure 13-1.)
- Provide space for extended comments. Every time the data recorder enters a code, the software should provide space for the recorder to add information about the event or to type the specific comments that the participant or a team member is making. During the working part of a test, that space should allow for at least 300 characters per comment. During interviewing sessions, it should allow for about 900 characters per comment.
- Time-stamp each event using the computer's system clock.
- Compute the duration of whatever events are important for a particular test. That is, the software should allow the test team to create separate codes for starting and stopping events and be able to give the time between those codes. For example, you might want to know how long it takes participants to recover from an error or how long they spend looking through the table of contents of a manual.
- Keep track of multiple events that are happening in parallel. Show visually on the screen when one event in a multiple set has been activated. Figure 13-2 shows this situation for a particular test in the AIR laboratory.
- Allow easy text entry and simple editing of the text field while the data recorder is working. For example, the text field should word-wra p. The backspace and delete keys should work. The arrow keys should allow movement through the text.

```
                    Blinking dots indicate the item is in progress
                         /
Usability Lab Data Logger                               DATE: 01/01/90
┌──────────────────────────────────────────────────────────────────────┐
│    S...Stop the test              B    Take a break                    │
│    T...Stop the task              A    Assist                          │
│                                                                        │
│    M    Menu error                H    Help desk                       │
│    S    Select from list err      F    Frustration                     │
│    E    Other error               N    Observations                    │
│    R    Repeat tasks              Q    Interview question              │
│    O...Online help                V    Look at tape!                   │
│                                                                        │
│                                                                        │
│    Event: │O                                         09:27:33          │
│  Comment: │    Looking at online help for To: field                    │
│           └──────────────────────────────────────────────┐            │
│                                                           │            │
└──────────────────────────────────────────────────────────────────────┘
```

Figure 13-2. The main screen of AIR's data-logging program with a task in progress

- Have a separate editing function that allows more extensive editing after the test. This should include being able to delete or change codes as well as edit the text.
- Allow easy backup and easy movement of the data into a file that can be given a recognizable name. These functions must be extremely reliable. Losing the logged data from a test is a disaster.
- Compute simple statistics itself and also be exportable as an ASCII file to a more powerful statistics program. To be compatible with other programs, the logging program should be able to write a file where each test participant is a row and each code is a column.
- Be able to both display on the screen and to print the log itself and the statistics, including for each task
  — the duration of the task
  — the frequency of each event code
  — the duration and average for each timed event
  — the text of the comments and observations and a summary over participants for each task of
  — the mean and standard deviation of task times
  — the mean and standard deviation of frequencies for each code
- Be able to show times in different formats. In particular, it should be able to show both hours, minutes, seconds, and total seconds (for ease in seeing and computing duration).

We discuss data-logging programs again in Chapter 15 on "Preparing the Test Environment."

What Can You Do If You Don't Have a Computer-based Logging Program?

A computer-based logging program keeps track of time and adds up the frequencies of the codes automatically. A data recorder who is comfortable with the software will be able to capture much more of the test than a single person could do without the software.

The computer-based program, however, is not essential. You can collect performance data with a stopwatch and a paper log. You could set up a form like the one in Figure 13-3 and then just enter the times and tick the appropriate box each time the user does something you are coding.

Usability test of electronic mail program									
Participant #		M = menu error				O = online help			
Date:		S = select from list error				H = help desk			
Recorder:		E = other error				F = frustration			
Task	Time	M	S	E	O	H	F	Participant's comments	Notes
Task 1. Log in	start: stop:								

Figure 13-3. Part of a paper logging form

Should You Measure Positive Behaviors?

The goal of a usability test is to find the product's weaknesses and problems so that you can improve the product before it goes out to users. Therefore, in a usability test, you usually concentrate on measuring areas of concern and counting indicators that your goals are not being met. That means collecting data on time, errors, and frustrations.

Not all the performance measures have to be negative, however. You could, for example, set a code for positive comments or expressions of satisfaction as well as one for frustrations.

In the typical performance measures, such as time and errors, you are also hoping to find low rates, which would indicate that the product is working well for users.

Some of your goals may relate to elements that you have built into the product to help people. If the product has online help, you want people to use it. You might measure the number of times people go to the online help. Your goal for this measure would be that people will use the online help, but that they will not spend a lot of time on each online help screen and that they will not keep going back to read the same help screen many times. Using online help is a positive performance measure. Repeated uses of the same help screen or a long time in help are negative measures.

As we will discuss in the next part of the book, attending a usability test is an emotional challenge for the product's developers, as is reading a test report or viewing a highlight tape. The developers have put their creativity and energy into the product that you are testing. While the focus of the test must be on the problems that participants have, you can help the developers to feel good about themselves and to accept your negative findings if you can also show them that some of the features of the product are working well for users.

Later in this chapter we discuss setting quantitative criteria for each task. One of the values of setting these criteria is that they allow you to find—and show developers—when the product is meeting the criteria. Thus, sometimes positive findings are the absence of the problems that you were concerned enough to want to measure.

Matching Measures to the Product's Stage of Development

As you plan for performance measures, consider where the product is in the development cycle. Some of the measures you might want to use won't make sense because you are testing a prototype or a partially developed product. Here are two examples in which the stage of development will influence what you measure:

- If you are testing a prototype to see whether the product's menu structure matches users' expectations, performance measures such as wrong menu choice, repeated error, and frustration make sense. Time probably does not, especially if the prototype is on a different system from the one that the final product will be on. If the prototype has only a small database behind it for the test, but the real product will be used on a network with many users and a very large database, times for the tasks in the prototype may well not match times in the real product.
- If the manual will have an index, but you are testing a draft and the index isn't ready yet, it doesn't make sense to collect data on time to find information in the manual. You can collect information on how often participants go to the manual, whether they say they would use an index, how useful they find the table of contents, how much time they spend reading the information in the manual, whether they make fewer errors when they use the manual than when they don't use it, and so on. But if you collect data on time to

find information, you must realize you are finding out only about using the table of contents or flipping through the pages, and not about how quickly people who prefer to use an index will get to what they need.

As you conduct iterative tests at different stages in the development cycle, you may want to repeat some measures to gauge improvements. You may also want to collect some different measures because you are concentrating on different concerns or because the product has reached a stage of development where new measures make sense.

Setting Quantitative Criteria for Each Measure and Each Task

How are you going to interpret the data that you get from the performance measures? We urge you to think about that before the usability test as well as after you have the data. This is another aspect of one of our main points, namely that it is not very useful to just say that the product should be "usable" or "easy to use." You have to define that much more explicitly and quantitatively to develop a successful product.

Let's say that you are testing a product that allows users to set a VCR from menus that come up on the TV. One of the tasks you'll have users do is set the VCR to record a program tomorrow night at 7 p.m. from Channel 5. You've also decided that one relevant measure of the product's usability is "time to complete the task." How will you understand the data that you get? If users take an average of half an hour to do the task, will you be satisfied that the product is "easy to use"? What if they take 15 minutes? 10 minutes? 5 minutes?

If you have set quantitative usability goals at the predesign stage, you already have done most of the work for this part of a usability test. If you didn't, this is the time that you'll have to think about what "usability" means for this product, these tasks, and the representative users who will be helping to evaluate the product.

How Do You Set Criteria for Performance Measures?

Usability means making users productive and happy. In setting quantitative criteria for a usability test, therefore, you must focus on users and not on the system or the product.

Don't base your criteria on what you know the product or system

Focus on what will make users say, "This is a great product! It's so easy to use!"

will allow. You could get good test results and still fail in the market-place.

> Don't say "It's going to take people 20 minutes to work their way
> through this menu structure and all the fields they have to fill out."
> That's focusing on the product. If users will get frustrated by that task
> taking 20 minutes, the product isn't easy to use.

If you have information from job and task analyses, contextual interviews, performance tests in focus groups, earlier usability tests, or other interactions with users, they can all help you set criteria for what you are measuring in the usability test you are now planning.

If you are testing usability late in the cycle without the benefit of a process that has included a focus on usability from the beginning, how can you set criteria for a usability test? For many performance measures, your own common sense and putting yourself in the place of users may allow you to set realistic criteria. For example:

- If one of the goals for a product is to reduce support costs, you'd probably measure calls for help and say the product is easy to use only if participants make no calls for help.
- If one of the goals for a product is to have icons that are easy to use, you'd probably measure wrong icon choices. You might want to say the product is easy to use if people make one or two wrong icon choices the first time they have to select a particular icon, but make no wrong icon choices in a later task that requires selecting the same icon.

The measure that is hardest to gauge if you have no user-based data is the time to complete a task. Common sense tells you that 30 minutes to set a VCR to record a program is too long. Users will give up before that. But what is reasonable? That is, what will make users say, "That was easy to do"? What will give you confidence that people will use the product to do that task?

If you or the designers have never set quantitative criteria before, you will find that, at first, the process feels like guesswork. It will probably heighten your realization of how important it is to watch typical users. Your intuition and common sense will get you only so far. If the task you are testing is a new one that has never been included in an application, you are only guessing at how long it "should" take. Only the users can tell you that, and only after they have tried it.

Users' self-reports of how long they think a task should take are also often unreliable. People do not have a good sense of how long a given period of time is. They have to try the task to give you good time estimates of their tolerance for working at it.

A technique that is sometimes helpful is to time an expert doing the task. This will provide you with a baseline from which to judge the times that participants take. If an expert takes 3 minutes to do one task and 30 seconds to do another, you know that the first task is more time-consuming. This may help you interpret the task times of participants. However, you do not necessarily want to set your time criteria for the task for novices as the time that an expert took to complete it.

What Are Typical Criteria for Performance Measures?

You may find it useful to think about three levels for each performance measure for each task:

• Excellent	The product is really easy to use according to this performance measure in this task.
• Acceptable or OK	Users will be satisfied with this level of performance on this measure in this task.
• Unacceptable	The product is not OK. According to this measure, people are having problems using the product for this task.

In setting criteria for performance measures, it may help to remember that you will be looking at the data across users and across measures. You will generally be reporting means (averages), not individual scores. (See Chapter 20, "Tabulating and Analyzing Data," for more on using the data.)

- You are not necessarily going to say that a product has problems if one participant makes more errors than expected in trying to do a particular task but all the other participants did the task without difficulty. You *would* want to look more deeply into what happened in that session. You *would* want to ask: What were the errors? Why did that participant make those errors? Which users does that participant represent?
- You are not necessarily going to say that a product has problems if the participants take slightly longer on the average to do a task than you expected. If they don't make errors and they don't express any frustrations, you may say your expectations of time were off rather than saying the product needs fixing.

Your goal is not to have the product pass your criteria. It is to help develop a product that people will love to use.

- On the other hand, you are not going to say the product is fine even if your criteria for some measures are met. If you say that 15 minutes, three wrong menu choices, and four other errors are OK for a task, and people meet your expectations but their comments indicate that they won't use the product, you'd want to revise your criteria.

Selecting Performance Measures

Before you can set criteria for the performance that you expect participants to achieve with the product, you have to choose the performance measures you are going to count. Remember that each measure that you choose should give you useful information about your concerns or goals for the product.

Here is an example of the performance measures that you might count for two tasks in testing an electronic mail program. We list only some of the general and specific concerns that you might have about this product.

Product:
General concerns

Electronic mail
- ease of use for users who have never used e-mail
- ease of use for people who know other e-mail systems
- Will new users be able to navigate through the menus quickly and easily?
- Will new users be able to select items from lists on the screen quickly and easily?
- Will the online help be useful?
- Will users get enough feedback to know what the system is doing?

Specific concerns:

- Will new users be able to read a specific piece of mail and skip over mail they don't want to read at this moment?
- Will new users be able to find and select people's addresses to send them mail?
- Will new users be able to find the right menu path to read a message? write and send a message?

Task 1:	*Read a message*

Measures:
- time to complete task
- time in online help
- time recovering from errors
- M = chooses incorrect menu option
- S = uses incorrect procedure for selecting from a list
- R = repeats task after completing it successfully
- O = goes to online help
- H = calls help desk
- F = expresses frustration

Task 2:   *Write and send a message*

Measures:
- time to complete task
- time in online help
- time recovering from errors
- M = chooses incorrect menu option
- S = uses incorrect procedure for selecting from a list (for example, from a list of addresses)
- E = other error (for example: tries to type message in wrong place on screen or fills out fields incorrectly)
- R = repeats task after completing it successfully
- O = goes to online help
- H = calls help desk
- F = expresses frustration

Setting Criteria for These Measures

Now you are ready to set criteria. Remember the point is always to ask yourself: "What behavior on each of these measures will make users be productive and happy with the product?"

You might set these criteria for the measures in our example. (You can also put these criteria into spreadsheets that you can later use for recording and analyzing the data.) (See Figure 13-4.)

Measure	Excellent	Acceptable	Unacceptable
Task 1: Read message			
Time for task	< 3 minutes	3 - 5 min.	> 5 minutes
Time in online help	< 1 minute	1 - 2 minutes	> 2 minutes
Time recovering fr. errors	0	< 1 minute	> 1 minute
M = menu error	0	0	1 or more
S = selection error	0	1 - 2	more than 2
R = repeats task	0	0	1 or more
O = uses of online help	1	2 - 3	more than 3
H = help desk calls	0	0	1 or more
F = frustrations	0	0	1 or more
Task 2: Write and send			
Time for task	< 10 minutes	10 - 15 min.	> 15 minutes
Time in online help	< 2 minutes	2 - 4 minutes	> 4 minutes
Time recovering fr. errors	0	< 3 minute	> 3 minutes
M = menu error	0	0	1 or more
S = selection error	0	1 - 2	more than 2
E = other errors	0	1 - 2	more than 2
R = repeats task	0	0	1 or more
O = uses of online help	1 - 2	3	more than 3
H = help desk calls	0	0	1 or more
F = frustrations	0	0	1 or more

Figure 13-4.   Setting criteria for measuring usability

Are the Measures the Same for All Tasks in a Given Test?

For most tasks in the same test, you'll want to follow the same performance measures, that is, you'll be observing the same aspects of what users do. However, all the performance measures may not be relevant for all tasks. If one of the tasks is getting into a program, menus and online help may not be available at that point. You won't count wrong menu choices or uses of online help for that task.

In the example we've just given, we included a measure of "other errors" to capture problems participants have in finding where on the screen to type a message or filling out fields incorrectly. That measure is relevant for tasks like writing messages, forwarding messages, and replying to messages. It isn't relevant for the task of reading a message.

Are the Criteria of Performance the Same For All Tasks?

No. Your expectations for the same measure may vary from task to task. The criterion you set for time will surely vary with the task. The criterion for how many times participants go to online help might also vary with the number of choices people have to make and the number of fields they have to fill out. If you are looking at how easy the product is to learn, you might set criteria for the first time participants do a task that differ from the criteria you set for subsequent scenarios that essentially repeat the same task.

How Do You Take the Test Situation into Account in Setting Criteria?

Most people become accustomed to the lab environment very quickly, and it does not affect their performance. If anything, they'll work longer and harder at the tasks in the lab setting than they would at their desks or in their homes.

However, you may want to add a small amount of time to account for the fact that participants have to read the scenario for each task. (If you keep the scenarios short, this extra time will be trivial for most tasks.)

> In one test, the first scenario asked the participants to get into the program. This required typing a user ID and a password. The test team decided that if the product were really easy to use, people would be able to complete this task in less than 15 seconds. In fact, we found that participants in the test who did the task with no problems and were happy with the way the product handled this task took an average of 30 seconds. When we reviewed the tapes, we realized that reading the few lines of this first scenario and looking over the screen for the first time accounted for most of the difference between the expectation and the reality.

You would not double the time for each task, but adding 15 seconds to read the scenario is certainly reasonable.

Should You Count System Response Time in Setting the Criteria?

This question is more difficult to answer than the previous one. Slow system response time may frustrate users and make them unwilling to use the product. If speeding up the system response time is not possible, a different product design is probably needed to compensate for the slow system.

If you set your expectation for time to include all the time the system will need in a particular task, the product may meet your criterion and still fail in the marketplace.

We come back at the end of this section to the point that we started with: In deciding on measures and criteria for them, you must focus on *users*, not on the *product* or the *system*.

In setting criteria for measures like time and error rates, you must not ask, "What will it take to do this task with this product?" You must ask, "What will make users say, 'This is fast enough for me. This is easy for me. I'll use this feature all the time.'?"

There are two other issues about response time to consider:

One problem is that response time is difficult to estimate with a prototype. In Chapter 5, we discussed the fidelity of prototypes and mentioned that even prototypes that look quite crude can help you to assess the usability of a design. When it comes to "look and feel," prototypes can give you an accurate sense of usability, but one of the weaknesses of prototypes is their inability to give you an accurate estimate of response time.

Sometimes the prototype will run much faster than the real product and you will underestimate the problems users will have waiting for a response. Just as often, the prototype runs slower than the real product and biases users against the product. Some prototyping tools become very slow when screens contain complex graphics. If you are concerned about response time and you can't simulate it, you must wait until you have the real product to verify the influence of system response time on usability. (Don't wait, however, to test the usability of other aspects of the interface or documentation!)

A second problem is that it is difficult to estimate how response time will affect usability after the product is in use for some time. A slow response time that is acceptable to new users may become intolerable after a few weeks. To assess this problem, you would need to have participants use the product for many hours. While it is possible to run tests of long-term use, they are time-consuming and can be expensive. Therefore, not many design teams are willing to take the time to assess long-term, response-time issues. Usability tests are usually limited to investigating initial ease of learning problems and those ease of use problems that do not change over time. This limitation is not with the usability testing process itself, but with how it is most commonly used today.

Now that we have decided on the tasks that the participants will do during the test and on how we will measure participants' performance with the product, we can turn to the other materials that you will want to have ready for the usability tests. Some of these materials are questionnaires you can use to gather the subjective measures that we discussed at the beginning of this chapter. Other materials are consent forms, information about the help desk, and questionnaires for gathering more detailed background data about the participants.

14

Preparing Test Materials

For every usability test there are materials you will need to prepare in addition to the product you are testing. These include:

- legal forms to protect the rights of your organization and the participant
- questionnaires for the test participant to fill out
- a training script to bring all participants to the same level of experience (if you need it)
- task scenarios for the participant to attempt
- checklists for testing to keep the test team organized
- manuals and other types of product documentation that will be included in the test

You need to have these materials ready for the pilot test, but don't make copies for the full test until *after* the pilot test.

In the remaining sections of this chapter, we describe each of these types of materials and give you examples to help you create them. At the end of the chapter, there are example paragraphs for legal forms and example pretest, posttask, and posttest questionnaires.

The Legal Form

In a usability test, both the organization conducting the test and the test participant have rights they need to protect. As a tester, it is your responsibility to

- create a form that correctly states each party's rights
- ensure that test participants have read and understood what the form says
- observe or witness participants signing the form

You and your company need to create and follow procedures for the proper treatment of human test participants.

We recommend that you follow at least the minimum requirements we describe here even if your organization does not receive federal funds for testing or research. As a tester, you have an obligation to understand the practices that the federal government mandates for organizations that conduct federally funded research. The government scientists who have helped establish these practices have worked from a foundation of ethical principles that usability testers should understand and adopt as they see fit.

Even when such a suit has no merit, you and your organization are vulnerable to giving the appearance of negligence if you have no written policies and procedures for the treatment of human participants.

If you wish to learn more about the federal policy for the treatment of human participants, the best place to start is in the Notice of Proposed Rulemaking in the Federal Register, 1988, Vol. 53, No., 218, pp. 45661–45682. The notice contains a brief history of risk and informed consent, a glossary of definitions, and the details of the federal policy.

The Concept of Minimal Risk

At the heart of any policy on the treatment of human participants is the concept of minimal risk. As defined in the Federal Register, *minimal risk* means that "the probability and magnitude of harm or discomfort anticipated in the test are not greater, in and of themselves, than those ordinarily encountered in daily life or during the performance of routine physical or psychological examinations or tests."

Usability tests should never put participants at more than minimal risk. Tests of software and documentation would rarely present a physical risk to participants. Tests of hardware, particularly installation tests, could put participants at risk if there is any potential for shock or for injury due to lifting heavy objects.

One type of risk that can occur in a usability test is more subtle. It happens when the test participants work for the organization developing the product being tested. Test participants who are watched by their bosses or friends of their bosses, could feel that they are at risk of jeopardizing their jobs if they are critical of the product.

If, in your judgment, any usability test could put participants at risk, you have three options:

1. Eliminate the risk.
2. Follow the federal policies for such tests.
3. Don't do the test.

The federal policies for conducting a test that puts participants at risk are so elaborate that eliminating the risk is your best option.

Informed Consent

The key to protecting both the participant's and your organization's rights is to obtain an informed consent. Respect for persons requires that participants be given the opportunity to *choose* what will or will not happen to them. You provide participants with this opportunity when you obtain their informed consent.

There are three elements to any informed consent:

1. Information—Your consent form should explain
   - the procedures you will follow
   - the purpose of the test
   - any risks to the participant
   - the opportunity to ask questions
   - the opportunity to withdraw at any time

2. Comprehension—You must convey the information in the consent form clearly and completely. Rushing through the consent procedure, making the consent procedure seem unimportant, or not allowing the opportunity for questions will adversely affect the participant's ability to make an informed choice.
3. Voluntariness—The participants must be free from coercion and undue influence when you ask for their consent. Unjustifiable pressures usually occur when you are in a position of authority over the participant. For example, if you know the boss of participants who work in your company and the participants felt that you suggested that you would tell their boss about withdrawing from the test, they might not give their consent voluntarily. When participants are considering withdrawing from a test, remain calm and neutral in your manner so that you do not unduly influence them.

If you include these three elements in your procedure, the consent you obtain should be informed.

Explaining rights to test participants and obtaining their signature can be an awkward moment. By its nature, the process must occur very early in the test, often within the first 15 minutes. At that point, test participants are still understandably uneasy. As we describe in Chapter 18, "Caring for Test Participants," it is essential that you develop a rapport with participants from the minute they appear at the test site, and keep that rapport going.

Use the serious issues that are covered in the legal form to your advantage. Filling out the form provides a transition from the greetings and "small talk" that precede to the test events that follow.

Convey to the participant in your professional handling of these issues that the test is an important event for you and for the designers of the product. You expect the test participant to follow instructions and to use this opportunity to help future users be more productive.

If you are videotaping the test, have the camera(s) on while you are going over the form. The videotape shows that the participant was properly informed and voluntarily signed the form without pressure.

The best approach to explaining the legal form and why they are important is to use a neutral, but friendly tone. Convey to the test participant that the test is an important event to the testing organization. A typical opening might be:

"The purpose of this test is to make the product (computer program, manual) easy to use for people like you. We have chosen you for this test because you meet our special qualifications to be an evaluator. We want you to help us improve this product. To make this test work for

both of us, you need to keep what you learn today confidential and you
need to be aware of you rights as an evaluator. The purpose of these
forms is to make your rights and responsibilities clear. Let's go over
them, step by step, so that you understand them . . ."

At this point, go through the legal issues one at a time making sure
the participant understands each one.
 The major legal issues are:

- *Nondisclosure*—when the product is under development or
  in any way confidential, you need to tell participants they
  cannot talk about the product or their opinions of it to
  anyone, including their closest friend or spouse. It helps to
  suggest to participants what they *can* say. They need some
  explanation of how they spent their time. Tell them
  something like "you can tell people that you were evaluating
  a new product (computer program, manual) by using it and
  giving your opinions of it, but you cannot tell them anything
  about the product because it is confidential."
- *Waivers*—when you make a videotape of the test, and when
  you have participants fill out questionnaires, you need their
  permission to use these questionnaires and tapes. Companies
  have different policies and wordings for the scope of the
  permission they seek. Typically, you will ask for permission
  to use this material for the purposes of evaluating the
  product and educating product designers about usability
  issues. However, you need to inform participants that
  whenever this material is used, their names will not be
  included. You should instruct them *not* to put their name on
  any form, except the legal forms, which will not be available
  to anyone but the test administrator.
- *Participants' rights*—organizations that watch over the use of
  people in research and evaluations agree that these people
  have a set of rights. As we have seen, one of these rights is
  the right to be informed about their rights.

We assume that you will never be putting your participant at more
than minimal risk. The rights that are the most relevant to a usability
test are

*Every test lab
needs to have and
enforce a policy
on human rights.*

- the right to withdraw at any time without penalty
- the right to ask for a break at any time
- the right to the protection of privacy by not using their
  names
- the right to know what the test is about and what they will
  be doing

After you have carefully explained each of the paragraphs in the legal form, ask the participant to read them further if he or she wishes and then sign and date them. Do not fidget while the participant is going over the form. This is a silent moment that conveys the seriousness of what's at stake and reinforces your professionalism and your willingness to be patient throughout the test. If you project an attitude of "let's get this over with," even if it's just with your body language, participants will feel pressured into signing quickly. You may want to leave the test area while the participant reads the form. When you see the participant signing the form, you can go back in and ask if he or she has any additional questions.

The form at the end of this chapter contains sample paragraphs you may want to modify to meet your organization's needs.

Questionnaires

There are several points during a test when you will want to ask participants questions about a variety of topics, such as their backgrounds, their opinions about a particular task, and their opinions about the overall ease of use of the product. You need to anticipate every question you might ask and put them in written form.

There are two reasons for having written questionnaires:

1. So that you ask every participant the same question.
2. So that you will not forget to ask the question.

It isn't enough just to put the question in writing. You also need to put the question into the most specific and appropriate form. The answers to an open-ended question, such as "was this product easy or difficult to use?" won't be as useful as the more specific information you'd get if you format the question as a structured rating. For example: Using the software was:

1	2	3	4	5
Very Easy	Easy	Neither Easy Nor Difficult	Difficult	Very Difficult

Comment:_____
_____

The following are some sources on how to create effective questions:

Dillman, D. (1985). *Mail and telephone surveys: The total design method*. New York: John Wiley and Sons.
Labaw, P. (1981). *Advanced questionnaire design*. Cambridge, MA: Abt Books.
Payne, S.L. (1979). *The art of asking questions*. Princeton, NJ: Princeton University Press.
Sudman, M., & Bradbum, A. (1982). *Asking questions: A practical guide to questionnaire design*. San Francisco: Jossey-Bass.

There are three points during a test when you might need to have test participants answer questions: before the start of the tasks, after each task, and after they complete all of the tasks. More specifically, there may be a:

- pretest questionnaire to gather information about the background of the participant
- posttask questionnaire to gather judgments and ratings after each task
- posttest questionnaire to gather judgments and ratings after participants have completed all of the tasks

In the following paragraphs we discuss creating each of these questionnaires and make suggestions about the best formats for questions. The forms at the end of the chapter contain examples of all three types of questionnaires.

Pretest Questionnaire

The purpose of a pretest questionnaire is usually to (a) gather background information to help you interpret the data from the test, and (b) to verify the qualifications of the test participant in cases when you have not already done so. Even when you have qualified the participants by having them complete a questionnaire during recruitment, there may be additional information you'll need to know.

For example, if you are testing the user interface to an electronic mail application, you may want to know how much experience the participant has using microcomputer software. People who use microcomputers frequently are familiar with common function key mappings, such as pressing the ESC key to move back to the previous screen. Conversely, people with little microcomputer experience may not know these mappings and, therefore, perform more poorly using electronic mail. When you conduct your analysis, you may, therefore, find wide differences in performance that are related to microcomputer experience, and these differences may highlight weaknesses in the interface for inexperienced microcomputer users. Therefore, you should ask about microcomputer experience on a pretest questionnaire for a microcomputer product.

Do not use a pretest questionnaire to go fishing for every potential confounding factor.

Every question you include should have a purpose. Ask yourself, "What will I do with the information I get from this question?" and "How will I use this information in the test report?" If the question will help you diagnose problems with the product, it is a candidate to be in the questionnaire. If not, eliminate it.

Most of our pretest questionnaires are about one page or less. What follows are examples of the types of questions we most frequently ask. We have not listed the alternative answer options as they vary with each test.

- What is your job title?
- How would you describe yourself? ("programmer," "computer operator," etc.)
- How long have you been doing this kind of work?
- How long have you worked with this product?
- How long have you been using personal computers?
- How often do you use a personal computer?
- Which of the following software products have you used?
- What features of _____ do you use most often?

Posttask Questionnaire

In usability tests that try to simulate having the user working alone with the product, you will normally wait until participants have completed all of the tasks or reached the time limit before you interview them. However, there are tests in which you want to get a reaction immediately after a particular task or a scenario, or after every task or scenario was completed.

- You might want to obtain an immediate reaction to the participant's experience during an important task. For example, you may have a task you have designed to see if users can find information in the manual or to see if they can navigate through an online help system. In these cases, you can get an immediate rating by the participant of how easy it was to use the manual or help system by including a posttask questionnaire that participants fill out as soon as they have completed the task.
- You might want to measure changes in perceptions over time. For example, different types of software often have major barriers to usability that appear at different levels of experience with them. Barriers to using communications

software often occur early in use, while barriers to using a database management system may not occur until the user is faced with understanding concepts such as what a "view" of a database is. You can track users' changing perceptions of ease of learning by asking for ratings *during* the test.

In almost all cases, you will also want to cover these issues with the posttest questionnaire and interview.

Consequently, when you have a posttask questionnaire, make it short, usually one page or five to six questions at most, with a few questions and room for the participant to make a comment. Having a short set of questions can actually be an advantage when the test team is new to testing. They may need a minute or two after each task to finish writing notes or typing into the data log. When you have the participant wait until these activities are completed, there is an awkward "dead" time for the participant. The posttask questions give the participant something to do during this time.

At the end of this chapter, we have included an example posttask questionnaire.

The tradeoff in a posttask questionnaire is between sampling the participants' perceptions over time and breaking up the flow of the tasks.

Posttest Questionnaire

After participants have completed the tasks, you have one final opportunity to gather data. After spending time, often two to three hours, using the product, participants have had an opportunity to gain some perspective about their impressions of its usability. The posttest questionnaire provides you with a vehicle to gather those impressions.

In our tests, we begin the debriefing by clarifying any ambiguities that may have occurred during the test. Frequently, events happen at a fast pace, and you need to clarify something that the participant did or said before you both forget about it. Then you present the posttest questionnaire. The debriefer should leave the room while the participant works on the questions. Participants pay more attention to the questions when they are left alone. After several hours of work both the test team and the participant are anxious to finish. It is almost impossible for the debriefer to avoid squirming and subtly hurrying the participant when the debriefer stays with participants while they fill out the questionnaire. After the participant is finished with the questionnaire, the debriefer goes over it with the participant to clarify the questionnaire responses.

In most posttest questionnaires there are usually two types of questions:

1. General questions that could apply to any product
2. Specific questions that apply only to the tested product

General Questions.   In our posttest questionnaire, we ask participants to answer questions such as:

- How do you rate the overall ease of use or difficulty of the product?
- How easy or difficult was it to find information in the manual?
- What do you like least about the product?
- What do you like best about the product?
- What one thing would you tell the designers to change?
- Would you use this product if your company bought it?
- Would you recommend that your company buy this product?

As with all questionnaires, structure as many as you can into formats such as ratings or YES/NO questions.

Specific Questions.   In many cases, you will have usability concerns about the design of the product you are testing. When you know that you will want to focus on these concerns during the debriefing, put as many as you can in the form of structured questions. Even when you know that you will be covering a topic during the debriefing, put structured questions about it in the questionnaire. It is much easier to tabulate the answers to questions than it is to piece together the debriefer's notes from all the test participants.

Training Scripts

There are usually two reasons for providing training during a usability test:

1. To ensure that all participants have the same level of skill or knowledge before they begin the tasks
2. To provide some groups of participants with training that others do not get

Whatever the purpose of the training, it is critical to the validity of the test that you conduct the training with a script. The script is for you. It is not something you give the test participant. The script is an aid to ensure that every participant receives the same training.

If you don't have a script, you will be inconsistent in the way you train.

There are too many details you need to attend to during a test to follow the same training procedure flawlessly without a script. It is rare to conduct a test in which no training is given to participants. While there are some tests that specifically require that participants not be shown *anything* about the product or its environment, most products exist in an environment that requires some orientation. When you are not testing the environment, you often simply want to get participants familiar with it so that they can begin to use the product. In effect, you want to "control" this variable by making sure that everyone is familiar with the environment before they begin.

Beware of training that is mislabeled as "participant orientation." For example, in preparing for a test of a new software development tool, you decide that you want to make sure that each programmer you test understands how to manipulate the windows and use the mouse buttons that the operating system environment requires. Do not be casual about how you will teach these skills. You will be tempted to make the training informal and unstructured. If you give in to this temptation, your training will be inconsistent. Some test participants will begin the tasks without the skills other participants have.

To provide effective training, you need to decide:

- the purpose of the training
- what skills and knowledge you want participants to learn
- how you will conduct the training
- what criteria of success you will use to measure the effectiveness of training

When you have made these decisions, create a training script to conduct the training and to measure its success.

Use the training script to list each of the procedures the briefer needs to follow to train the participant. In some cases, the script is simply a short checklist of procedures. The briefer checks off each item as the training proceeds.

For some tests, however, training becomes a more critical issue. For example, we once conducted a comparison test of four competitive devices. We wanted to make sure that the participants, who were engineers, knew how to perform five basic tasks with each of the devices. Our briefer was an expert in usability testing, but not in the detailed operation of all four of the devices. Creating a five- to eight-page training script for each device was essential to ensuring that our test was not biased toward one or another of the devices. In addition, it freed our briefer from having to memorize and then remember the detailed steps to follow for each device.

The Task Scenarios

In Chapter 12 we describe how to create task scenarios from the tasks you want participants to attempt. As you prepare for the test, you need to package the scenarios into a format that will allow you to observe participants and record data on each task. The purpose of scenarios is to make the tasks realistic and plausible to test participants. However, the way that you organize the scenarios on the pages of instructions to participants determines how easy it will be for you to partition the test data by task.

There must be a clear beginning and ending for each task or groups of tasks you want to time. In addition, the test participant needs to know when to pause and when to proceed. A typical set of scenarios will contain a cover page to keep participants from looking at the first scenario followed by a series of pages with one task per page.

As the test proceeds, the test administrator tells participants when to start each task by turning the page. When participants feel they have completed the task, they announce that fact and wait for instructions to proceed to the next task.

Do not string the tasks together on the same page; provide clear breaks between them. If you do put tasks one after the other, you allow participants to look ahead at future tasks, and you make it difficult for them to stop between tasks.

Frequently, when a task is completed, the test team is still catching up with events. The data recorder in particular is often still typing comments and logging other test events and, therefore, needs some time before the start of the next task. Putting the tasks on separate pages and making participants wait for instructions to go on to the next task allows time for everyone to be at the same starting point.

Each page can have a note at the bottom, such as "Do not turn to the next page until we tell you to." However, these instructions are generally effective only if the briefer also reminds participants about them after each of the first few tasks.

Checklists for Testing

In Chapter 16 we describe the roles that each of the members of the test team plays during a test. Each role carries with it a set of duties and a time to perform each duty. Each member of the test team needs a checklist to follow on each day of the test.

Usability testing has a tendency to deteriorate with time without aids, such as these checklists, to help you maintain discipline.

The test administrator may have test team members create their own checklists, but the administrator is responsible for checking their accuracy and completeness. In addition, administrators need to have an item on *their* checklist to ensure that the other team members complete their checklists and keep them up to date. We describe the details of what goes into these checklists in Chapter 16.

In the next chapter, we discuss how to prepare the testing environment.

Examples of a Legal Form and Questionnaires

The following pages contain figures that show examples of

- paragraphs for legal forms (Figure 14-1)
- a signature block for a confidentiality form (Figure 14-2)
- a pretest questionnaire (Figure 14-3)
- a posttask questionnaire (Figure 14-4)
- a posttest questionnaire (Figure 14-5)

Purpose	Ajax Industries is asking you to participate in a study of computer software. By participating in this study you will help us make the software easy to learn and use.
Study Environment	The study takes place in Ajax's laboratory, where you will be observed as you use the product.
Information Collected	We will record information about how you use the software. We will ask you to fill out questionnaires, and we will interview you. We will use the information you give us, along with the information we collect from other people, to recommend ways to improve the software.
Videotape Waiver	All or some of your work with the software and the interviews will be videotaped. By signing this form, you give your consent to Ajax to use your voice, verbal statements, and videotaped pictures, but not your name for the purpose of evaluating the software and showing the results of our testing.
Non-disclosure Agreement	During this study, we will ask you to work with an unannounced product and publication. Any information you acquire relating to this product and publication is confidential and proprietary, and is being disclosed to you only so that you can participate in this study. By signing this form, you agree that you will not tell any of this information or anything about this product to anyone else.
Comfort	We have scheduled breaks for you, but you may take a break at any other time you wish. Merely inform the test administrator that you would like to do so.
Freedom to Withdraw	You may withdraw from this study at any time.
Freedom to Ask Questions	If you have any questions, you may ask the test administrator now or at any time during the test.

Figure 14-1.   Example paragraphs for legal forms*

If you agree with these terms, please indicate your acceptance by signing below.

Signature:_____

Printed name:_____

Date:_____   _ _ _____

Figure 14-2.   Example of a signature block for a legal form

---

*This form should be reviewed by your legal department, but do not let them put it into legalese.

Participant #_____
Date _____

1. What is your job title?

    ____ Computer programmer/Software engineer
    ____ Systems Analyst
    ____ Project engineer
    ____ Senior engineer
    ____ Member of technical staff
    ____ Test engineer
    ____ Project manager
    ____ Other _____

2. What do you actually do? (Check all that apply.)

    ____ Design and code software
    ____ Maintain/debug software code
    ____ Quality assurance for software products
    ____ Other _____

3. How long have you been doing this work?

    ____ Less than 6 months
    ____ 6 months - 2 years
    ____ More than 2 years

4. Which programming languages are you proficient in? (Check all that apply.)

    ____ C, C+ or C++
    ____ Pascal
    ____ FORTRAN
    ____ COBOL
    ____ Basic
    ____ Assembly
    ____ Other _____

5. If you programmed in the C language, did you do so in a UNIX environment?

____ Yes ____ No

If Yes, for how long? ____ years ____ months

6. Which operating systems are you proficient in using? (Check all that apply.)

    ___ AIX
    ___ Mac Operating System
    ___ MS-DOS
    ___ OS/2
    ___ SunOS
    ___ UNIX
    ___ Other _____

7. Have you ever worked on a computer that had a windowing environment?

___ Yes   ___ No

If Yes, which environments? (Check all that apply.)

    ___ DEC Windows
    ___ MS-Windows
    ___ NeXTStep
    ___ Presentation Manager
    ___ Sun/Open Look or SunView
    ___ Window Manager
    ___ X-Windows
    ___ Other _____

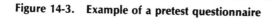

Figure 14-3. Example of a pretest questionnaire

PostTask Questionnaire
(For a test of a manual)

Participant #_____
Date_____

1. How easy or difficult was it to complete the task? (Circle your answer)

1	2	3	4	5
Very Easy	Easy	Neither Easy Nor Difficult	Difficult	Very Difficult

Comment:_____

2. Did you use the manual to complete the task? Yes _____   No _____

If No, tell us you are ready for the next task.

3. When you used the manual, was the information easy or difficult to find?

1	2	3	4	5
Very Easy	Easy	Neither Easy Nor Difficult	Difficult	Very Difficult

Comment:_____

4. When you used the manual, was the information easy or difficult to understand?

1	2	3	4	5
Very Easy	Easy	Neither Easy Nor Difficult	Difficult	Very Difficult

Comment:_____

Please tell us you are ready for the next task.

Figure 14-4.   Example of a posttask questionnaire

PostTest Questionnaire
(For software and a manual)

Participant #___
Date:_____

This questionnaire is designed to tell us how you feel about the product you used today. Please circle the number that most clearly expresses how you feel about a particular statement. Write in any comments you have below each question.

1. Using the software was:

1	2	3	4	5
Very Easy	Easy	Neither Easy Nor Difficult	Difficult	Very Difficult

    Comment:_____

2. Finding the features I wanted in the menus was:

1	2	3	4	5
Very Easy	Easy	Neither Easy Nor Difficult	Difficult	Very Difficult

    Comment:_____

3. Understanding the instructions in the prompts was:

1	2	3	4	5
Very Easy	Easy	Neither Easy Nor Difficult	Difficult	Very Difficult

    Comment:_____

4. Recovering from errors was:

1	2	3	4	5
Very Easy	Easy	Neither Easy Nor Difficult	Difficult	Very Difficult

    Comment:_____

5. Using the software <u>manual</u> was:

1	2	3	4	5
Very Easy	Easy	Neither Easy Nor Difficult	Difficult	Very Difficult

       Comment:_____

6. Did the manual allow you to grasp the scope of the capabilities of the software?

___Yes   ___No

       Comment:_____

7. If your company were buying this product, and the software and documentation were sold separately, would you recommend buying the manual?

___Yes   ___No

       Explain why you would or wouldn't recommend buying the manual.

       _____
       _____
       _____

8. Would you recommend that your company buy this software.

___Yes   ___No

       Explain why you would or wouldn't recommend buying the software.

       _____
       _____
       _____

9.   List any other comments you had about the software or the manual.

       _____
       _____
       _____
       _____

Figure 14-5. Example of a posttest questionnaire

15

Preparing the Testing Environment

Before you are ready to conduct the pilot test, which is the last step before conducting the usability test, you must prepare the physical test environment and the people who will conduct the test. In this chapter we discuss preparing the testing environment; in the next one, we discuss preparing the team.

If you are conducting the test in a usability lab, you will need to prepare the test room and the observation room. If you are not using a lab to run the test, you will still need to prepare the area where you will make your observations.

To be ready for the test, you will go through the process of

- arranging the equipment and the props
- preparing the product
- adjusting the audio and video controls
- preparing the data-logging materials or software
- labeling tapes and disks

Arranging the Equipment and the Props

If you have done your test planning properly, you already know what equipment you need to run the test. Now is the time to set it up and make sure it works.

The test equipment may include the hardware the participant uses as well as other equipment you need to interact with the participant's equipment. For example, if you are testing our example electronic mail application, you may need to have an additional terminal in the test room so that you can communicate electronically with the participants. Set up both terminals and make sure they really do communicate.

To take another example, if you are interested in testing a networking application that uses a printer at another node on the network, hook the printer into the network and make sure it works properly.

You may also need to set up the test room to simulate the real environment in which the product will be used. For example, to test an application that uses reservations information and will be installed at airports, you may want to set up the room with a typical reservations desk.

Simulating the real environment may be as simple as moving a plant and a picture into the area for the test.

Preparing the Product

The development team is responsible for getting the product ready for the test; you may have to prepare any special hardware, software, or data.

Creating Sample Data

When you analyze each task as a candidate for the test, you list the resources that you need to run the task. (See Chapter 11, "Selecting and Organizing Tasks to Test".) Now you need to gather or create those resources. For most usability tests, this means creating data. For example, you may need to create a letter for the participants to send or mail accounts for fictitious people the participant will send mail to.

You can obtain or create most of these resources in a few minutes. Occasionally, the task is more time consuming, such as building a database for the participant to browse. To complete these longer tasks, you will need more lead time if you want to avoid working late into the night just before the pilot test.

Planning for Disaster

Plan for situations in which the software you are testing will malfunction. This is especially important if you are testing an early prototype.

You can save yourself and participants time and frustration by creating several versions of the test data in successive stages of use. For example, suppose you are testing a spreadsheet, and participants will do 15 tasks. Some of these tasks will use work done in earlier tasks. Many of the tasks will ask participants to modify the spreadsheet. Suppose that the third task asks participants to total the columns in the spreadsheet. A later task asks participants to make a graph of this new line. If the software crashes after the third task, and you have to go back to the data as it was at the beginning of the test, participants will have to do Task 3 again. Instead, you could have a second spreadsheet file that includes the work participants did in Task 3 and load that file after the crash. Using the same logic, you might have five different versions of the data, each version allowing you to recover gracefully from a software crash.

Preparing Manuals

If the test involves manuals, you will need to make sure that they are ready for the test or that the writers will have them ready. Getting manuals ready means

- having them produced with legible type and graphics
- writing large page numbers on the bottom, outer corner of each page
- if the documentation is still in draft form, putting it in a high-quality binder or binding it so that it looks as professional as possible
- if you are near to having the final version of the documentation, making it look professional and putting in tabs (even if they are handwritten), a table of contents, cross-references, and an index

Adjusting the Audio and Video Controls

The quality of the videotapes you make during the test depends on having the best viewing angles from the cameras you are using and the clearest sound from the microphones.

It usually takes us about 30 minutes to make these adjustments in our lab. We will first discuss the video adjustments, then the audio adjustments.

Video Adjustments

In a typical setup, we use three cameras: one to focus on the screen, one to focus on the participant, and one to focus on the documentation. We adjust each camera to get the sharpest picture. The following are a few hints about making these adjustments:

- There are 3 common problems with getting a clear view of the screen:
    1. Glare from the lights in the room, which can be corrected by simply moving the screen to a better position in the room. Typically having the screen perpendicular to ceiling fluorescent lights helps.
    2. A poor viewing angle that exaggerates parallax problems. This distortion is common when the cameras are mounted close to the ceiling in the room. You can correct or minimize the problem by adjusting the angle of the screen or by raising the screen by placing something such as a book under it. Be sure to check that the participant can see the screen when you make these adjustments.
    3. The participant's head blocks the view of the screen. Have a colleague sit where the participant will and make sure you can see the screen. It also helps to have the colleague move around a bit to see how much latitude you will have, because every participant will not sit exactly where you want.

       None of these adjustments are necessary if you have the equipment to take a feed from the screen and display it directly onto a monitor in the observation room. If you will be conducting tests with similar hardware, it may be worth the price to be able to take such a feed. With a good system, you can get a nice clear picture and you don't have any of the problems with camera adjustments. But look at the quality of the hardware you are buying, because some products we have seen that give you a direct feed from the screen give you a poor quality picture.

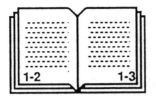

Figure 15-1. The page numbers have been written in large characters to allow you to see what page the participant is looking at

- Getting a clear view of the documentation requires that you be able to see the whole page, including the page number. We usually rewrite the page number with a large black marker in the bottom outer corner of the page (Figure 15-1). We also put a piece of tape down on the spot where we want the participant to place the document (Figure 15-2). The top of the tape should line up with the bottom of the document. Because participants will move the document around as they use it, the tape helps us to tell them where to put it so that we can see it.

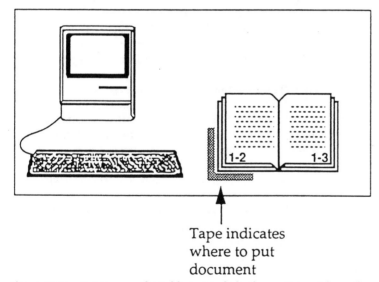

Tape indicates
where to put
document

Figure 15-2. Put tape on the table top to help the participant keep the documentation where you can see it with a camera

- Getting a clear view of the participant is usually quite easy. The objective of this view, when you have three cameras, is to provide a long shot that shows both the participant and the equipment. We often use this shot when the participant is talking, to provide some variety from the close-ups of the screen or the documentation. We also have the ability to mix views from two cameras on our monitor and consequently on our videotape. We often will put the view of the participant's head on one corner of the picture and leave it there while the rest of the picture shows the equipment screen or the document (Figure 15-3).

To get this shot, we adjust the camera that is focused on the participant so that his or her head is in the upper right-hand corner of the picture.

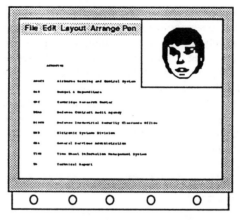

Figure 15-3. Viewing the screen and the participant on the same monitor

If you are not using a laboratory to conduct the test, you still will need to make video adjustments. If you have one camera, you have to decide where to focus it. It is impossible to move the camera quickly enough between views to make any sense out of what you see. For example, by the time you move the camera from viewing the participant to viewing the screen, the participant has already typed a response or pointed and clicked to select a menu item. You will have to focus the camera and leave it there.

If you are testing software, you can focus on the screen, but you will not be able to see the keyboard or mouse or what the participant is doing with the documentation. If the participant is good at talking out loud, you may be able to tell what is happening. But if the participant is quiet, you will find yourself wanting to know what the participant is doing as you hear pages being rattled.

If you have two cameras, you can see more. If you are testing software, you can focus on the keyboard and the screen or on the participant and the screen. If you are testing documentation, you can focus on the document and on the screen. But unless you have a way to mix the two views together or switch between them, you will have to watch the two tapes through two VCRs and monitors to see what was happening with both views at any one time.

Audio Adjustments

You need to adjust the audio levels so that you can communicate with participants and hear them clearly on the videotape. Most VCRs allow you to adjust the audio level. Have a colleague talk as a participant would and watch the audio level needle to see that you are getting it loud enough on the tape as well as on the speaker you hear in the observation room. If you are not using a lapel microphone, have your colleague talk from different positions so that you can see where the limits of good sound quality are. Then, talk to the colleague in the test room to see that you can be heard without startling the participant with a loud voice.

If you are not using a laboratory to conduct the test, your only concern is to make sure the sound is loud enough on the videotape.

Preparing the Data-Logging Materials or Software

The key to having quantitative measures of performance is recording the duration and frequency of events during the test. Most of the labs we have seen have either written their own data-logging software or bought a commercial package. We first discuss setting up data-logging software to record test events; then we discuss what you can do if you do not have data-logging software.

Preparing Data-logging Software

A data logger is simply a tool to record both events and the time at which they occur. Figure 15-4 shows a screen from our data logger.

This is the screen that the data recorder uses to log events. For each event, such as starting a test, the recorder types the event code, such as "S", and then some text, such as "Participant 3, Ajax tutorial." The software then saves the event code, the time, the date, and the text. The software also changes the event code description to "Stop the test" and puts a line of moving dots before the description to indicate that that item is being timed. In a similar fashion, the label for "Start a task" changes to "Stop a task" when the data recorder presses "T", at the beginnning of a task.

As the test progresses, the recorder selects the appropriate event codes and types informative text. The software saves these along with the date and time. When we are finished with each participant, we can get a printout of all of the events as well as tabulations of the duration and frequency of each event.

There are two types of event codes on the screen. Near the top are the three mandatory codes, beginning with "Start a test." The data recorder must use these codes for every test. The codes for "Start a test," "Start a task," and "Take a break" are toggles. When you select

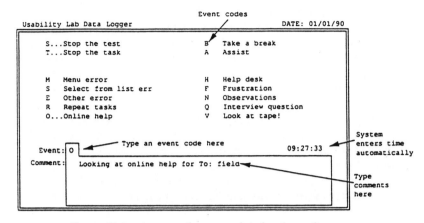

Figure 15-4.   A screen from our data-logging software

them by typing the code, they change to "Stop a test," "Stop a task," and "Resume a test." We use "Take a break" for any situation when we suspend the test without ending it. For example, if something goes wrong with the equipment or the software, we stop the test so that the time it takes us to fix the problem is not added to the time for the test.

The rest of the event codes are optional, that is, they can be changed for each test. The codes we show here are ones we would use for a test focusing primarily on documentation but including major problems with the user interface to software.

Some of these optional codes just record an event, such as "H" for "Comment." Others, such as "F" for "Flipping pages," are toggles that record the start of an event that the recorder will stop at a later time. Consequently, the toggles allow us to record both the frequency and duration of an event. Philips and Dumas (1990) discuss the need for such toggles and some of the other requirements for data-logging software.

To use the data logger for a test, we must give each test a unique name and then set up the optional codes we want for the test. Some codes are commonly used for most tests, such as codes for when the participant makes a comment or an error. Others are unique to the test, because you use them to record potential usability problems with the product. For example, if you expect that users will have difficulty finding their way through a menu hierarchy, you might add a code for "Navigating menus." If you are concerned that users will have a problem remembering what function keys do, you can add a code for "Wrong function key."

The codes you see in the graphic are appropriate for a test that focuses primarily on the documentation, but they also allow you to record some of the problems with the user interface to the software. With this setup, we can record

- where participants look to find the information they need, such as in the table of contents or index
- how long they spend reading about concepts and how long they take reading task instructions
- how often they look at graphics or the glossary to understand information

We can also record major problems with the software, such as when participants make or repeat an error, and the time participants spend working on the computer, that is, using the software, which would be an interesting measure if you have one group of participants that use the documentation and another group that does not.

At the end of this chapter, we show you data-logging screens for other common types of tests, such as tests of software, hardware, and a combination in which the focus is on the software, but the documentation is also included.

Recording With Other Types of Data-logging Tools

If you do not have data-logging software, you can still record events with a stopwatch and a sheet of paper that lists the task numbers. If you assume that you can get this information from timing the tasks from the videotape, keep in mind that it will take you twice as long to run the test and then watch the entire tape. See Figure 13-3 in Chapter 13 for an example.

Labeling Tapes and Disks

It is critical that you label every item you use to record information during a test. There are some items that you can label before the test starts, such as the videotapes and computer disks. In Chapter 19, "Conducting the Test", we talk more about labeling other materials.

The best strategy for staying organized during the test is to label all of the tapes and disks before the test begins. For example, if you know that you are going to have 16 participants in the test and that each participant will spend 3 to 4 hours doing the test, label the 32 videotapes you will need for the test and the 2 you will need for the pilot test ahead of time.

We label each tape with the test name, the participant number, and the number of the tape for that participant, such as "E-Mail, Participant 3; Tape 1." For tests in which we keep a tape from more than one camera, we also indicate what that camera was viewing, such as "Screen" or "Document."

You can add other information if it will not change. For example, if you have decided that participant 3 will be in the "no documentation" group, you can add that information. But be careful about adding information that could change. For example, you may plan to run the third participant in the morning on Thursday, so you'd want to add the day and "a.m." to the label. But what if the third participant is a no-show who is then rescheduled for Monday morning? It is best to only put information that will not change on the label at this point. You can always add more information later.

The same logic applies to labels for disks you may need for data-logging files. For example, if you use diskettes to back up the data files for your data-logging software, label them before the test so you can't forget to label them in the rush to do a backup at the end of a long day.

Now that we have covered how to prepare the physical environment, let's move on to preparing the test team.

Examples of Data-Logging Screens

Figures 15-5, 15-6, and 15-7 show the setup of our data-logging software for a test of :

- hardware
- software
- documentation

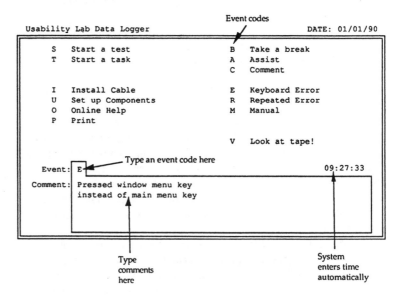

Figure 15-5. Setup of data-logging software for a usability test of hardware

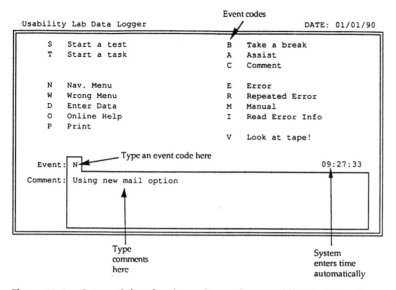

Figure 15-6. Setup of data-logging software for a usability test of software

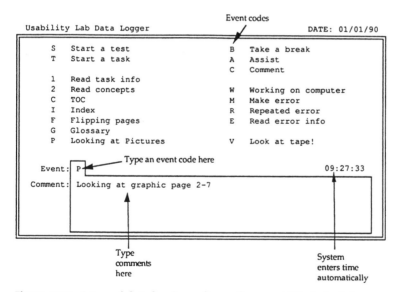

Figure 15-7   Setup of data-logging software for a usability test of documentation

16

Preparing the Test Team

The people who are going to run the usability test need to understand and practice their roles before the first participant arrives.

In this chapter, we first discuss these four questions that you may have about the team that actually conducts a usability test:

- How many people do you need to run a test?
- Should people switch roles during the test?
- Who should be on the test team?
- How can other people participate in a test?

Then we give detailed information about roles for test team members. We talk about seven roles, but these are *roles*, not *people*. We know of no group that has seven different people on their test teams. One person may take several or even all of these roles, or some may not be applicable to the type of test that you are conducting. Everyone combines at least some of these roles in some way, and we talk about different ways to distribute the roles across the people on your test team.

At the end of the chapter, you'll find a checklist for each of the roles that we cover. You'll want to consider all the items on all the checklists. However, you will probably want to reorganize the checklists for your own team. Your checklists will depend on how many people you have on the team, the way that your lab—or whatever space you are using—is set up, and the roles that are or are not appropriate to your situation.

How Many People Do You Need to Run a Test?

Three people make a good usability test team. At AIR, we usually have two usability specialists and one member of the client's technical staff as the team.

Some labs have as many as five people on each test team, usually including more of the product's technical staff. Most labs don't have room for more than five people to be actively involved in conducting the test. You don't want to be tripping over each other in the test team's room.

Two people can make up a test team if both are skilled usability specialists and the participant does not move around much during the test, which is generally the case for tests of software products.

What About a One-person Test Team?
Some usability groups can only afford to have one usability specialist conducting each test. If you are in that position, you will have many

roles to fill and may have to sacrifice some of the types of data that other teams collect.

You will probably want to videotape the test to review actions that go by too fast for you to capture in your notes. Sometimes, you can set up camera angles before the test so that you do not have to do much camera work while watching the participant. If you have a console in which you can quickly change which camera is actually being recorded on the videotape, you can set up two or three camera shots—for example, the screen, the participant's face, and the document—and then move among them with the press of a button. If you have a console in which you can have a split screen, you can set up to record two cameras at the same time and, perhaps, not worry about camera work at all during the test.

Unless you are a skilled user of a particular data-logging program, it may be difficult for you to both observe the participant and enter data into the log. It may also be difficult to shift quickly between interacting with the participant and entering data into the log. If a "help desk" is part of your test plan, you would have no log entries during the time you, as the single test team member, are assisting the user.

Without a data log, you will probably not have detailed measurements of participants' behaviors. You could collect gross times for tasks by noting the start time and end time for each task, taking the time from the video screen or from a watch or stopwatch. It might be difficult to reliably mark down more detailed times, such as whenever a participant goes down an incorrect path and then finds the correct one. You might only write down the time for events that you want to later check in the tape.

If you know the steps that users will take to do the task correctly and have some idea of the types of errors that users are likely to make, you might be able to create "scoring sheets" or "checklists" before the test to make note taking easier. You might even have a column for time for the beginning, end, and each major step in a task, as well as a column for comments. You might set up a paper-based log like the example in Figure 13-3 in Chapter 13 on "Deciding How to Measure Usability."

If you are the lone test team member, you will have to take very good notes of what the participants do and say. As a tradeoff for no help during the test, you may have to spend more time after the test sessions reviewing the videotape, which can be very time-consuming.

Trying to conduct any type of usability test by yourself has another disadvantage. If you are the only person who has observed the participants, you will have no one else's observations and insights to help you interpret the data.

If a test team of one person is the only choice you have, of course, you will do the best you can with it. However, you will be trading off the richness of the data you can collect and the time you may need to spend before and after the test sessions themselves for the lack of help.

What If You Don't Have a Laboratory?

If you do not have a laboratory and the test team will be in the same room as the user who is working on the product, you definitely want to keep the team small. More than two observers in a room with one or even two participants is likely to be intimidating.

If you are conducting a design walkthrough, a user edit of a document, or an active intervention test of a prototype in which one test team member is sitting with the participant, you might have one other team member unobtrusively in the corner of the room. (Of course, if you do have a laboratory with one-way glass, you can have other team members behind the glass, even when someone is working with the participant.)

Should People Switch Roles During the Test?

No. It is best if the same people carry out the same roles for all participants. Otherwise, you are introducing the possibility that differences in the data will be due to differences in what the test team does rather than what the participants do.

Who Should Be on the Test Team?

Everyone who conducts the test should be on the planning team. However, not everyone on the planning team has to conduct the test.

A major question that companies face in setting up usability testing is deciding how to staff a usability test laboratory and who should be on the team that conducts each test. Should all test team members be professional usability specialists? Should the test teams be entirely made up of the people who own or are working on the product? Should the test team be a combination of usability specialists and developers or writers?

We know of at least one company or group that has chosen each of these three staffing patterns:

- In Company A, usability testing is done entirely by usability professionals who act just like other quality assurance teams. Product developers must send their products to usability testing, but may not participate in the usability testing. They are encouraged to observe the test from a third room that is set up with one-way glass or with a video monitor. The product developers get feedback from usability testing in the form of "bug" reports to which they must respond, just as they get "bug" reports from the people responsible for function testing.

- In Company B, usability testing is done entirely by product developers. One professional usability specialist runs the laboratory and serves as consultant to each product team that brings their product through the lab. Product developers go through a two-day, hands-on training course before they test their products.
- Company C is an independent usability testing group. Professional usability specialists conduct the test, but they work closely with the product developers as they plan the test. They require that one product developer be present to answer questions and maintain the product. They encourage other product developers and managers to attend and observe the testing.

Staffing patterns like these generally reflect the corporate style of the organization. (See Chapter 6, "Establishing a Usability Program in Your Organization," for more about how corporate style affects usability programs.) Another pattern may fit best into your company's culture.

What are the advantages and disadvantages of having professional usability specialists as testers compared to having developers as testers?

Professional Usability Specialists as Testers

Advantages:	*Disadvantages:*
They know how to plan and conduct tests. They focus on users and tasks.	They are not experts in each product.
They know what to look for. They are trained in reviewing products and observing users.	They are not experts in how users for each product do their jobs.
They know how to analyze data, find the underlying problems, and suggest fixes.	
They become experts at using the lab equipment and software.	

The only major disadvantage of having a professional usability team in charge of the testing is that they are not experts in every product that comes through the laboratory. Of course, that is an advantage in that they can more easily see the product through the eyes of the new user.

Someone on the test team has to know the product well enough to know when users are having problems with it. In the AIR laboratory, we get the product to be tested beforehand so that the test team can practice with it, can see which pathways participants should take to do the tasks, make educated guesses about wrong pathways participants are likely to take, and develop more specific concerns about what to focus on during the test.

Product Developers as Usability Testers

Advantages:	*Disadvantages:*
Developers see users trying out their product.	The developers must learn new tools, such as the data-logging software. No one becomes expert at it. The company gets no benefit of learning from one test to the next.
Developers are forced to think about usability, users, tasks, measurements.	Developers are not trained observers. They do not know how to move from observations to an understanding of what users' problems really are. They may deny that a problem exists. They may not know how to fix the problems they see.
Developers already know the product. They may understand how users for the product do their jobs (or they may not).	Testing takes time away from the work for which they are trained.
The company does not have to hire more people.	The costs may be higher.

The major advantage of having developers as testers is that they get to see how users work with their product. As Grudin (1991) writes, one problem with many products is that developers aren't forced to see the pain they cause. However, developers don't have to do all the work of usability testing for the company to gain that advantage. They can be observers rather than be on the test team. In the AIR laboratory, we always ask that the developers be present to observe the test so that they can see for themselves the problems that ordinary users have with the product.

Another reason to have developers present is to have someone with intimate knowledge of the product available in case the user gets very far off track or something else goes wrong—for example, in case the software crashes. This is the role of "product expert" that we discuss later in this chapter.

However, there are many disadvantages to having developers take on responsibilities as usability testers. The cost is likely to be higher to the company, because each development team has to go through the learning curve of doing a usability test, and because it takes untrained developers longer to do each part of the process than it takes a trained usability specialist.

Developers may not be good at finding the usability problems in a product. It is very difficult to be objective about your own work. Developers may also not know how to recognize problems.

In a recent study, software engineers who were given guidelines to use when reviewing their product found fewer than half the usability problems that usability specialists found. They predicted only 16% of the problems that showed up in a usability test of the product (Desurvire et al., 1992). (See Chapter 5, "Evaluating Usability Throughout Design and Development," for more on this research.)

How Can Other People Participate in a Test?

People who are not part of the test team can still participate by observing. There are several ways to arrange this.

You can set up a video monitor in a conference room that is connected to your audiovisual equipment so that the observers see what you are recording on the videotape at the same time that you are recording it. You can use this method even if you do not have a laboratory with one-way glass. Observers can come and go without disturbing you or the participant. However, they see only what is being recorded. They miss the ambiance of the test and actions or expressions that don't happen to be caught by the camera.

If you have a laboratory with two rooms, separated by one-way glass, you can allow observers to stand in the back of the test team's room. They can see the entire test just as you do. If they have doubts or concerns about the test or start to jump to conclusions about the product, you may hear them and be able to deal with them. (See the section on "Dealing with Managers and Developers" in Chapter 19, "Conducting the Test.") However, the observers' comings and goings and whispering may disturb the test team. If the test team's room is small, too many observers may make it very cramped.

Some groups have built laboratories with a third room for observers, either behind the test team's room or to the side of the participant's room. In either case, the third room is separated from the others by its own one-way glass. The observers can view the test just as the test team does, but they are not physically with the test team.

If the third room is behind the test team's room, the observers see the test from the same angle as the test team. It is also easier, in that case, for the test administrator to know who is observing and to be alert to concerns that visiting developers or managers may have. Figure 16-1 shows this configuration for a usability test laboratory. (See Appendix B for information and pictures of other laboratory configurations.)

If the third room is on a different side of the participant's room, the observers are seeing the test from a different angle. In this case, you would have to consider the observers' needs in setting up the participant's room. You might want to have a video connection, too, so that observers can also see what you are recording.

In any case, developers, writers, managers, and others who are interested in the product should be encouraged to come observe. Nothing is as effective at convincing people of the need to change a product as watching people have problems with it. The experience can be sobering, fascinating, humiliating, or thrilling. It is bound to be enlightening.

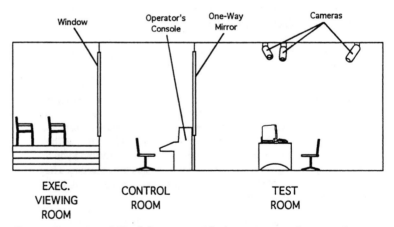
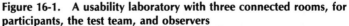

Figure 16-1. A usability laboratory with three connected rooms, for participants, the test team, and observers

What Roles are There for Test Team Members?

For a usability test, you want to consider the following seven roles:

- test administrator
- briefer
- camera operator
- data recorder
- help desk operator
- product expert
- narrator

As we said earlier in the chapter, you will almost certainly want to combine these roles in some way.

The test administrator's functions don't require activities while the participant is working, so the test administrator usually also takes on at least one other role. In many cases, the test administrator is also the briefer.

The product expert may be a member of the development team who is primarily present in the back of the room as an observer, but who is available as needed to get the software back up or to answer a technical question. Another possibility is to have the product expert also be the help desk operator.

If the participant will not be moving around, which is usually the case in testing software, the camera operator may be able to take on other roles as well, such as being the briefer or the help desk operator. Depending on the nature of the test and the skills of the team, you may want to combine the roles of test administrator, briefer, camera operator, and help desk operator.

Some usability teams include a narrator whose job is to tell the story of what the participant is doing throughout the test. Others forego this role during the test, relying on the participant's talking out loud to tell the story of what is going on. Some teams plan to add narration later, in the form of "voice over," to the parts of the videotape that they include in an edited tape of the highlights from the test.

The narrator's role becomes more critical for companies in which developers do their own testing. It is very difficult for someone who is not skilled at using a data-logging software program to both observe the test and log what is happening at the same time. In this case, one person (the narrator) watches the participant and tells the other person (the data recorder) what to put in the log.

On the following pages, you'll find more information about each of the roles. At the end of the chapter, we've included checklists for the tasks that we describe.

Test Administrator

The test administrator is the team leader. The test administrator

- assigns roles and delegates responsibilities to other team members
- acts as spokesperson for the team
- is responsible for making sure that the hardware, software, and data are properly set up for each test session.
  This may mean deleting files that the previous participant created; reestablishing files that the previous participant deleted; reinstalling software; repackaging the product— whatever it takes to undo what the previous participant did so that each participant starts with the same setup.
- leads the review sessions that the test team holds at the end of each day of testing
- leads the analysis of the test data and the interpretations of what the results mean
- often writes the report of the usability test and presents it to senior management or to the client

The test administrator has overall responsibility for making sure that the test runs smoothly and produces useful information. Therefore, the test administrator is usually the senior person on the team—the person with the authority to take or delegate responsibility.

The test administrator is usually the project leader for the entire testing project with responsibility for planning as well as for conducting the test. In some cases, the leader of the overall project may delegate responsibility for the data collection part of the test.

On many teams, the test administrator is also the briefer. The one role that is difficult to combine with being the test administrator is the role of data recorder.

Briefer

The briefer is the only person who interacts with the participant. A primary part of this person's role is to make the participants feel welcome and comfortable. The briefer, therefore, should be someone who enjoys being with people.

Briefing means talking to the participants before they begin working. Briefing may involve asking the participants about themselves, showing them the test room, informing them about the test situation, answering their questions, and conducting training, if that is part of the test plan.

At the end of the test, the briefer becomes the "debriefer," talking to the participants after they have finished working through the scenarios. An effective debriefer has good interviewing skills and is a good listener.

Before each test session, the briefer must make sure that

- the test room is properly set up
- all of the materials for the test session are in a folder that is marked for that participant

When the participant comes, the briefer

- greets the participant, if the lab does not have a receptionist who can assume that function
- brings the participant into the test room
- makes the participant feel comfortable in the room
- gives the participant the "Understanding Your Participation" form to read and sign
  (Some usability test groups have a policy that the briefer leaves the room while the participant is reading this form so that the participant does not feel rushed or harassed into signing it. Other groups have a policy that the briefer stays in the room so that the participant can ask questions before signing the form. Consider the tradeoffs and set a consistent policy for your organization.)
- gives the participant the pretest questionnaire, if you are using one
- explains the test and conducts whatever training is part of the test plan
- makes sure the participant has the appropriate telephone number if you have set up a "help desk" by telephone
- gives the participant the booklet of task scenarios and reminds the participant
  - to think out loud
  - to do the tasks one at a time; stopping at the end of each page and waiting to be told to continue

During the test session, the briefer is the only person who talks to the participant, unless the participant calls the help desk. If you have a laboratory with a one-way mirror, you probably also have an intercom connection between the test team's room and the participant's room. In most situations, while the participant is doing the scenarios, the briefer communicates with the participant over the intercom, not by going back into the room.

The briefer may need to remind the participant to think out loud, but, otherwise, the briefer usually only talks to the participant in between tasks. (See Chapter 18, "Caring for the Participants," for more on the briefer's role and for hints on getting participants to think out loud.)

During the test session, the briefer is also an observer, taking notes that will lead to interesting questions during the debriefing and that will be useful insights for the team when they analyze the data.

After the last scenario, the briefer (now debriefer)

- asks participants to complete the posttest questionnaire, if you are using one
- goes back into the test room when participants have finished filling out the questionnaire
- interviews participants about their responses to the questionnaire and their experiences during the test
- thanks participants and sees them out

If you are paying participants directly or giving them something for coming to the test, the briefer is usually responsible for taking care of that. An appropriate time would be at the end of the debriefing interview. You may want to invite the participants to meet the rest of the test team and see the laboratory set up on the way out. If so, the briefer escorts the participant.

After each test session, the briefer must make sure that

- all the forms, questionnaires, and notes for that participant are properly labeled and are in the participant's folder
- the test room is back the way it should be for the next participant
- if it is the end of the day, the test room is shut down for the night

Camera Operator

The camera operator is responsible for the audiovisual record of the test session. You don't need to be an AV specialist to fill the camera operator's role in a usability test, but you do need to learn to operate whatever camera equipment the test team will be using.

Usability laboratory video equipment ranges from a single camera on a tripod to three cameras and an automatic feed from the participant's computer, all of which are controlled on a very elaborate console.

The camera operator does not have to be a specialist in the product being tested, but the camera operator has to understand the purpose of the particular usability test in order to know what to focus on during the sessions. In fact, the test team, including the camera operator, should plan the types of shots to capture on the videotape before any participants come.

For example, if you are interested in how people use the documentation, the camera operator should know to focus in on the manual when the participants go to it. If you have cameras that can be zoomed in for close-up shots, the camera operator should know that you are interested in showing whether the participant is using the table of contents or the index or reading a particular page.

Before each test session, the camera operator must make sure that

- the cameras and all the recording equipment in the laboratory are set up and working properly
- the cameras are in the right positions for this particular test
- there are videotapes, properly labeled, in each VCR, and enough extras ready and labeled if the test lasts long enough for a second tape
- all the equipment is turned on and ready to go
- the timers on the AV console and the computer are synchro-nized so that the videotape and the computer record show the same clock time and elapsed time

During the test session, the camera operator

- runs the audio and video equipment
- adjusts the cameras as needed to get the desired input onto tape
- adjusts the sound as needed
- selects the shot or shots to record
- changes the tapes in the VCRs as needed

After the test session, the camera operator

- rewinds the tapes
- turns off the equipment

Data Recorder

The data recorder is the person who creates a coded record of the participant's actions and comments, usually with data-logging software. Data logging is the most time-consuming and pressured role on the test team. Therefore, the data recorder should be someone who likes to focus on details, is a good typist, and works well under pressure.

Logging is a full-time responsibility. The data recorder is very busy during most test sessions and has no time to take on other roles. Actions happen quickly in a test, but if you want accurate quantitative information from the test, the data recorder has to capture all the actions that relate to what you are counting, for example, wrong menu choices, incorrect field entries, or references to online help.

You might ask: "Why not just go back and log later at leisure from the videotape?" If you were doing research and had the time to do detailed analyses of the tapes, you could do that. Usability testing, however, is not research. You won't have the time. Your clients or managers want answers yesterday, but watching the videotape would take at least as long as conducting the test.

You may want to have a code in your log that alerts you to look at the tape for a particular action or segment; but if you use it too often, you'll be duplicating time and effort. You'll also be missing important information for your quantitative analysis. Furthermore, the test team may not have captured all the participant's actions on the tape.

If you are interested in accurate and reliable quantitative measures, therefore, you should seriously consider who will be best able to take on the role of data recorder.

The data recorder must become familiar with and comfortable with the logging software, if you are using that, with the specific codes for this test, the test team's concerns, and the planned task scenarios. Here are two ways that data logging can work:

1. The data recorder is a member of the usability lab staff who is an expert at data logging. The data recorder is trained to be able to observe a test and record the appropriate codes at the same time. As a usability test specialist, the data recorder has experience from many previous tests to use in deciding when a participant's actions and comments should be logged.

   In that situation, a separate narrator may not be needed. However, the data recorder must have the time to prepare for the particular test by learning how the product is supposed to work, how participants should go through the task scenarios, the errors they are likely to make, and the specific areas of concern that the test team is looking at.

2. The usability test laboratory staff is not large enough to provide a data recorder for each test. Each test team provides their own data recorder, who has time to develop only minimal proficiency with logging. If you are using data-logging software, this person should be someone who types well and fast. Whether you are logging with software or with paper and pencil, this person should be someone who works rapidly and accurately, works well under pressure, and likes to pay attention to detail. Although the person does not have to be a product expert, it helps if the person understands enough about the product to make sense of what is happening and of the words he or she hears during the test.

   If the data recorder is not proficient with logging, the data recorder is not likely to be able to observe and log at the same time. The team might then include both a data recorder and a narrator. The narrator should know the product well and learn the codes that are being used for logging this test. The narrator watches the participant and tells the logger what is happening. The data recorder's role becomes somewhat like a secretary taking dictation. The data recorder and the narrator need to take the time to establish a good working rapport and rhythm.

Before the test begins, the data recorder must

- learn to use the data-logging procedure
- set up the codes for the specific test

Before each participant comes, a data recorder who uses data-logging software must

- turn on the data-logging software
- check that the appropriate codes are on the screen
- create the file for the particular test session

During the test session, the data recorder

- codes all actions that are being measured
- includes relevant comments from the participant and the test team

After the test session, the data recorder who is using data-logging software

- reviews and edits the log
- runs and prints preliminary analyses for this participant
- prints the entire log for this participant
- creates a backup copy

Help Desk Operator

In most usability tests, you want to see how easy the product is for people to use on their own. However, you cannot just abandon the participants with no recourse if they are truly stuck. You have to develop some way to let them ask for assistance.

You also have to decide who will give help and how much help you will give. The first of these issues is relevant here in our discussion of roles for the test team. The second, which is a difficult issue for many usability test teams, will be relevant to our discussion of conducting the test; you'll find that in Chapter 19, "Conducting the Test."

Who will give help? You can have the briefer also be the help desk operator, or you can have a separate help desk operator, that is, someone other than the briefer who answers a help desk telephone number in the test team's room.

If you want to see how often users are likely to actually pick up the telephone and call for help, it is probably best to have two people in the two roles. If participants realize that the briefer is also the help desk operator, they are likely to start asking for help informally without picking up the telephone. As users, they may feel more comfortable doing that, and you may not get a good sense of how much support users will call for.

If you don't combine the help desk and briefer roles, you could combine the help desk operator's role with others, such as camera operator, product expert, or narrator.

In a typical usability test, while participants are working with the product, the briefer's role is primarily to acknowledge that participants have finished a task and to tell participants when to go on to the next task. To keep the atmosphere cordial and supportive, the briefer may add comments at these times to keep participants relaxed and feeling good about themselves. But the briefer does not usually answer substantive questions about the product or the tasks. If you allow participants to seek help by just asking the briefer over the intercom, rather than by taking the extra step of calling a help desk, you may get into a situation in which participants try to rely on the briefer like a colleague in the next office. That won't give you the insights you need to know if people are going to be able to learn to use the product on their own.

Note that the situation may be different in a design walkthrough or an early usability test of a prototype in which there may be much more interaction between the briefer and the participant. In that case you will probably be combining the roles of briefer and help desk operator, having one person act both as interviewer and as the source of assistance.

Whoever fills the role of help desk operator on the usability test team should know the product well enough to help but must also understand the goals of a usability test. Unlike a real help desk at which the goal is to give the answer and get the person back to work as quickly as possible, in a usability test, the goal is to give the least amount of help that you can. The goal is to get the participants to reveal how they are approaching the task and what is not working well for them, and then to get them back on track just enough for them to go on.

If you are using a telephone connection, before each test session, the help desk operator must make sure that

- the telephone connection is working properly
- the telephone number is available to the participant

During the test session, the help desk operator

- waits for the participant to ask for assistance; does not volunteer help
- answers the phone as if it were a real help desk
- tries to elicit the participant's insights
- gives the minimal amount of advice needed to help the participant move on

For a discussion of how to be an effective help person for a usability test, see the checklist at the end of this chapter and also Chapter 19, "Conducting the Test."

Product Expert

Having a product expert present during the usability test serves at least two useful functions: maintaining the product, and offering technical advice.

In many cases, you will be testing software that is still in development. It may be buggy; it may crash if participants do something unusual. But time is precious in usability testing. If the software crashes, you want to be able to bring it up quickly again. Having a product expert available may be critical to keeping the software going during the test. (Crashes are discomforting to participants. In Chapter 18, "Caring for Participants," we talk about how to handle situations in which the product crashes during a test.)

If you are a team of professional usability specialists, even if you learn the product before the test, go through the scenarios, and try out alternative paths and errors you think participants will make, you will still not know everything about the product. Participants may get themselves so far off the expected path or into parts of the product you haven't tried that when they call the help desk, you can't help them. Having a product expert available at these times is very useful.

The product expert may take on other roles on the usability test team or may otherwise be an observer.

Narrator

Some test teams have a separate role for an observer who narrates the test.

If the data recorder is not proficient at the software, the narrator's primary function may be to act as the data recorder's eyes, observing the participant's actions and telling the data recorder what to code. This is a difficult role. The narrator has to be able to pay attention to both the data recorder and the participant at the same time, all the time. In this function, the narrator will be busy and under pressure throughout the test.

The narrator must know the product well to explain what the participant is doing and to give the data recorder the correct codes. That is, if you are measuring the number of wrong menu choices that participants make, the narrator is the one who must know when the participant chooses incorrectly from a menu.

But the narrator also must maintain a neutral position. The narrator must be absolutely factual and objective about what is happening in the test. You will get good value from a usability test, only if the narrator watches participants with an open mind and tells the data recorder exactly what the participants do. This may be difficult for developers, programmers, or writers watching their own products being tested.

Even if you do not need the narrator to work closely with the data recorder, you may want a narrator to tell the story of what is happening so that you have words to accompany the pictures on the videotape. Narrators who record observations for the tape have to be comfortable talking out loud, loudly enough to be heard on the tape.

They also have to have a good sense of when to talk and when not to. They have to talk only in between the participants' comments. Thus, if a participant is talking out loud, giving a good verbal protocol, the narrator will have less time and need to record observations. Many people find narrating in this situation to be awkward; a good narrator is often difficult to find.

If you do not need a narrator to help the data recorder, and if you choose not to have a narrator who speaks for the taped record, you may still want to assign someone the role of observer/note taker.

This could be the briefer or it could be a separate role for another test team member. An observer/note taker needs to be familiar enough with the product and the task scenarios to know when participants are making mistakes, but he or she need not be the product developer, programmer, or writer. This is a good role for a usability specialist who will be able to add insights from his or her expertise and experience.

On the next several pages, you will find checklists for the different roles we have discussed. With the test materials, the test environment, and the test team prepared, you are ready to put them all together and conduct a pilot test—a dry run or dress rehearsal for the usability test. That's the topic of the next chapter.

Checklists for Each Role on a Usability Test Team

On the next several pages you will find checklists to help whoever is taking on the roles of

- test administrator
- briefer
- camera operator
- data recorder
- help desk operator
- product expert
- narrator who works with the data recorder
- narrator who records on the tape
- observer who takes notes

These are sample checklists only. Remember that in an actual test, people will almost certainly be combining these roles. Change or rearrange these lists to match the roles that the individuals on your test team will have.

Checklist for the Test Administrator

Before each participant comes:

_____ Make sure that each test team member has a copy of the scenarios, the documentation, and anything else they need.

_____ Make sure that all test team members have their checklists and are following them.

_____ Greet guest observers.

During each test session:

_____ Manage any problems that arise.

_____ Be sensitive to concerns of visiting developers or managers. Discuss test as necessary with developers and managers. (See the section on "Dealing with Managers and Developers" in Chapter 19, "Conducting the Test.")

_____ Observe and take notes, looking for the real problems, for the big picture of how the product is doing.

After each test session:

_____ Escort guest observers out.

_____ Make sure that someone is responsible for setting everything up again for the next test session.

At the end of each day of testing:

_____ Lead a review session in which the test team discusses the day's findings.

Checklist for the Briefer

Before each participant comes:

_____ Make sure the test room is properly set up. Turn on test equipment. Get the product ready. This may mean turning on the computer and bringing up the product. It may mean turning on another type of machine.

_____ Make sure the documentation is in place, if appropriate.

_____ Have a pad and pens or pencils for taking notes.

_____ Have an ink pen ready for the participant to use in signing the "Understanding Your Participation" form in case the participant does not have one.

_____ Check the folder for that participant. These materials should be in the folder:

    __ the release form, "Understanding Your Participation"

    __ the pretest questionnaire or background form

    __ the training script, if there is one

    __ the scenarios

    __ the posttask questionnaires, if you are using them

    __ the posttest questionnaire

    __ the payment or incentive, if appropriate

At the beginning of each test session:

_____ Greet the participant.

_____ Check the participant's name to be sure that this is the person whom you expect.

_____ Make the participant comfortable. Offer coffee.

_____ Bring the participant into the test room.

_____ Let the participant see the cameras and other equipment.

_____ Show the participant where to sit.

_____ Give the participant a brief introduction to the test session.

_____ Ask the participant to read and sign the "Understanding your Participation" form.

_____ Ask the participant to fill out the pretest questionnaire.

_____ Give the training according to the training script, if appropriate.

_____ Ask if the participant has any questions. Answer honestly, but do not give away any test-related information.

_____ Make sure that the participant has the number for the help desk, if appropriate. Remind the participant to use the help desk in whatever way the team has decided to do this. That is, you might say: "Call the help desk whenever you would if you were really using this product in your office." Or you might say: "Try to work through the tasks yourself. If you have problems, try the online help. If you really get stuck, call the help desk." Whatever you say must be appropriate for the test and the same for all participants in that test.

_____ Remind the participant to think out loud.

_____ Remind the participant to wait for you to say when to start the first task, to tell you when he or she has finished the first task, and then to wait for you to say when to start the second task.

_____ Put the "Testing in Progress" sign on the door, if appropriate.

At the end of each test session:

_____ Ask the participant to fill out the posttest questionnaire.

_____ Go in to the test room and thank the participant for his or her help.

_____ Debrief the participant. Go over the participant's responses to the posttest questionnaire. Depending on the situation, you might go over specific problems that you noticed the participant had, call up situations that you saw and have the participant walk through them, show the participant alternatives and ask for opinions, and follow up on comments the participant made.

_____ Give the participant the payment or other incentive.

_____ Offer to show the participant the test team's room. If the participant accepts, show the equipment and introduce the team.

_____ Thank the participant and show him or her out.

After the participant leaves:

_____ Put all the forms in the participant's folder.

_____ Turn off the equipment in the test room.

Checklist for the Camera Operator

Before each participant comes:

_____ Turn on the equipment.

_____ Make sure the cameras are properly set.

_____ Make sure the sound is working properly.

_____ Prepare labels for tapes with the project name, participant number, date, and time.

_____ Label enough tapes for the session.

_____ Load a tape into each VCR.

During each test session:

_____ Synchronize starting time with the data recorder.

_____ Run the equipment.

_____ Select which picture to record and handle the recording.

_____ Adjust cameras as needed to get desired input onto tape.

_____ Adjust sound as needed.

_____ Change the videotapes when needed.

After the participant leaves:

_____ Rewind all the tapes used in that session.

_____ Check to be sure all tapes are properly labeled.

_____ Put the tapes away so they will be easy to locate.

_____ Turn off the equipment.

Checklist for the Data Recorder

Before the test begins:

_____ Learn to use the data-logging software.

_____ Set up codes that are appropriate for this test.

Before each participant comes:

_____ Turn on the data-logging software.

_____ Make sure it is properly set up for this test.

During each test session:

_____ Code each action appropriately in the data-logging software.

_____ Add information to help understand exactly what happened in each action. For example, if you are counting "wrong icon choices," don't just enter the code, add a description, such as "chose chart icon, not text icon."

_____ Type in the participant's comments.

_____ Type in team comments that will help elucidate the log later.

After each participant leaves:

_____ Review and edit the log.

_____ Correct typos.

_____ Elaborate on comments now while you remember them.

_____ Correct any codes that you know are wrong.

_____ Back up the log.

_____ Run a preliminary analysis and print it out.

_____ Print out the log.

_____ Label all the printouts with the project name, participant number, date, and time.

_____ Make copies for each team member and for the participant's folder.

_____ Distribute the copies, remembering to put one in the participant's folder.

Checklist for the Help Desk Operator

Before the test begins:

_____ Make sure the help desk phone is working properly.

_____ Make sure the correct phone number is taped to the participant's phone.

_____ If the participant will get a piece of paper with the help desk phone number on it, make sure the number on the paper is correct.

During each test session:

_____ Answer the help desk phone if participants call.

_____ Answer the phone pretending that you really are the help desk operator.

_____ Act as if you cannot see what participants have done. Have the participants tell you what they are trying to do and what actions they have taken so far.

_____ Be friendly and courteous even if participants make disparaging remarks about the software.

_____ Don't just give the answer. Try to elicit what the participants think is happening and what choices seem logical to them.

_____ Give the minimal amount of advice that participants need to help them move on. Don't stay on the telephone and walk participants through the task.

EXCEPTION: If a participant has worked at the task longer than you expected, you have seen the problems participants are having, and the participant is frustrated or about to break down, forget the previous point and ACT LIKE A REAL HELP DESK OPERATOR. Give the answer, walk the participant through the task, and stay on the telephone until the task is done. The participant's well being is your most important consideration.

Checklist for the Product Expert

Before the test begins:

_____ Get the product up and running, if appropriate.

During each test session:

_____ Bring the product backup if needed.

_____ Answer technical questions from the test team.

Checklist for the Narrator Who Works with the Data Recorder

Before the test begins:

_____ Know the product well.

_____ Know the objectives of the test.

_____ Know the scenarios.

_____ Know what the team wants to capture on the tapes and in the data logs

_____ Coordinate with the data recorder on how you are going to work together.

During each test session:

_____ Feed information to the data recorder.

_____ Make sure that the data recorder accurately captures actions and comments.

Checklist for the Narrator who Records on the Tape

Before each participant comes:

_____   Check with the camera operator to make sure that the sound is recording properly from the narrator's microphone.

During each test session:

_____   Narrate the test.

_____   A narration should be strictly factual, objective observations.

_____   The narrator should not talk when the participant is talking.

Checklist for the Observer who Takes Notes

Before each participant comes:

_____ Make sure that there is paper and pencil to take notes.

_____ Label each page of the notes with the project name, participant number, date, and time.

During each test session:

_____ Take notes on problems and other observations.

After each participant leaves:

_____ Review and edit notes so that they are legible and clear.

_____ Put notes in that participant's folder.

17

Conducting a Pilot Test

A pilot test is nothing more than a dry run or a dress rehearsal for the usability test to follow. In a pilot test, you treat the participant or participants exactly as you would treat the first participants in the usability test. You follow all the procedures you will use in the test, and you collect the same data you will collect during the test. But you do not analyze the data or include it with the rest of the data you will collect during the test.

Though usability tests differ in their formality and when they occur in the development process, we recommend that you always do a pilot test before you begin the test proper.

If you eliminate the pilot test, you will waste more time than you save.

You will be tempted to cut the pilot test out to save your team a day or two of valuable time during the hectic days immediately before the test begins. Don't give in to that temptation. Every pilot test we have run has found significant problems that would have caused us to throw out the data from at least the first participant. As you will see from our examples, it is virtually impossible to conduct a flawless usability test unless you run a pilot test first.

You should consider eliminating the pilot test only if you are conducting a *retest* of a product using the same tasks and procedures.

In this chapter, we discuss

- why you should run a pilot test
- when to run the test
- how to run the test

Why Run a Pilot Test?

The most important objective of a pilot test is to "debug" the equipment, software, materials, and procedures you will use for the test. A secondary objective is to give the test team a chance to practice the activities they will be using during the usability test.

The following are some typical examples of the types of problems a pilot test will uncover. For each problem, we also describe at least one solution.

Problems with Test Methods

- The participant cannot save the file TEST.DOC as instructed. The software displays an error message saying that TEST.DOC is a "duplicate name." The problem here is that there is already a file with the name TEST.DOC. A likely cause of this problem is that you forgot that all participants cannot use the same file name when they save the file they created. There are two solutions to this problem:

1. Change the scenario so that each participant gets a unique name to use for their file.
2. Change your testing checklist to remind you to delete the file after each participant finishes the test.

- The pilot participant uses a procedure you did not anticipate. The new procedure gets the task done, but it does not force the participant to navigate down a menu tree, which is the procedure you wanted to test.
  There are at least two solutions to this problem:
  1. Change the instructions to force participants to use the procedure you want to observe.
  2. Find a new task that will make participants use the procedure you want to observe. Don't forget to pilot test the new task.

- The pilot participant completes only 6 of 10 tasks and, therefore, does not get to 2 important tasks. When you run one pilot participant, you have to make a guess about how representative that participant is. There is no way to estimate the distribution of times from one participant. Consequently, your best strategy is to be conservative and assume that most participants will not complete all 10 tasks.
  There are at least three solutions to this problem:
  1. Increase the time for each participant.
  2. Change the order of tasks so that the two important tasks come earlier.
  3. Eliminate some early tasks that take a long time to do.

- The pilot participant keeps making the mistake of pressing the wrong function keys. Your data-logging program or procedure does not have a code for this specific type of error. The data recorder spends too much time typing the specific cause of the error.
  The solution is to add a code that tabulates function key errors.

Problems with Testing Materials

- The answer options to a question on the posttest questionnaire are poorly worded. One option is "0–6 months"; the next one is "6 months–1 year." The pilot participant has 6 months experience and doesn't know which option to select. This is only one example of the many details that go wrong when you make up a questionnaire in a hurry.
  The solution is to fix this problem and then carefully go over all the questions to check for additional problems.
- Participants cannot do a task because they do not understand the words you have used to describe it.

The solution is to talk with participants about what words would make sense and then change the wording. You can see why it is important to have a pilot participant who represents the users. If you use a colleague down the hall who is convenient to recruit, but more computer literate than the user of the product, you will be hard pressed to find wording that will work for the test participants.

Of course, you will not have this problem in the pilot test if you use a colleague as a test participant. They are likely to be as familiar with the terminolgy as you are. You may, however, uncover the problem when you run the test with the first real participant, because you did not use a participant who represents the users.

- The participant cannot start a task, because a member of the test team forgets to leave a cable connector on the table in front of the participant. You might think that this is a problem with the test method rather than the test materials, but it is really a problem with the testing checklist.

  The solution to this problem is to add an item to someone's testing checklist. That team member is then responsible for ensuring that the connector gets on the table.

Problems with the Product or the Documentation

You expect that there will be problems with whatever you are testing, otherwise there would be no need to do the test. But, some problems with the product will cause you to have to make decisions about how to deal with them or whether to continue with the test. The following are some examples:

- There is a problem that keeps the participant from completing the task, but it is trivial to fix. (In the terminology we will use in Chapter 20 "Tabulating and Analyzing Data," this is a local problem.) For example, there is a step missing in the description of a procedure in a manual. The writers assure you that they will fix this problem. You must make the decision regarding what to do about the missing step. If you do not let the writers fix it now, you will waste your time watching each participant struggle with a problem you know will be fixed.

  In this situation, we recommend that you fix the problem and record both the problem and the solution. It is a waste of time to make every participant struggle with a problem that will be fixed unless you have set strict pass–fail criteria for the product. Of course, you should verify that you have really fixed the problem.

- There is a serious problem that keeps the participant from completing a task. (In the terminology of Chapter 20,

"Tabulating and Analyzing Data," this is a global problem.) For example, your review of the menu hierarchy for a software application shows that it is designed around the structure of the software, rather than the user's tasks. The pilot participant, more than once, has difficulty finding where things are in the hierarchy and, in one case, cannot complete a task without help.

In this case, you should continue with the test as is, but you should tell the designers about the problem. Because you have only one sample of behavior, you cannot guarantee that other participants will confirm your opinion about the poorly designed hierarchy. It is best to wait for some more participants to confirm the finding.

At that point, you may want to ask the designers whether they want to have you and, perhaps, themselves watch every participant fail at the task. It can be extremely frustrating to watch participant after participant spend a long time, such as 20 minutes, trying to do a task that you know they will need help to complete.

- The software crashes during one of the tasks, but otherwise seems to work fine.

  You will want to consider eliminating or revising the task. You can never be sure that participants will not find other bugs that cause crashes, but when you find one you know about, it is best to avoid it. If the task is critical to the test, you can ask the designers to fix it, even if you have to postpone the test, or you can go ahead with it and explain the problem to the participant when it happens. In our experience, if the crash ends up being truly a one-time event during the test, participants treat it as an exception, and it doesn't appear to influence their performance or ratings of the product.

- There are many bugs in the product and many basic usability problems that frustrate the pilot participant.

  The decision you have to make here is whether to run the test at all, because the product is not ready for testing. It may be better to start the redesign effort right away than to run the test to uncover more of the less severe problems. When the test participants have trouble doing simple tasks and are frustrated by their difficulties, they do not use enough of the product to uncover as many other problems as when the product is in better shape. It is more efficient to fix the serious problems first and then conduct the usability test.

As you can see from these examples, the pilot test often generates its own little drama. Besides allowing the test team to debug the test materials and procedures, the pilot test begins the process of uncovering problems with the product. It will give you an opportunity to begin to think about where the problems are and how they might be fixed. You cannot generalize from one participant, but you can be ready to confirm what you see in the pilot test when the usability test begins.

If any members of the design team or visitors such as managers attend the pilot test, it helps to warn them to expect the pilot to be a bit chaotic. The purpose of a pilot test is to find the problems (you might call them bugs) in the test materials, test procedures, and the readiness of the test team. A chaotic pilot test can preceed a smothly run test. Observers and visitors should not draw the conclusion that the test team doesn't know what it is doing from the fact that problems occcur in the pilot test.

When to Run a Pilot Test

When you can only run one pilot participant, your natural tendency will be to wait until the last possible minute, which usually means the day before you have scheduled the first "real" participant. If you follow that practice, you will more often than not find yourself and your test team working late into the night to make all the adjustments you will need for the next day of testing. As you can see from the examples in the previous section, many problems may show up during the pilot.

Schedule the pilot test two days before the usability test. This will give you a day to make all the changes you need to make and will allow you to be more relaxed when the first test participant arrives.

Try to schedule the pilot test at least two days before the beginning of the usability test.

If you are testing only part of a product and you have conducted tests of other parts of the product, you may be able to get away with having the pilot test one day before the real test.

There are some testing groups that continually test parts of the same product. In our discussions with them, they tell us that they do not conduct a pilot test, but consider the first test participant as the pilot. If there are not problems with that participant, they count the pilot participant as the first participant of the test. These testers have conducted many similar tests, and they also know that they are taking a small risk by not running a pilot test. We recommend that you *always* conduct a pilot test unless you are a very experienced tester testing a familiar product.

How to Run a Pilot Test

As you can see from the examples of the problems that a pilot test can uncover, it is critical that you

- conduct the pilot test exactly as you will conduct the full usability test
- use a test participant who represents the users you are concerned about

Do not take shortcuts to make it easier to run the pilot test. You will be tempted to use a pilot participant who you can conveniently recruit, such as the person in the cubicle next to yours. If you give in to this temptation, you will very likely have to throw out the data from the first usability test participant when you uncover problems. You and your test team will then be up late at night fixing the problems before you run the second participant.

What happens when you have limited time to run the pilot test, but you have more than one type of participant in the test? For example, if you have planned to have two groups of participants, one that lacks computer experience and one that has at least one year of computer experience, how many pilot participants do you run? Obviously, the best answer is to run one participant from each group. If you have to make a choice, you should select the pilot participant from the group with no computer experience. Most of the members of the test team will be computer literate. They are more likely to have problems developing procedures and wording questions for the participants with no computer experience. The rule here is to select the pilot from whichever group has the least experience or is the most naive about some area.

This chapter ends our discussion about planning and preparing for a usability test. In the next part, we discuss conducting the test and using the results to change the product and the process of design.

Part III

Conducting and Using the Results of a Usability Test

In this part, we describe how to conduct a test, how to use the data you collect to identify the usability problems with the product, and how to recommend changes, communicate your findings, and get your changes implemented.

There is so much information about conducting a test, that we have broken it up into two chapters.

Chapter 18, "Caring for Test Participants," discusses how to view the test from the participant's point of view. We describe the rights of test participants and how to deal with participants when there are problems with them or with their participation in the test.

Chapter 19, "Conducting the Test," discusses the additional activities that occur during the test. We describe the events of a typical test day and how to be organized, interact with participants, deal with visitors, and look for usability problems.

The final five chapters cover posttest activities.

Chapter 20, "Tabulating and Analyzing Data," discusses how to organize and summarize the data you collect from a test. We describe how to triangulate on problems by integrating the quantitative and qualitative data with the list of problems you started during the test.

Chapter 21, "Recommending Changes," discusses the nature of usability problems—the fact that one cause can have many manifestations and that global problems are difficult to fix. We describe the importance of solving problems as a team and using experts in human–computer interaction to help the test team find ways to improve the usability of the product that was tested.

Chapter 22, "Communicating the Results," discusses the media you can use to tell people about the test. We describe communicating test finding in a variety of ways from meetings to preparing a complete description of a test.

Chapter 23, "Preparing a Highlight Tape," discusses the value of the video medium for communicating findings and recommendations. We describe deciding what to include in a highlight tape, selecting tape segments, and making the tape. We also discuss how to use videotape to communicate more than just the highlights from the test.

Chapter 24, "Changing the Product and the Process," discusses ensuring that the results from a test are used by the people who designed the product and the people who manage the design process. We describe getting changes into the product, making changes to the process of design, and viewing yourself as a change agent rather than a usability gatekeeper.

Following Part III is a list of references to the literature about usability testing. The reference section includes both research studies and descriptions of the practice of usability testing.

18

Caring for the Test
Participants

In the next two chapters, we describe conducting a usability test. In this chapter we focus on the test participants, especially communicating with them before the test and helping them deal with some difficult situations that occur during testing. In the next chapter we focus more on events that occur once the test begins.

The people who participate in the test are helping you. Even if you are paying them, they are likely to be taking time away from other work or from their own time. They are also likely to be nervous and uncomfortable, at least at first. Making them comfortable and caring about them and for them throughout the test is part of the test team's job.

In this chapter, we offer suggestions for how to interact with the test participants. We discuss

- seeing the test from the participant's point of view
- understanding participant's rights
- getting participants to think out loud
- being sensitive when events go awry

For some additional points about the treatment of test participants see Schrier (1992).

Seeing the Test From the Participant's Point of View

Participants tell us that they are a bit apprehensive when they come to a test. The vast majority of them have never been part of a test before. The test is an unusual experience for them. They've never been in a similar facility. When they hear words like "usability," "test," "videotape," and "one-way mirror" from the recruiter, they realize the experience will be different, but they aren't sure what it will be like. They may connect "testing" with trying something out, but their model for that may be test driving a car, not being under the scrutiny of a team of people behind a one-way mirror.

The way you treat participants during the first few minutes they are at your facility has a major impact on their level of anxiety.

If you are the person who greets the participants, you need to realize that they may be anxious and have only the sketchiest knowledge of what will be happening to them. It's your job to calm them and make them feel comfortable.

The participants do not understand, nor should they have to, that you were up late the night before getting the test ready or that you are worried that something will go wrong. If you act distracted or impersonal or worried, the participants will pick up your mood. Furthermore, if they see the members of the test team running around and whispering things to each other that participants are not supposed to hear, it will, at best, add to their concern.

To get the most out of participants, you must be calm and focused on them when you greet them and have a quiet place to talk with them before the test. Your first objective should be to develop a rapport with them. They need to feel that they are safe and that you will take care of them.

It helps to have a checklist for the person who greets the participant. The checklist should cover activities, such as offering the participant coffee, and issues to be discussed with the participant, such as what the participant can expect the test to be like.

Some lab facilities have a separate room where the test participants wait before the test and during breaks. Most organizations, however, cannot provide the space for such a room. In that case, find a place to be with participants that is out of sight of the testing area. Your office or cubicle, no matter how small, is better than a place where participants can see the test team hurrying between the observation and the testing rooms or areas.

Be prepared for participants to arrive early for the test. There seems to be a law that participants arrive earliest when you are least prepared. Have a plan for early arrivals.

You need a place for them to wait and something for them to do. Don't make them wait at the reception area with no one to talk to and nothing to do. Go to them and establish who they are. Bring them to the waiting area, tell them you are not quite ready, and give them something interesting to read. Offer them coffee or tea or a soft drink and show them where the rest rooms are located. Make them feel they are important.

Do not let participants wait for the test without being greeted and cared for.

When you, the person responsible for briefing participants, do get to talk with them, use your time wisely. Calm any fears they may have and begin to introduce the topic of testing. To help them to be calm, begin your conversation with neutral topics that they are likely to be willing to talk about. *It is important that they talk.* Some typical opening topics are

- how they found your facility
- the weather
- what they do in their jobs
- the organization they work for
- local issues, such as parking problems or traffic congestion

Within a few minutes, you need to begin to tell them what the test will be like for them. At this point they have not signed a nondisclosure form. So you typically cannot talk about the specifics of the test. But you need to help them make the transition to the testing environment.

Do not refer to participants as "subjects." They are co-evaluators with you, not interchangeable subjects in a research study.

You should not refer to participants as "subjects."

A good start is to ask them if the recruiter told them what they will be doing today. Even if they say that they were told all about the test, you should go over the basics with them. You need to convey two attitudes early and reinforce them often:

1. They are co-evaluators of the product.
2. You are testing the product, but not them.

Convey this feeling of equality to them as you describe the testing experience and how your organization conducts tests. For example,

> Here we study how people learn to use computer programs. We are interested in making our programs as easy as possible to learn. We select people with your background to come in and work with us to evaluate our programs. We need your help because you are the type of person who will be using the programs we sell. We built our usability lab to be a special place to learn how to make our products better. People like you can teach us how to make what we sell easier to learn and use. We have people like you use our programs in the lab where we can watch how the program is acting and ask you about your reactions to it. Did the person who first called you tell you that we would be videotaping you today?

As you get into the topic of testing, it is time to move into the testing environment itself. Make a point of always ending your introduction to testing by reminding participants again that you test products not them.

Introducing the Testing Environment

Usability testers have typically recognized the importance of having participants feel comfortable in the testing environment. Consequently, three different approaches have emerged for helping participants understand the testing environment:

1. Talking with participants about the environment
2. Showing a videotape
3. Showing participants the observation room

Talking with Participants About the Environment

With this method the briefer deals directly with participants' anxiety about being watched. If the test is in a lab, the first things the participants will notice are the camera(s) and the one-way mirror. The administrator tells them that the people who are developing the product need to study the videotapes to see how they can improve the product, and that some of the developers are watching the test to understand how their product is working.

Some other issues the administrator may want to cover now are:

- the cameras may make noise as they move to get a better angle to see the product
- where the briefer will be during the test
- how the briefer will talk with them
- how long they will be working and when a break is scheduled

Showing a Videotape

Some labs have created a videotape for test participants to view before the test. The videotape explains what a usability test is and shows the test room and the observation room. It may also show them how to think out loud (see discussion later in the chapter). Having such a tape ensures that all test participants come to the test with the same understanding about what a test is like, and it also solves the problem of what to do with the test participant until the test starts.

Showing Participants the Observation Room

Some test teams believe that it is important to have the test participant see the observation room and meet some of the people who will be watching them. By allowing the participant to see the monitors and view the test room through the one-way mirror, these test teams believe that they are taking the mystery out of the situation and calming the test participant. Other test teams believe that showing the observation room to participants will *increase* their anxiety. Both of these test teams may be correct. Some people may be less nervous when they see who is watching them, while others may be more nervous. The testers who show participants the observation room believe that, on balance, it is better to do so than to just talk about the environment or show it on tape.

Research issue:	What effects do activities that occur before the test starts have on test participants? Do test participants work more effectively when they get to see a videotape showing what the test will be like? Are test participants less nervous when they are shown the observation room and the audience before the participants begin the test? Are there other things we could be doing before the test starts that would allow us to conduct a more valid test?

Understanding Participants' Rights

In Chapter 14, "Preparing Test Materials," we discussed the importance of obtaining an informed consent from test participants and of the participants' rights. We also mentioned the test team's responsibility to fully explain to participants both what will be happening to them and about their rights.

Because you need to obtain participants' informed consent before you even begin the test, you can see how important it is to develop trust and rapport with participants before you bring them into the lab or the test environment. If you rush participants from the entrance to your building right into the test environment without communicating with them, you will be asking them to make some important decisions before they have developed any trust that the test environment is a place at which they are to be themselves.

In order to obtain participants' informed consent, hand them the form or forms that describe their rights and responsibilities and go over the forms with them item by item. As you explain each item, make sure that you allow them an opportunity to ask questions. The key items to cover are:

- any waiver you are asking for
- a general description of the procedures you will be following
- the purpose of the test
- any risks to them
- the opportunity to ask questions
- the right to withdraw at any time

As you go over these items, keep in mind that you are helping participants to make another transition. This transition is from the light chatter you have been having with them to the serious business of testing a product. The professional way that you handle the items covered in the legal forms provides participants with cues that the real work is beginning.

If the participants happen to be employees of your organization, you may not have to ask them for waivers. You should, however, ask for their consent to be in the test and inform them of their rights.

Getting Participants to Think Out Loud

For many tests, we ask participants to think out loud so we can hear and record their reactions to the product we are testing. People do not normally think out loud while they work.

Test participants vary in their ability to tell you what they are thinking while they work. The best talkers sound as if they are giving you an unedited stream of consciousness and they also add their interpretation of events. The worst talkers say almost nothing or, worse, mumble. Most participants fall somewhere in between.

Does Thinking Out Loud Change Performance?

Whether you ask participants to think out loud or simply record their
spontaneous remarks, you want to use what they say as data to help
you understand how users respond to the product. Asking someone to
think out loud when doing a task is sometimes called *taking a verbal
protocol* and using verbal protocols as data is called *protocol analysis.*
Flower, Hayes, and Swarts (1983) and Schriver (1991) have shown
that protocol analysis can be very useful in revising documents.
Ericcson and Simon (1984) have shown that protocols accurately
reflect the contents of people's short-term memories.

There have been a number of studies looking at whether thinking
out loud changes the way participants solve problems or perform
tasks. Rhenius and Deffner (1990) showed that when participants
think out loud it takes them longer to perform tasks. Not all studies
show this effect, however. In addition, participants who think out loud
are less flexible at changing problem solving strategies when they
first start talking. With time, however, problem-solving strategies are
no different whether participants think out loud or remain silent.

Is Retrospective Thinking Out Loud Better?

Bowers and Snyder (1990) did an interesting study of concurrent
and retrospective thinking out loud. In the concurrent condition,
participants talked aloud while they did 12 window management
tasks. In the retrospective condition, participants remained silent
while they performed these tasks, but were then shown a videotaped
version of their performance and asked to describe what they were
doing and thinking while they performed the tasks.

The most interesting difference between the retrospective and
concurrent conditions was in the *types of statements* the two groups
made. Those participants who talked concurrently while working on
the tasks tended to read what was on the screen and to describe the
procedures they were following. Those participants who talked
retrospectively tended to use more statements that gave explanations
for why they acted as they did and to make suggestions about how to
improve the product.

This study shows that when participants talk retrospectively, they
provide more diagnostic information about the problems they had
and make more suggestions for changing the product. However, it
does take participants about 80% longer to first do the tasks and then
view a tape of their performance. For usability tests you conduct
early in the design process and for which you only run a few
participants, you may want to use retrospective thinking out loud.

A recent study by Wright and Converse (1992) introduces a caution
about the impact of thinking out loud on the performance of test
participants. These authors compared test participants who were

required to think out loud with participants who did not think out loud. It is important to note that Wright and Converse specifically asked the participants who thought out loud to give *an explanation* for each action they did. They were not encouraged to simply describe what they were doing, but to try to explain it. The results show that the participants who thought out loud were faster and committed fewer errors than the participants who were silent.

If you think about this finding, you will see that it makes sense. How often have you understood something you were doing as soon as you talked out loud about it.

The fact that thinking out loud improves performance should not discourage you from using it. The value of the information you get from participants who think out loud usually outweighs the bias this procedure may cause. It would be interesting to see if thinking out loud results in fewer calls to the help line in a usability test. If so, a test in which participants think out loud about what they are doing and why they are doing it may underestimate the number of customer support calls that will occur with the real product.

Teaching Participants How to Think Out Loud

As part of the instructions to participants during the pretest briefing, tell them you are interested in what they are thinking, because you value their reactions to using the product. Ask them to think out loud as they work.

A good strategy is to give participants think-out-loud instructions and one or two warm-up exercises. Ericcson and Simon (1984, p. 376) recommend these instructions for getting participants to think out loud:

> In this test, we are interested in what you say to yourself as you perform some tasks that we give you. In order to do this, we will ask you to think aloud as you work on the tasks. What I mean by think aloud is that I want you to say out loud everything that you say to yourself silently. Just act as if you are alone in the room speaking to yourself. If you are silent for any length of time, I will remind you to keep thinking aloud. Do you understand what I want you to do?

When participants understand the instructions, give them a practice problem to get them started thinking out loud. We do not like to use abstract exercises such as multiplying two numbers or adding two 3-digit numbers. Instead, we have the briefer give an example of talking out loud and then ask the participant to do it. For example, we often will show the participant how we would think out loud as we open a stapler to insert new staples. As we think out loud, we use statements that do more than just describe what we are doing. We say things like, "I see that it says press on the lever I use to open the stapler. I like that." We also give an example of something we do not like. Using these two examples shows participants that we want them to give us both positive and critical statements and to do more than just describe what they are doing. We then give them a ballpoint pen with a reusable ink cartridge and ask them to disassemble it while thinking out loud. Again, we reinforce participants when they use evaluative statements.

We believe that it is important to have the participants actually think out loud in this exercise rather than just see a videotape of someone else thinking out loud.

Reminding Participants to Think Out Loud

Some participants will forget that they were asked to think out loud. They have many things to remember as they begin the tasks. You will have to remind these participants during the first few tasks to think out loud. Even the best talkers forget that they are not talking as they get involved in tasks.

Some helpful prompts to get people thinking out loud again are:

- "Mary, could you tell us what you are thinking now?"
- "John, could you tell us why you pressed the enter key?"
- "Abigail, what were you looking for in the index?"
- "Jim, we couldn't hear what you said just then."

Most participants will pick up on your gentle reminders and start talking. Some participants will not. When participants are just too shy to talk, the briefer may have to change strategies by asking them questions rather than continuing to prompt them to talk. Be careful, however, about biasing the participants with the form of questions they are asked. (See the discussion in the next chapter about how to avoid bias.)

Being Sensitive When Events Go Awry

There are several events that occur infrequently in testing but have the potential to be difficult situations:

- The test participant refuses to participate in the test.
- The test participant is nervous and cannot continue.
- The test participant is not qualified to be in the test.
- The test participant exceeds the time limit for a task without finishing it.

- You must stop the test because of equipment or software malfunction.
- The participant gets frustrated or anxious because the product is so difficult to use.

Let's look at each of these situations in detail.

The Test Participant Refuses to Participate in the Test

In all of the tests we have run, we have had only one case in which the test participant refused to start the test after being told what the test would be like. Participants do, of course, have the right to refuse to participate. When they make their feelings known, the administrator may ask them if they would feel more comfortable if the administrator sat with them during the test. This strategy is not appropriate for all types of tests. If you are trying to estimate how users will perform when they are working alone, don't offer to sit with participants during the test.

When participants do refuse, you have three tasks to accomplish:

1. Make sure that you understand *why* the participant does not want to be in the test. Could you or some member of the test team have prevented this refusal? Did the participant understand what would happen during the test? Sometimes there is nothing you can do to prevent a person from deciding against participating. On the other hand, the refusal may be a signal that you need to change your recruiting or greeting procedures.
2. Allow the participants to leave without putting any pressure on them or making them feel they have failed. It is imperative that you remain neutral or positive toward the participant. Tell them that they have the right to refuse and that you understand their position. Do not under any circumstances press them to continue. Pressing them is a violation of their rights as participants.
3. Decide how to handle the compensation they expected to receive. In the case of the one participant who refused to participate in our test, we agreed to pay her half of the amount that the temporary agency would have paid her for the test. We gave her credit for two of the four hours. You do not, of course, have to give participants any compensation, but you must not use the compensation as a tool to try to get them to participate. Again, remain neutral or positive in your attitude toward them and their action.

The Test Participant is Nervous and Cannot Continue

Occasionally, you will have participants who are so nervous that they cannot complete any tasks. It is usually clear right away when this happens. The participants will not think out loud and, when you talk to them, they do not seem to have the slightest idea how to accomplish the task. They are literally paralyzed with fear. When this occurs, you may want to take a short break and talk with them for a while. However, in our experience, these people seldom recover enough to give you much feedback about their reactions to the product. If you stop the test at this point, you need to decide whether to compensate the participant. Because you are taking the action to stop, you may want to be more generous than you would to someone who refuses to participate in the test.

The Test Participant is Not Qualified to Be in the Test
No matter how careful you are about recruiting, you will occasionally have a participant who comes to the test, but is not qualified. There are usually two reasons why this happens:

1. Participants do not understand what you have asked them about their qualifications.
2. Participants lie or stretch the truth about their qualifications.

When participants are not qualified, you will usually find out when they fill out their background questionnaire. Consequently, it is important to repeat the qualification questions you used for recruiting and to go over each one with participants after they have filled out the questionnaire.

This is a potential source of embarrassment for both you and the participants. The participants may have thought they were qualified when they came, and they were expecting to get some reward for participating. You will have to decide how to handle whether they get all or any part of the incentive you would have given them for the test. If the participants came to you through a temporary agency, you have the right to not compensate them or the agency. However, you will want to consider the time and effort it took to come to the test and whether, in your judgment, there was a legitimate misunderstanding about the qualifications.

It helps in this situation if your organization has a policy on compensating participants who are not qualified. The policy may allow you to negotiate some of its terms.

On rare occasions, you will find out after the test has begun that a participant is not qualified. We once ran a test that required participants to have one year's experience programming in the C language. We began the test after the participant had said that she had the appropriate experience. The first task was a simple one for a C programmer, but our participant could not do it. We then probed further and discovered that she was a writer who wrote manuals for applications written in C. No wonder her comments on the manual were so perceptive! She had assumed that she had enough knowledge about programming to get by. She was embarrassed when she had to reveal her deceit. We thanked her for her enthusiasm and sent her on her way.

The Test Participant Exceeds the Time Limit for a Task Without Finishing It

When you plan a test, you should have an estimate for how long it should take to complete each task. You may also have set a time criterion for an unacceptable time for a task, as we discussed in Chapter 13. There is, however, no hard and fast rule for when to *stop* a task. When you are running a test to get as much diagnostic information as possible from the test, you can often learn about usability problems as the participant tries alternative strategies. But at some point, you will want to move the participant along to new tasks so that you can observe what happens during them.

In our tests, we use a flexible rule of thumb: If the time we expect participants to take for a task is longer than 10 minutes, we allow at least twice that time before we stop the task; if the time we expect participants to take is shorter than 10 minutes, we allow at least three times the expected time before we stop the task.

Eventually, a participant will exceed the limit, and you will have to stop the task. This is usually a sensitive time for the test participant. No matter how many times you tell them that you are not testing them, most participants will feel that they have failed when they do not complete a task. You need to make them feel that the product has failed, not them.

It helps if you deal with this issue in your pretest instructions. You can tell participants:

> At times, I may ask you to go on before you have finished a task. When this happens, it does not mean that *you* have failed to complete the task. Sometimes we have learned all we need about how the software works for that task. We would rather you go on to the next task than to waste your time.

During your test planning you should be prepared to deal with the consequences of the participant not completing a task. If later tasks depend on the terminated task, you may have to intervene. For example, if the task involves creating and filing a mail message and a later task uses this message, you need to have a message ready to file for the participant or be able to modify the later task.

> *Research issue:* Should you help the participant finish a task to make them feel better, or should you just go on to the next task? What if you give participants information that will help them to do a future task? Are you biasing the test in favor of the product? On the other hand, if you do not help participants finish, will they perform differently? Will they be more discouraged and bias the test against the product? In our tests, we have moved more toward *not* helping participants finish tasks to avoid the likelihood of biasing the test, but we know of no studies investigating this issue.

You Must Stop the Test Because of Equipment or Software Malfunction

When something goes wrong that forces you to stop the test, it is a frustrating moment for all concerned.

You'll tend to ignore the participants while you figure out what's wrong. Don't just leave them sitting there. The best approach is to move the participants to another room and explain to them what is happening. If you decide to stop the test, you must decide whether to reschedule them and how you will compensate them. Because the problem was not their fault, you owe them something for their time if you are not going to reschedule them.

Do not forget about the participants' feelings in your frustration over getting equipment or software working.

The Participant Gets Frustrated or Anxious Because the Product is so Difficult to Use

On occasion, you will test a product that is so poorly designed that participants have a very hard time getting started and are continually frustrated by their inability to complete a task without many false starts. When this happens, participants have different ways of reacting. Some will get angry; others will blame themselves and become nervous.

When participants' emotional reactions begin to interfere with their performance, you need to intervene. Try taking a break and talking with them for a few minutes. If they are angry, talk with them about the important role they have in improving the product so that future users will not have to go through what they are going through. If they are nervous, remind them that you are testing the product not their ability to use it. Even though it may be natural for them to feel that their failure to complete tasks is unique, other participants have had similar problems.

If participants' emotional responses continue when you begin the test again, you will have to decide whether to complete the test. In this case, your decision should be based on your concern for the participants. If you feel that participants are experiencing too much stress or that they cannot respond appropriately to tasks, stop the test and talk with the designers about canceling future participants.

As you can see, caring for test participants takes effort and sensitivity. In most tests, the members of the test team will be focused on the product. They want to know how it is doing and how it can be improved. When you are responsible for interacting with test participants, you need to pay attention to both the product and the participants' reactions to it. You need to view the test through their eyes to help them to both get prepared to be test participants and be co-evaluators of the product with you.

In the next chapter, we continue our description of conducting a test.

19

Conducting the Test

In this chapter, we continue our discussion of events that happen on the day of the test. We begin by describing a typical test day, and then go on to discuss:

- being organized
- observing problems and creating a problem list
- interacting with participants
- dealing with managers and developers

A Typical Test Day

While no two days of a usability test are the same, it is informative to walk through the events of a typical day of testing. The following is a description of a typical day of testing in our usability lab. On this day, two participants are scheduled, one from 9:00–12:00 and the other from 1:00–4:00. We also expect several members of the client's development team as visitors. The product is a software application. The tasks we describe are performed by the three members of the test team.

8:15–8:30	Arrive at work. Make coffee. Turn copier on. Make copies of test materials for participant. Put participant number on materials.
8:30–9:00	Notify receptionist that visitors and participant are scheduled. Unlock lab rooms. Turn on lights in test and observation room. Power up prototype hardware and software. Power up audio and video equipment. Power up computer and open the data logger. Label videotapes for morning and afternoon. Record color bars at beginning of tapes. Load first tape, advance 10 seconds. Do sound check and video check for cameras. Set camera angles for test. Get refreshments ready. Greet visitors as they arrive, give them copies of materials, and get them seated in observation room. Greet participant, offer coffee, indicate when test will begin, offer materials to read.
9:00–9:25	Check observation room, lower lights, close door. Check test room.

Lead participant to test room.
Start video recording.
Start data log.
Adjust camera angles.
Give participant orientation, nondisclosure form, and pretest questionnaire.
Give participant brief training on use of mouse.

9:25–10:30   Run first set of tasks, while recording video and data log.
Write observations on the problem sheet.

10:30–10:40   Give participant a break, take participant to conference room for coffee.
Stop recording.
Set up prototype software for second set of tasks.
Put in a new videotape, advance 10 seconds.
Order lunch for team and visitors.

10:40–11:30   Bring participant back to test room.
Start recording video.
Run second set of tasks.
Run remaining tasks, while recording video and data log.
Write observations on the problem sheet.

11:30–12:00   Stop test.
Give participant posttest questionnaire.
Go over answers with participant.
Conduct posttest debriefing.
Pay participant and escort out.
Put participant number on all observations.
Put all participant materials in folder.

12:00–1:00   Eat lunch with visitors, discuss morning's observations.
Go to bank to get payment for next two participants.
Edit the data log to fix errors, clean up.
Make copies of materials for next participant.
Put participant number on materials.
Greet participant.
Get visitors back into observation room.
Prepare prototype software for first set of tasks.

1:00–1:25   Lead participant to test room.
Start tape, advance 10 seconds.

Initialize data logger.
Adjust camera angles.
Give participant orientation, nondisclosure form, and pretest questionnaire.
Give participant brief training on use of mouse.

1:25–2:30   Run first set of tasks, while recording video and data log.
Write observations on the problem sheet.

2:30–2:40   Give participant a break, take participant to conference room for coffee.
Stop recording.
Set up prototype software for second set of tasks.
Put in a new videotape, advance 10 seconds.

2:40–3:30   Bring participant back to test room.
Start recording video.
Run remaining tasks, while recording video and data log.
Write observations on the problem sheet.

3:30–4:00   Stop test.
Give participant posttest questionnaire.
Go over answers with participant.
Conduct posttest briefing.
Pay participant and escort out.
Put participant number on all observations.
Put all participant materials in folder.

4:00–5:00   Discuss observations with visitors.
Escort them out.
Discuss observations with test team.
Go over problem sheet.
Put all observation sheets in participant folder.
Edit the data log to fix errors, clean up.
Print data logs for both participants.
Put logs into participant folders.
Back up data-log files for both participants.
Check for blank tapes for tomorrow.
Clean up rooms.
Put trash out.
Shut off all equipment.
Shut off lights, lock up.

As you can see, there are many activities to accomplish on a test day. Running a test makes for a very full day, even when there are no major problems. Of course, not all of these tasks are done by the same person. Each of the members of the test team is responsible for some of the tasks. As we discussed in Chapter 16, "Preparing the Test Team," the activities each person is responsible for should be on their testing checklist.

Being Organized

Conducting a usability test is a demanding physical and emotional exercise. As the days go by, you begin to lose track of which participant did what. There is not enough time to pause and let all that is happening "sink in." Yet, keeping your concentration on what is happening as each participant performs is critical to achieving the goal of creating a more usable product. You need to keep yourself and your team members focused on the participant and on looking for the most basic causes of usability problems.

Make a label for each test participant with the name of the test, the participant's number, and any other identifying information you may need. Put the label on every form and every piece of paper you create during the test.

Other keys to remaining an effective test team are to use the checklists you created and keep file folders for materials and notes.

We discuss these tools in this section. In the next section, we describe the problem list, which is an important tool for keeping track of usability problems.

Using Checklists

The quality of a usability test will deteriorate over the course of a few days if your test team does not use their checklists. As with many stressful activities, you begin to fall back on old, learned habits as time under stress increases. As you need to concentrate harder to keep focused on the important tasks, you forget about or ignore details and less important tasks. If you have to think about or remember these details, you cannot concentrate on observing the usability problems with the product.

We know of no other way to maintain the quality of the test than to compulsively follow your checklists every day.

You can't beat Mother Nature. Human beings forget details when they have to concentrate over long periods of time. Without checklists, you will forget simple activities such as turning on a printer or filling the participant's glass with water.

When the slips and mistakes happen, you end up apologizing to participants and hoping that they keep thinking that you consider the test as important as you have told them to consider it.

Keeping Materials Together

For each participant who comes to the test you will have quite a large pile of materials. A typical list of materials includes:

- a recruiting questionnaire and the recruiter's notes
- a nondisclosure form
- a pretest questionnaire
- the task scenarios
- a posttest questionnaire
- notes the test team makes during the test
- the debriefer's notes from the posttest interview
- a printout of the test log
- a receipt for the participant's incentive

On your checklists, you should have items for putting the number of the test participant on all printed materials.

If you make notes on what is happening during the test, you must put the participant's number on them. If you do not, you will soon forget which participant the notes are for.

Keep a file folder for each participant and put all of the materials into that folder.

You must put the participant's number on every piece of paper that is related to the participant.

Observing Problems and Creating a Problem List

As with any empirical method, the keys to success in a usability test are the observations and measurements you make during it. In order to keep your observations organized, you need some means for tabulating events, either a software-based or a manual datalog. But you also need to record what you are seeing at another level. When participants have problems of any kind with the product, you need to record that problem and, in some cases, its frequency. We recommend that from the first minute of the first participant to the last minute of the last participant, the person responsible, usually test administrator or the briefer, keep a running list of the problems they see. When other members of the test team see problems, they should have the responsible person add them to the list.

In our tests, the test administrator has a pad of paper with the pages still attached. The participant's number goes on the top of page 1, and the administrator keeps a running list of problems as the participant proceeds through the tasks.

What we record on this list are observations (what we actually see) and inferences (our hypotheses and interpretations). What we want to understand at the end of a usability test are the real, underlying problems—the ones that have to be fixed. The behaviors we observe may be symptoms of these problems. Our hypotheses and interpretations help us understand the scope and severity of these problems—and give us insights for recommending good solutions.

Amanda Prail of Hewlett-Packard has captured many of these points very well in an article in the newsletter *Common Ground* (Prail, 1991). Figure 19-1 quotes Prail's suggestions on collecting observational data.

Suggestions on collecting observational data

Before observing
- Know the product that the user is using.
- Know the goals of the task the user is performing.
- Get into the observer role:
  - Respect the user.
  - Assume there are lots of opportunities to improve the design.
  - Be very curious.
  - Become detached, uninvested in the outcome.
  - Think of yourself as an anthropologist.

While observing
- Keep 100% of your attention on the user.
- Observe actively. Think of all potential user actions and construct hypotheses about observed actions.
- Write down both observations and your hypotheses and interpretations.
- If design ideas occur to you, write them down, but save design discussion for after the session.
- Stay away from your own thoughts. Censor any tendencies to rationalize or defend the design or to dismiss problems that "can't be fixed."
- Record all the user problems, whether they are part of your design or not.

After observing
- Discuss your interpretations of user problems with others to discover differences.
- Ask questions of the user during debriefing to confirm unsupported or debated interpretations.
- Make sure you have support from the user for all of your interpretations before examining potential design solutions.

Figure 19-1. Suggestions for observing – and looking for problems – during a usability test (Prail, 1991)

We recommend that if you are new to testing, you should focus on making observations first and leave the interpretations until after the participant is done and you have time to think and talk about what you have seen.

With practice, you will be able to move from observations to problems more quickly, and you will spend less time in your end-of-day discussion of the day's problems. Having an understanding of the context of research and experience with human-computer interaction helps you to interpret the meaning of observations.

Eventually, you want to get to the basic causes of the problems you see. But you must become skilled at making the observations before you learn how to interpret them. For example, as you watch a participant try to complete a task, you see that he says that he does not understand the word *toggle* in an instruction and makes an error by following the wrong procedure. Your observation, then, is the fact that there was a statement by the participant about not understanding the word *toggle* and that the wrong procedure was followed.

What interpretations and hypotheses can you make from this observation? There are several that are possible, and part of the skill of a good tester is seeing the range of possibilities and then deciding which one explains the most observations.

For example, this observation may only be the first of a series of observations about the wording of messages. There may be several other cases that would eventually lead you to believe that the interface is filled with jargon. You might hypothesize from this first instance that there may be jargon in other messages. You would then be on the lookout for future observations about problems participants have with words.

You might also hypothesize that the messages were written by software engineers not writers, and that there may be other evidence of this fact, such as awkwardly written messages and online help text. You would want to look for these instances and ask the developers who wrote the messages.

Experienced testers can write down observations and also some hypotheses or even keep the hypotheses in their heads. They also know that there is a danger in forming hypotheses early, because hypotheses can bias observations when they influence what is observed, and because they can make you miss observations that you would otherwise see. In our example, testers may be more likely to see difficulties with wording when there really are none, or they may be so focused on language that they miss problems with graphics.

As we will see in the next chapter, the problem list you create during the test becomes a tool for structuring the way you analyze the data. Some test teams take the first day's hurriedly written notes and create a more organized, formal list of problems. After the second day, the team adds any new problems to the formal list. They also look to see whether the second day's participants had any of the same problems as the first day's participants. If so, the team increases the frequency of the first day's problems by one.

When you keep this organized problem list up to date, you have a major part of your data analysis done when you have finished conducting the test. Keeping a formal problem list is a good practice when you are new to testing.

Interacting with Participants

In the last chapter, "Caring for the Test Participants," we discussed how the briefer gets the participant settled into the test and some of the problems that may arise in testing, so that you can develop policies for handling those situations.

In this chapter, we are concerned with who interacts with the participant and how to deal with normal interactions with the participant during the test. In particular, we discuss five issues that you may need to think about as you conduct the test:

- Who interacts with the participant during the test?
- When and how should you interrupt the participant?
- How do you avoid biasing test participants?
- Who decides when a participant has finished a task?
- What makes an effective help desk in a usability test?

Who Interacts with the Participant During the Test?

Even if you have several people on your test team, you want to keep the number of people with whom the participant has to interact to a minimum.

If you have a test team member acting as the help desk, that person talks to the participant—if and only if the participant calls.

If you have different people delivering the scenarios as if they were customers, either in person or over the phone, of course, you'll have more people interacting with the participant. That is a fairly unusual circumstance, however.

In most tests in which there are separate observation and test rooms, the participant works alone in the test room. Other than calls to the help desk, only the briefer interacts with the participant during the test. While the participant is working on the tasks, the briefer does not go back into the room. The briefer can talk to the participant over the intercom when one is available. In tests in which there is a member of the test team in the room with the participant, that person will be the one who interacts with the participant.

When and How Should You Interrupt the Participant?

When to interrupt a test participant is a matter of some controversy. Some organizations keep interruptions to a minimum, while others talk freely with the participant. The difference between the two styles depends, to some extent, on the goals of the test. If it is important that the test simulate a situation in which users will be working alone without help, keep interruptions to a minimum. For example, for some organizations it is important to find problems that will cause users to call the company's customer support line. In tests for these organizations, therefore, the test team takes a hands-off approach when participants have problems with the product. The test team provides help to the participant only through a help line that the participant calls from the test room.

In tests of early prototypes, on the other hand, the designers usually want to get as much diagnostic information as possible. In these tests, there is more interaction with the participants. For example, the briefer may ask participants to repeat a task using a different method or to describe why they did a task the way they did.

In general, you want to let the participants do each task at their own pace and in their own way. That's what you are there to observe.

It may be very difficult to sit behind the one-way mirror and watch participants struggle. You may find yourself desperately wanting to help. Don't give in to the impulse to jump in. You are there to watch what will most likely happen in people's offices and homes.

You will not be there in users' offices and homes to jump in and offer help.

In the first few tasks, the briefer may need to interrupt to encourage the participant to think out loud. (See Chapter 18, "Caring for Test Participants," for suggestions on getting quiet participants to verbalize their thoughts.)

If the participant does not stop between tasks, the briefer must quickly interrupt and remind the participant to say when he or she finishes one task and then wait to be told when to turn the page for the next task. Other than those two circumstances, encouraging participants to think out loud and making sure they stop between tasks, you should normally not have any need to interrupt unless you have decided to probe for diagnostic information.

In some tests of early prototypes, we create a set of probes to ask participants when they do not comment on a procedure or when they do not do the task the way we want them to. For example, we might be concerned about what participants would look for in online help during a particular task. If participants do not use online help during the task, we might ask them what they would have looked for. The probe is a reminder to the briefer to ask the question when the participant completes the task without using online help.

At the end or the beginning of tasks, you may want to add words of support or encouragement to your acknowledgment that the task is completed or to your instruction to go on to the next task. That support can be words such as:

"Thank you. The comments you are making are very helpful. We appreciate them. Please continue to think out loud like that."

"OK. Jim, how are you doing? Are you ready to do the next task?" [Participant says, "Yes, I'm ready."] "Good, let's start Task 5, and please continue to think out loud."

Your friendly tone and few words of encouragement can make a difference in how comfortable participants feel in the test situation.

How Do You Avoid Biasing Test Participants?

In the last chapter, we talked about how to encourage participants to think out loud and how to reduce their stress. Here, we want to discuss how to talk with participants in a way that allows you to get the most information you can from them without biasing them or giving them information that may help them with tasks.

During the 1960s and 1970s, researchers discovered that many participants in research studies try to figure out what the experimenter wants them to do and then they do it. In addition, experimenters bias studies by influencing what participants say and do (Rosenthal, 1976). Translated into the usability testing environment, these discoveries suggest two points:

1. Test participants are recruited specifically for the test and are usually reimbursed. Consequently, some participants will be looking for ways to be "good" participants. They want to know what the test administrator wants them to do. Our impression from what we see in our lab is that participants assume that the test team is somehow involved in the design of the product and wants the participant to like the product. This may cause them to make positive comments or refrain from negative comments about the product or to give it higher ratings than they ordinarily would. These expectations can change, however, if the tester reinforces the participants for making negative comments.
2. Testers can influence the way participants act and what participants say by biasing them with leading questions and encouraging either positive or negative statements.

The usability testing environment is a place in which these sources of bias exist. You need to be careful to avoid them. You will need to exercise caution when:

1. you ask questions of the participant
2. you respond to participants' questions and comments

How to Ask Questions

There are many times when you want to ask questions of the participants in a test. You may be probing them for additional information, or you may be asking about something they did or said.

When you ask these questions, you need to use neutral words. A good way to know whether you may be biasing the participant is to *examine how you use adjectives and adverbs in your questions*[1]. In English, adjectives and adverbs often carry an evaluative component with them. For example, if you ask the participant whether they found a procedure "easy," or whether they performed a task "easily," you may be biasing them by focusing on the positive end of the evaluative dimension from easy to difficult. It is better to question them in a more neutral way, such as "How was it performing that procedure?" or "Did you find that procedure easy or difficult?" The first form of the question contains no adjectives or adverbs. Sometimes, you may find that you need to use the second form so that participants describe their experience along a specific dimension, in this case the ease or difficulty of a task. Table 19-1 contains a list of useful neutral questions to ask, biased questions to avoid, and a short explanation of why the neutral questions are preferable.

How to Respond to Participants' Questions and Comments

Sometimes the participant asks *you* a question. These questions can make you feel uncomfortable, because you feel pressured into giving the participant information you do not want to give them. There are some strategies you can use in these situations.

Turn the question around. Participants might ask, "Do I use Help to find that out?" The participants may be asking you to give them the answer, or they may just be unsure. In either case, you do not want to lead them. You might say, "What do you think you should do?" or "Do whatever you think you should do," or "I would like you to figure that out," or "I can't tell you what you should do, but I'd like you to keep trying."

Participants might ask, "Did I do that right?" An appropriate response would be, "Do you think you did it right?" Knowing how confident participants are can be useful information. If they are not confident, the software may not provide enough feedback to their actions.

Don't answer the question directly. Participants might ask, "Did everyone else have as much trouble as I did?" You might respond, "Did you have more trouble than you expected?"

Participants might ask, "Do you want me to tell you when I don't like something?" You might respond, "Tell me what you like and what you don't like," or "I'd like to hear any reactions you have about the product, good or bad."

---

[1] We call this rule *Coleman's Rule* in honor of Marilyn Coleman who first brought it to our attention.

Table 19-1 Neutral questions to ask, biased questions to avoid, and why the neutral questions are preferable

Ask:	Instead of:	Why:
Can you tell me what you are thinking right now? What are you trying to do?	Are you thinking ___ ? Are you trying to ___ ?	Even though you may think you know what they are thinking (that may be why you are asking the question), you do not want to put words into their mouths, because you may be wrong. Remember, you do not want participants to know your opinions about what you are questioning them on.
What are you thinking? Can you explain to me what you are trying to do? Can you explain to me your train of thought right now? (After the task is ended) Why did you try to ___ ?	Why are you ___ ? Are you trying to ___ because ___ ? Are you trying to ___ ?	By asking participants why they are doing something, they may feel that you are asking them to justify their actions, and, therefore, think that they are going about the task incorrectly. It is, however, acceptable to ask a participant why they went about a task in a certain way after the task has been ended, or at the end of the test if future tasks have components similar to the task you are questioning them about.
Did you find the product easy or difficult to use? Were the instructions clear or confusing? Were error messages helpful or hindering?	Did you find the product easy to use? Did you find the product difficult to use? Were the error messages helpful?	Trying to get someone to express an opinion on a specific usability attribute is not always easy. Therefore, you may find that you need to guide participants by specifying the attribute you want them to react to. It is important to use both ends of the spectrum when you do this so that they do not perceive you as encouraging either a positive or negative answer. Also, by doing so, you will encourage a more informative response. Instead of responding "No (it was not easy)," they are more likely to say "I found it very difficult to use," or "it was pretty easy." You then can follow up by asking them "why?"
What are you feeling? How did you feel when you were doing ___ ?	Are you feeling confused? Are you feeling frustrated?	Sometimes, participants need to stop and think – maybe to try to remember how a similar product worked. Though they may appear confused or frustrated, they may just be contemplating. Everyone expresses themselves differently, so we take a risk by trying to guess what they are thinking.

(continued on next page)

Table 19-1 (continued)

Ask:	Instead of:	Why:
Would you change anything about this (product, screen, design, etc.)?	Do you think ___ would improve the product?	Unless the design team is considering a particular design change, you should never suggest what changes participants should talk about.
Are there any changes you would make to ___ to make it easier to use?	If we changed ___ to ___ do you think that it would be easier to use?	Always let participants express their own ideas. And, if there is a design change that the design team feels will improve the product, ask them to react to it only after they have made their suggestions and only after you let them know that their input is considered valuable.
How do you feel about (that error message, the organization of the screen, the way the procedure is described in the manual, etc.)?	Was the (error message, the organization of the screen, the description of the procedure, etc.) confusing?	Even though you may think you know what they are thinking (that may be why you are asking the question), you do not want to put words into their mouths, because you may be wrong.
Do you have any reactions to (that error message, the organization of the screen, the way the procedure is described in the manual, etc.)?	Are you confused by the (error message, the organization of the screen, the description of the procedure, etc.)?	Remember, you do not want participants to know your opinions about what you are questioning them on.
Do you have any comments on the (appearance, size, feel, feedback, etc.) of ___ ?	Do you like the (appearance, size, feel, feedback, etc.) of ___ ?	

Who Decides When a Participant has Finished a Task?

You want participants to tell you when they finish each task scenario. In most tests, you will be interested not only in whether participants can do each step in the process to complete a task, but in their own evaluation of whether the task was done. There are two circumstances that you have to consider:

1. The participant has done all the steps, but is not ready to say the task is done.
2. The participant says the task is done, but it is not.

When the Participant Isn't Ready to Say the Task is Done

In many tests, we have seen participants spend time wondering whether they really did the task, checking to see if it was done, or even redoing it several times because they are not sure. All of that is valuable information for you.

If users in their offices or homes are going to spend extra time trying to figure out if the message was really sent, if the file was really saved, or if the changes were really made, that's part of the time it will take them to do the tasks. Moreover, if users redo the task because they are not sure the software has actually carried out their instructions, the consequences could be more significant than just extra time.

> For example, in testing an electronic mail package, we were not comfortable with the way the product handled replying to a memo. While the memo they had received was on the screen, users correctly chose "Reply" from the menu, typed their reply, and then chose "Send" from the menu to send it. The computer did in fact send both their reply and the original memo, if they chose to include it with the reply.

> The system message that the reply was being sent flashed by so quickly on the screen, however, that very few users noticed it. They thought they had no word from the computer that the reply had been sent. Furthermore, after they chose "Send," the product reset the screen as it had been at the beginning of the task, with the original memo ready to be read but without the reply that the user had written.

> Users, after looking at this screen and completing the task correctly, concluded that they had somehow messed up and that their reply had been deleted or had somehow been sent off to oblivion. They redid the task. Some redid it three times before concluding that it must have worked even though they were still uncomfortable about it.

> Only by letting the users continue until they said they were done would the product developers see what a problem not having a readable message like "Reply sent" was to these users. This was an important problem to see, because the consequences are not just the extra time that users will spend redoing the task, but the embarrassment users might suffer from sending three identical replies to the same writer about the same memo and the confusion and time of the writer who receives the three identical replies.

If the test team, not users, had been the ones to decide when the task was done, they would not have learned about this important problem.

When the Participant Says the Task is Done, But It Is Not

One of the issues you will have to address is deciding when to ask participants to continue with a task that they either think they've completed or want to give up on. In setting policy for this issue, consider these three points:

- You must be consistent for all participants. Otherwise, you won't have data that you can compare.
- You should be compassionate. If you have seen enough to know the product needs work, don't push participants beyond endurance.
- But, you want to learn as much as you can.

If the situation isn't overly frustrating for the participants and if they haven't been working at the task an inordinate amount of time, you will usually learn more by asking them to continue to work on the task.

For example, in testing a new telephone with a small display screen, we asked participants to do a task that involved changing the setting for a feature. Participants did not connect the feature with the display and usually gave up after trying—and failing—to find a specific button to press or wheel to turn. We could have let them stop and told the developers that users don't expect to use the display to change that particular feature.

However, we didn't let the participants stop. We asked them to continue to work at the task. We were able to observe two other very important problems —that the quick reference card didn't help these participants, and that they couldn't make the change in the time that the system allowed them before automatically clearing the display.

These were both global problems that the client needed to fix before releasing the product. We may not have seen them if we had let participants give up on the task.

What Makes an Effective Help Desk in a Usability Test?

Deciding when to give help and what help to give is one of the most difficult parts of conducting a usability test. If you are counting error rates as one of your measurements, you need to let participants make errors. Those errors are among your most valuable pieces of data. If you let participants give up easily, you may be losing information that you need to keep other users from making the same errors with the final product. Therefore, you need to let the participant initiate the request for help, and you need to give the minimum amount of help that you can.

One of the reasons for having participants use the telephone to call a "help desk," rather than just letting the participant ask the briefer for help, is to see people's tolerances for working out problems before calling for help.

If one of your goals is to reduce calls to your help desk or customer support line, setting up a situation in which the participant actually calls for help on the telephone may give you some idea of how frequently, and at what points, users may call.

Don't be deceived into believing, however, that using a help line is somehow more "objective" than having the briefer interrupt participants to help them. Participants have their own criteria about when they will ask for help. Some participants will ask for help without really trying to do a task. Others will never ask for help. If you are the briefer, you will have to make decisions about when to interact with participants, whether they have a help line or not.

The following are some hints for being an effective help desk person on a usability test team:

- Act as if you were on a real help desk in these ways:
  - Pretend that you have not just been watching the participant.
  - Don't assume you know the participant's problem, even if you do know because you can see it. In a nontest situation, the help desk person would not know.
  - Ask the participant to tell you what he or she is trying to do.
  - Ask the participant to tell you what steps he or she has taken—and why.
- But then act quite differently from a real help desk:
  - Give the minimal amount of advice that you can to help the participant move on. For example, if there is on-screen help or labeled function keys that would help and the participant hasn't noticed them, you might ask the participant if there is anything on the screen that could be a clue as to how to proceed. Also, remember that you do not want to volunteer any information that might help participants on a future task.
  - If the product has online help, you might ask if the participant has tried it. If the participant has, you get the chance to ask what he or she looked at and why it didn't help. If the participant hasn't, you can suggest trying that first and calling back if necessary.
  - Try to get the participant to suggest how to proceed from a hint.
    For example, if you suggest online help and the participant asks, "How do I find it?" you might come back with, "Do you have an idea that you might try? Have you worked with another product that would give you an idea for getting to online help in this product?" That way, you get to observe the participant's expectations about which key

Do not volunteer information that is not directly related to the participant's question and do not volunteer information that will help the participant in a future task.

or key combination leads to online help.
- Do not let the participants stay on the line and expect you to walk them through the entire process. Once the participants have gotten over the immediate problem, suggest that they try to go on and call again if they need to.
- Don't be afraid to ask participants to keep trying if they have not given the task a fair effort.

These are two more general guidelines about giving help to participants:

- Be friendly and patient no matter what, even if the participant makes disparaging comments about the product or the test or you.
- Give the same level of advice for similar situations to all participants in the same test. It helps to develop guidelines for how to give advise and to follow them.

Dealing with Managers and Designers

In addition to the members of the test team, there are other people who will occasionally attend a test. The most important groups of visitors are members of the design team for the product you are testing and managers who work in the organization designing the product or in your own organization.

People who conduct usability tests have different approaches to handling these visitors. In some testing organizations, the people who conduct the tests try to keep visitors out of the observation room. In these labs, there is a separate room for visitors. From that room, visitors can see what participants are doing either through a one-way mirror, a window that looks through the observation room, or on a monitor.

Whether or not visitors are with you in the observation room, you will have to deal with them and their reactions to the test. In this section we discuss

- helping designers deal with their egos
- giving managers perspective
- maintaining discipline during test sessions

Helping Designers Deal with Their Egos

While designers often improve their attitudes when they attend a few tests, the process of change is difficult. A usability test is a highly charged experience for many designers. They have worked many weeks or months on the product. They know what the design goals are. In spite of all of the discussion in the literature about egoless design, most people cannot help being upset when the product they have designed is not working well for its users. Designing is a creative activity, and most designers are proud of what they have created.

We have watched many software engineers and writers struggle to keep their anger under control as they watch test participants have difficulty with a product. They want to yell out, and sometimes do, "Can't you see it on the screen! It is right in front of you." During these times, it helps to have a sound-proofed lab with a one-way mirror. You need to get these frustrated designers to talk about their frustration and to see how much better it is for them to find the problems in the test, rather than when the product is released and it is too late to make substantial changes.

It also helps if you can get designers to focus on the basic problem. Many of them have a narrow view of the causes of problems. If participants are having problems understanding an error message, the designers may say, "Let's rewrite that message."

The best solution, however, may not be to just rewrite the message. The problem may be more basic. Many of the messages may be poor, because the software designers wrote them. The design team may need to get a writer involved to rewrite all of the messages as well as the other text on the screen.

In this emotional situation, you have to act a little like a counselor. Let designers talk about their frustrations as long as it is not disruptive to the test team. If you feel the need, step outside of the observation room for a few minutes to talk with them. The attitude you want to convey is that there is no value in assigning blame for usability problems. Good design requires creativity and hard work. It also requires the flexibility to adjust as you learn more about the design and how users will react to it.

It may help to point out to software engineers that they would not expect to go through a code walkthrough or a quality control test without uncovering some problems. Finding problems is why you test a product.

Giving Managers Perspective

Managers are also likely to attend a test, especially when testing is new or the product is critical. The way that you handle visits from managers can strongly influence the future of both your recommendations from this test and of usability testing in general.

Managers are likely to come for only a short time. They may jump to conclusions from the little bit they saw, especially when the conclusions are consistent with their pretest intuitions about the product. You need to supplement what the managers see with a broader perspective of what has been happening throughout the test.

This is sometimes a difficult situation. Because judgments about the usability of a product come from an accumulation of data from several sources, you may not want to make a global statement during an early testing session. In that case, you should caution managers about making snap judgments or about the folly of predicting the final outcome based on early returns.

When managers attend a test, you can often use the opportunity to help them understand the underlying causes for both the good and poor performance of a test participant. Keep in mind that as you watch a test with a manager, you and the manager are often not seeing the same events. You may have the context of your knowledge of human–computer interaction and your experience conducting usability tests to help you see problems where others do not see them and to see the global rather than the specific causes of problems.

When managers come to see a usability test, it is these global underlying causes of problems that you need to spend time discussing, rather than just the solutions that only treat the symptom of the problem.

Maintaining Discipline During Test Sessions

Whenever you have visitors in the observation room there is the potential for disruption of your own work, which is recording and observing the behavior of the test participant. We have conducted many tests in which members of the design team and managers have observed with us for one day or for all of the days of the test. The pattern of their behavior is quite consistent. For the first day or two, they quietly watch and whisper when they speak. After they have watched a few participants perform the tasks, their attention begins to wander, and they begin to talk more to the test team. The most frequent topics of conversation are (a) what other participants have done, and (b) how to fix the usability problems they see.

At a point during the third day that visitors watch a test, they will begin to interfere with your ability to concentrate on what the participant is doing. The frequency of irrelevant conversations increases. Your test team will find it difficult to concentrate on keeping its notes and the test log up to date. It is usually necessary, when you see this happening, to say something politely to the visitors about the importance of watching the participant and not assuming that this participant will act exactly as other participants have.

If you are running the type of test in which you interact freely with the test participants, you will find that the visitors suggest questions for the briefer to ask the participants. You need to make it clear to the visitors that the test team administrator makes the decisions about what to ask and how to ask it. The visitors may make suggestions, but the test administrator may choose not to take them.

In this environment it helps to ask the visitors to designate a spokesperson. Only that person is allowed to talk with the test administrator.

In the next chapter, we move on to tabulating and analyzing the data you have collected during the test.

20

Tabulating and Analyzing Data

A usability test generates a substantial amount of data. When the test is over, you will probably have at least some of these:

- a list of problems that has been growing over the course of the test
- quantitative data on times, errors, and other performance measures
- quantitative data on subjective ratings and other questions from posttask and posttest questionnaires
- participants' comments from your logs or notes and from the questionnaires
- the test team's written notes or their comments that may have been typed into a log
- background data on the participants from the user profiles, recruiting questionnaire, or pretest questionnaire
- the videotapes, perhaps showing several views of the test

The point of a usability test is to find the *real problems* with the product—and with the process that was used to develop the product. The real problems are the ones that are going to cause difficulties for users when they get the product in their homes or offices to do their work. As we will discuss in the section on "Organizing Problems by Scope and Severity" later in this chapter, many of the problems that you see in a usability test are symptoms of larger problems and not the entire problem. How do you find the real problems in all the data that you have?

In a usability test, you usually have a great deal of data about a small number of participants. A useful technique for handling a rich supply of data from several sources is *triangulation*. You look at all the data together to see how each set of data supports the others. For

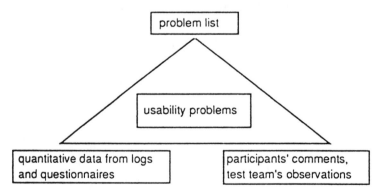

Figure 20-1. "Triangulating"—using multiple sources of data to find the usability problems with a product

example, a long task time, frequent errors, the participants' comments may all point to the same problem. When you triangulate three types of data, you will feel more confident that there is a problem and that you understand it.

The concept of triangulation gives you a framework for thinking about all of the data together. However, you still need a strategy to follow to make good use of all of these data quickly. There is almost always pressure to report on findings as soon as possible after the test. You don't often have the luxury of leisurely examining the data to look for findings that might emerge from it.

If you have been developing a problem list during the test, you will probably find that it can be a very useful key to your analysis. It gives you directions to search. That's why we've put it at the apex of the triangle in Figure 20-1. You must remain open and alert, however, to the information that your other sources reveal.

In this chapter, we describe a strategy for making use of all the data that you have gathered:

- tabulating and summarizing the quantitative data
- looking for trends and surprises in the data
- examining the data for problems
- using statistics
- organizing the problems by scope and severity

We end the chapter with lists of the common problems we have found in our usability tests of software and documentation.

Tabulating and Summarizing the Quantitative Data

The first step in getting a handle on the test data is to make summary sheets of the performance and subjective measures. For the performance measures you will need to begin by tabulating them for each task for each participant. For example, you will typically tabulate, for each task, the elapsed time, the number of errors of various types, and other important measures such as the number of assists the participants needed.

Table 20-1 shows task times for 16 participants in a fictitious test of the electronic mail example we have been using. The 8 participants in Group I were selected because they have no experience using electronic mail. The 8 participants in Group II were selected because they have previously used electronic mail software.

Table 20-1. Task times for eight participants in two groups from a hypothetical usability test

Group I

	PARTICIPANTS 1	2	3	4	5	6	7	8	Total	Ave.
Read new mail	5.47	14.04	5.87	7.26	14.58	6.45	8.19	10.24	72.10	9.01
T Create & send a message	10.50	36.00	3.50	36.50	15.87	12.00	13.50	34.00	161.87	20.23
A Forward, create a folder,file	17.24	25.50	5.18	6.50	14.19	12.52	3.05	8.74	92.92	11.62
S Find & delete	1.57	2.33	1.24	1.75	3.23	6.50	3.01	2.23	21.86	2.73
K Reply	17.57	13.20	6.53	13.08	8.65	16.72	23.07	12.63	111.45	13.93
S Attach a file	11.37	9.17	33.32	45.03	16.44	10.03	5.40	9.92	140.68	17.59
Create a dist. list	19.57	22.93	6.87	12.73	4.03	20.32	40.37	13.23	140.05	17.51
Set useful life & archive	9.48	3.54	19.31	4.34	13.24	18.03	11.30	7.05	86.29	10.79
Make a shared folder	20.34	13.57	6.72	23.17	9.37	8.53	21.22	5.16	108.08	13.51
Set priorities	14.34	10.28	31.33	18.39	29.21	20.51	N/A	18.64	142.70	20.39
Total	127.45	150.56	119.87	168.75	128.81	131.61	129.11	121.84		
Average	12.75	15.06	11.99	16.88	12.88	13.16	14.35	12.18		

Group II

	PARTICIPANTS 1	2	3	4	5	6	7	8	Total	Ave.
Read new mail	3.50	7.48	5.50	5.06	2.80	7.45	2.25	6.08	40.12	5.02
T Create & send a message	21.57	11.32	15.17	14.87	8.33	18.62	9.37	22.30	121.55	15.19
A Forward, create a folder,file	3.72	15.67	5.52	7.16	8.07	18.04	6.49	6.08	70.75	8.84
S Find & delete	1.37	2.25	2.87	4.06	5.22	5.29	2.24	1.21	24.51	3.06
K Reply	9.48	3.54	19.31	12.34	13.24	7.05	25.46	13.34	103.76	12.97
S Attach a file	8.36	23.57	7.29	14.59	43.13	6.60	11.34	28.42	143.30	17.91
Create a dist. list	8.19	21.25	16.24	15.50	12.63	35.76	19.96	10.90	140.43	17.55
Set useful life & archive	13.41	10.27	8.90	13.42	19.25	12.24	12.34	9.90	99.73	12.47
Make a shared folder	11.17	32.37	6.57	14.50	17.47	12.67	4.45	5.23	104.43	13.05
Set priorities	38.47	22.03	9.68	26.69	7.30	20.84	8.29	19.24	152.54	19.07
Total	119.24	149.75	97.05	128.19	137.44	144.56	102.19	122.70		
Average	11.92	14.98	9.71	12.82	13.74	14.46	10.22	12.27		

Spreadsheet software is a valuable tool for the kinds of summaries you need for usability test data.

As you can see in Table 20–1, in addition to the times for each task, we computed the total time and the average or mean time. We tabulated these time scores from a printout of the task times for each participant from our test logging software. But we could also have used times collected with a stopwatch. We entered the times into a spreadsheet on a personal computer and added the formulas to compute the totals, and averages.

Spreadsheet software allows you to compute simple statistics quickly, and spreadsheets are accepted as input by almost all of the more elaborate statistical packages as well as word processing software.

We also made separate spreadsheets for the pretest questionnaire items and for the posttask and posttest questionnaire items. The pretest items gave us a demographic profile of the participants. The posttask and posttest items gave us subjective measures that we can tabulate.

In addition, we made a list in a word processing file of the important comments the participants made. These comments come from the comment fields in the questionnaires and from the printouts from the data logs. Finally, we made a list of the comments that members of the test team made during the test. Some of these were on the problem sheets, and some were in the data log.

Looking for Trends and Surprises in the Data

A usability test is an empirical evaluation method. As such, you will have to justify the problems you report with the data you collected.

Before going back to the problem sheet, look at the tabulated data for trends that seem surprising. There may be findings that were not obvious as you watched each participant separately but that show up when you look at the numbers for several participants together.

For example, look at the average task times for the two groups of participants in Table 20-1. The average times for the first three tasks for Group I are quite a bit slower than the times for the same tasks for Group II. The times for the rest of the tasks are about the same for both groups. There seems to be something going on during these early tasks that is different for each group. Not only are the average times longer for Group I, but the spread of the scores is larger, which indicates that there are bigger differences in task times between the participants in Group I than there are in Group II.

These differences may be due to the level of experience of the two groups using electronic mail. But, there may be other differences between them, such as their level of experience using computers or using software applications. This is an instance in which to use triangulation to identify what the problem is. For example, you can see that participants #2 and #5 in Group I were particularly slow, especially during the first three tasks. If we look at their experience, we may find that they have the least experience using PC applications.

When we look at the specific cause of the slow times for these two participants, we may find that they spent time discovering how to use several function keys that the other participants found quickly. For example, these two participants may not have understood that they could use the ESC key to back up one screen. Thus, we have triangulated on a problem: Users who are new to PCs may have trouble using function keys during their first hour of using the electronic mail software.

Dealing with Outliers in the Data
Another place to look for interesting findings are *outliers*. An *outlier* is a value that is very different from the rest of the scores. In the case of usability data, outliers often show up as scores that are much smaller or larger than average scores. Looking at Table 20-1, there are several outliers. In Group I, there are two scores over 40 minutes: participant #4's time for "Attach a file," and participant #7's time for "Creating a distribution list." In Group II, there is one score over 40 minutes: participant # 5's time for "Attach a file."

It is worth examining each of these outliers to see what the cause may be. Sometimes the cause of scores like these may not be a usability problem. For example, the score may have been recorded incorrectly, or there may have been an equipment breakdown that took time that was not subtracted from the task time.

In other cases, these times may provide a clue to a usability problem. Notice that in our data set, two of the three times over 40 minutes occurred during the same task. Is there a problem here that happens infrequently, but disastrously?

In this case, both of these participants decided to go outside of the mail application to look at the file before they attached it. The mail software allows users to do this without logging out of mail. These two participants successfully found the menu item that allowed them to leave the mail software and go out to the operating system. They couldn't get back into the mail software, however, because they did not know the command for returning, and there was no online help available because they were not in the mail software. After repeated tries and becoming confused further by the commands they did try, both participants had to be told what the command was before they could complete the task.

Notice that in this case, there were three measures that all pointed to the same problem: the very long task times for two participants, the large number of errors from trying incorrect commands, and the assists both participants needed to complete the task. In this case, it was possible to find other measures that pointed to the same problem.

Taking Outliers Seriously

But, what happens when a problem shows up with only one participant? Do we ignore it because no one else had the problem? What if the one person who had the problem represents 20% of users?

Our approach is to seriously consider any problem that any participant had using the product. First we look for the reasons behind that person's unusual result. Was there something about one task or series of tasks that caused it? Is there something in the person's background that made that person susceptible?

Of course, it is possible that this participant does not represent many users. The risk you are taking if you dismiss the result, however, is not reporting a problem that turns out to be a real problem for the product and the company.

Our approach is to seriously consider any problem that any participant had using the product.

When you have so few participants in a test, however, the one participant who had that problem may represent a large subset of users who will also have the problem. Sometimes there is no way to know, without further testing, whether the outlier is an anomaly or an indicator of something serious.

This is one of the reasons why iterative testing is so valuable. If you find an outlier who might represent a large or important group of potential users, you can bring in more people who match that participant's background. If you fix problems that one or a few participants have, you can try the new version to make sure that the fix works for those people and does not cause problems for other users.

Examining the Data for Problems

After you have looked at the data to see if there are usability problems you did not anticipate, it is time to examine the data to see if it is consistent with the hypotheses you had before you started conducting the test. You want to look to see if the

- usability concerns you had about the product have been taken care of in the design
- usability goals you may have set have been achieved
- quantitative criteria you may have set for the tasks have been met or exceeded

Examining Your Usability Concerns

Consider what the data say about the concerns that you listed while planning the test. Because the concerns guided you in selecting the tasks for participants to do, each task is linked to one or more concerns. You can look at both the problem sheet and the tabulated data to see whether the concern is justified.

Let's consider a specific case from the hypothetical example we are using. One of our concerns about the electronic mail software was that users would have trouble identifying a new mail message to read. Figure 20-2 shows the screen from the mail system in its default configuration. As you can see, the newest message is highlighted with a highlight bar and with an arrow to its left.

In order to read the message titled "Meeting 5/9—minutes," you must move the highlight bar down to it with the Down Arrow key and then press the spacebar to identify it. Figure 20-3 shows what the screen looks like after these actions.

If you do not know enough to identify the message by pressing the spacebar, you will get the most recent new message when you select "Read" from the menu.

If you look at the top row of the data in Table 20-1, you can see that it took participants in Group I almost 10 minutes to complete this task, which is a long time for reading a one-sentence message. Participants assumed that all they had to do was move the highlight bar to the message and press ENTER. They were surprised when the software displayed the wrong message.

Two of the participants used the online help facility to look for the procedure for selecting a message to read. There is nothing, however, in the help text to explain how to mark a new message.

This example illustrates again how most usability problems reveal themselves in more than one measure. In this case, the problem shows up in several performance measures: long task times, number

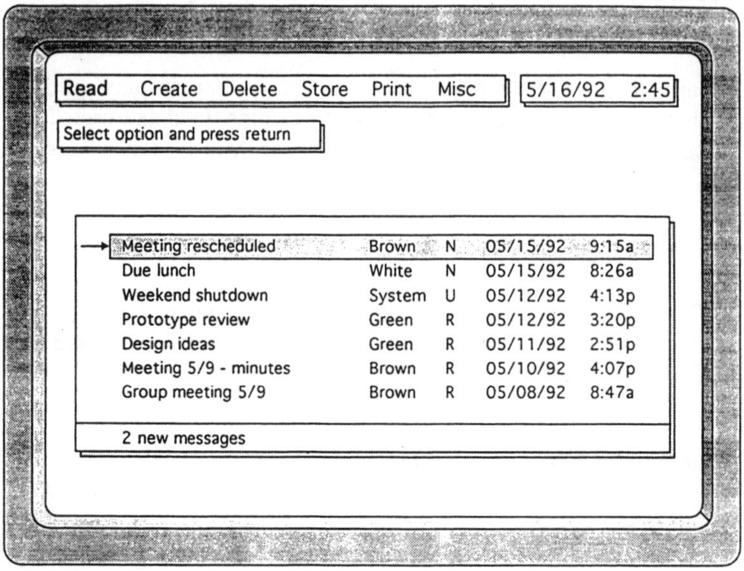

Figure 20-2. Screen showing a list of messages with the newest message highlighted

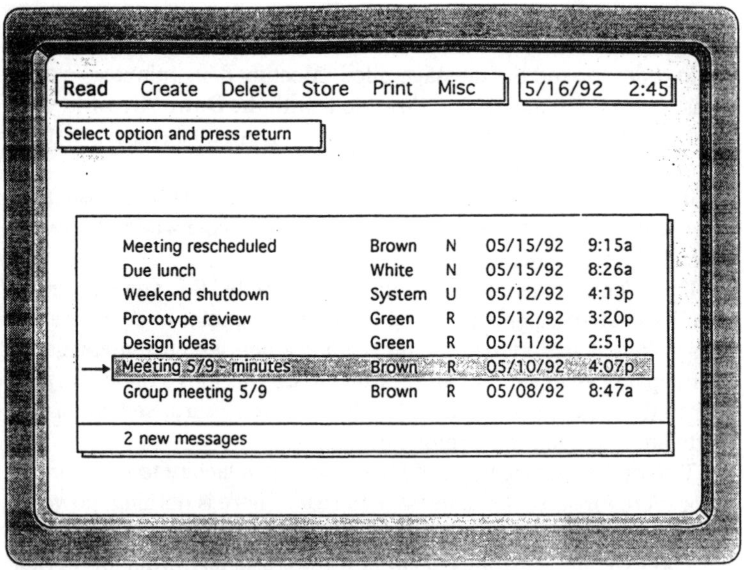

Figure 20-3. Screen after user has moved the highlight bar and pressed the space bar to identify the message to read

of errors, number of assists, and number of times using online help. There is also evidence in the comments the participants made while performing the task. For example, one participant said "If this first task is typical, I am not going to like this program at all."

When you look at all of the measures, there is no doubt that there is a serious problem here with selecting messages to read. We suspected that there might be a problem with this procedure, so we included a task to probe it, and we examined the data we recorded to provide empirical evidence for the problem. Later in this chapter, we discuss how to rate the seriousness of the problem.

This discussion of the problems with the first task also shows why usability testing is such a rich source of data on usability. It shows that participants

- took longer than expected to perform a task that was not intuitive
- had difficulty finding the information they looked for in online help
- were confused by jargon

You can see how much diagnostic information there is in just one task in a usability test.

Examining Usability Goals

If you have set quantitative usability goals for the product, it is now time to see whether the product has achieved these goals. For example, you may have decided that it should take users less than 5 minutes to read their first, short, mail message. Looking at the task times in Table 20-1, we see that the Group II participants were a bit over the 5 minutes on average, but that none of the Group I participants completed the task in less than five minutes. We now know that the criterion was exceeded and why.

You can see what an advantage it is to set quantitative usability goals. They make the analysis of the data much easier, because they allow you to isolate important problems without having to sift through the data to discover them.

Examining Quantitative Criteria

In Chapter 13, "Deciding How to Measure Usability," we discussed setting quantitative usability criteria for each task. If you have set criteria, now is the time to examine them.

The following is a set of hypothetical criteria for users who are new to electronic mail for the task of "Creating and sending a mail message":

- Excellent   less than 10 minutes
- Acceptable   less than 15 minutes
- Unacceptable   more than 15 minutes

These criteria apply to the data in Table 20-1 for the second task, "Creating and sending a message" for the very first time. Group I in the table had no previous experience with electronic mail. As you can see, the mean time for the task is 20.23 minutes, which is unacceptable according to our criteria. Only 3 of the 8 participants finished the task in less than 15 minutes, while 3 other participants took over 30 minutes.

There appears to be one or more usability problems with this task. You would need to look at the other quantitative measures, participant's ratings and comments, and your list of problems to triangulate on what the problems are.

Using Statistics

The statistics we have been discussing thus far in this chapter are called "descriptive" statistics. As the name says, you use descriptive statistics to *describe* the properties of a set of data. For example, the means of the task times in Table 20-1 describe the average (arithmetic mean) of times for each task.

The analysis of the data from any usability test always begins with describing the characteristics of the data. Typically, you would compute several measures that describe the data. There are measures of

- the frequency of scores, such as the number of errors that occur in a task
- typical scores, such as the average (mean) or median of the times for a task (The median is the middle score when you list the scores from lowest to highest.)
- the amount of variability of scores, such as the range of the times for a task

In most of the usability tests that we have conducted, we only need to use these simple descriptive statistics along with qualitative data, such as test participants' comments, to document the case for the presence of usability problems.

But what happens when the product manager, John, asks whether the values are "statistically significant"? John may not be sure what he is asking, but the answer to this question requires the use of a different type of statistic called "inferential" rather than "descriptive."

In inferential statistics, you look at your data as a sample from a larger set of data. You ask what you can *infer* about the larger set of data from the sample.

To take a concrete example, suppose that you had conducted a comparison test in which 10 test participants used 2 different prototypes to complete the same task, such as displaying a graph from a set of data in a spreadsheet. Assume that you had used the appropriate controls, such as having half of the participants begin with each of the two prototypes. Table 20-2 shows how long each participant took to complete the task with each prototype.

Table 20-2   Times (minutes) for completion of one task with Prototypes #1 and #2

Participants	Prototype #1	Prototype #2
1	1.9	3.3
2	3.2	8.0
3	5.0	7.6
4	4.4	8.3
5	5.9	9.2
6	2.7	9.4
7	6.2	8.2
8	3.7	7.8
9	4.3	5.3
10	2.8	8.2
Mean	4.0	7.5

At the bottom of the table are the mean times for the two prototypes. These means describe the average completion time for each prototype. The participants were, on average, faster with prototype #1.

But how do we deal with John's question about statistical significance? In a statistical sense, what John is asking is whether the two samples of task times come from the same larger set of data, in which case there is no statistical difference, or whether the two samples come from different sets of data and, therefore, are statistically different.

Before we proceed, let's consider what John may really be asking. He probably wants to know whether statistics confirm that there is a *real* difference between these two methods of displaying a graph. He may be worried about making a final decision on the method to display a graph from such a small sample of people. He may also feel that if the difference is "statistically significant," he has no choice but to make the change.

The reviewers of the manuscript of this book were split into two groups on the question of what to do at this point. We believe that this split reflects an important point of controversy about the use of inferential statistics in usability tests. One group would compute the appropriate statistic and carefully explain its meaning to John. The other group would not compute any inferential statistic, but would rather address John's concerns about whether the two prototypes differ in their usability and how compelling the case is from all of the available data for the superiority of prototype #1.

Let's spend a few minutes discussing the arguments on both sides of this issue.

There are three major arguments *for* computing inferential statistics:

1. There are some usability tests for which inferential statistics are appropriate. Our example comparison test between prototype #1 and #2 is a case in which inferential statistics are probably appropriate. In addition, some companies are willing to invest the resources to make a usability test of an important product into an applied research study with appropriate controls and numbers of test participants. In those cases, inferential statistics may also be appropriate.

2. An inferential statistic is just one piece of data testers use to diagnose usability problems. There is no reason to eliminate any useful tool from the kit of techniques we have to understand usability. *If properly interpreted*, testers can use inferential statistics and other data to help designers improve their products.

3. Whether we like it or not, the audiences to which we communicate the results of our tests will make judgments about the importance of a finding from the data we provide to them. For example, it is likely that John, the product manager, has "eyeballed" the difference between the two means for prototype #1 and #2 and decided whether the values are, in his eye, really different. If the difference between two means is smaller than John's "eyeball" value, he will see the means as not different, even though statistically they may be. Alternatively, if the difference between the two means exceeds John's "eyeball" value, he will see the means as different, even though statistically they may not be.

   Some usability specialists believe that because the audiences for a usability test will make their own judgments, whether we agree with these judgments or not, testers are better off providing audiences with the results of computing inferential statistics and helping them to interpret those results.

There are also three major arguments for *not* computing inferential statistics:

1. The potential for misusing inferential statistics is high and is probably increasing. The skill in using inferential statistics is in choosing the most appropriate statistic and being able to interpret it, that is, understand what it means. The answer to John's question about statistical significance is not as cut and

dried as it first appears. For example, there are several statistics that could be used to test the difference between prototypes #1 and #2. These statistics differ in their power, that is, how likely they are to find a difference. For some of these tests, their power depends on the size of the sample you are using. For example, the more participants we had use prototypes #1 and #2, the more likely it is that these statistical tests will show a statistically significant difference. There are, however, some statistical tests that were created to deal with small sample sizes.

The number of organizations who conduct usability tests is growing rapidly. We talk with and conduct workshops for an increasingly large number of people who want to conduct usability tests. The vast majority of these people do not have training in empirical data-gathering methods or statistics. These people do not know how to interpret inferential statistics. In most cases, these people know their limitations and do not want to be forced to use statistical tests.

2. Computing inferential statistics is not appropriate for many usability tests. Every statistical test has a set of assumptions that must be met before you can use the test properly. In many usability tests, there are no control conditions, and participants are not selected or assigned in any systematic way. In addition, when the number of test subjects is small, such as 3–5 in a group, most statistical tests are not appropriate.

   This problem about the conditions under which a statistical test is appropriate interacts with the lack of statistical training of testers. Testers who do not understand statistics cannot make informed decisions about which statistical tests are appropriate.

3. Most of the people who need to make decisions on the basis of a usability test, such as John, do not understand how to interpret the results of statistical tests. This is the other side of the argument we listed as *favoring* the use of statistics, namely, that John will apply his own "eyeball" test to the data. While that argument may be true, it is also true that John will probably not understand how to interpret the results of a statistical test. John, for example, may assume that the fact that a difference is significant *and* meets his "eyeball" test compels him to change his product no matter what the other evidence shows.

We have listened to the arguments for and against the use of inferential statistics. Our position is to avoid the use of these statistics in most cases. More specifically, our advice is to

- use inferential statistics only if you understand how to apply and interpret them
- explain carefully what the results of a statistical test mean when you use them
- describe your interpretation of key data values when you do not compute statistical tests so that the audience for your test will have some guidance on the accuracy of their "eyeball" tests

When we conduct usability tests for clients, we rarely compute inferential statistics, because the vast majority of our clients do not understand statistics, and we do not want to confuse them with carefully worded arguments about how to interpret the results of statistical tests. We do agree, however, that there are some usability tests for which inferential statistics are appropriate, and that test teams who understand how to use these statistics can use the outcomes of the statistical tests, along with other test results, to argue for or against changes in a product. (For more information on the use of statistics collected from people, see Bock, 1975; Conover, 1980; Hays, 1973; Hildebrand & Ott, 1987; and Ott & Mendenhall, 1985.)

Organizing Problems by Scope and Severity

You need a way to organize the problems that you find in a test. The organizing principle that makes sense is "importance." But what makes a problem important? Importance turns out to have two dimensions:

- *scope*—How widespread is the problem?
- *severity*—How critical is the problem?

Organizing Problems by Scope

The scope rule is the one we have been using throughout the book: Global problems are more important than local problems. The scope of local problems is restricted. In their simplest form, they apply to only one screen or dialog box or window or page of a manual. The following are examples of local problems:

- The wording of a menu option is not clear to users. When participants select it, they remark that they are guessing that it is the correct choice. If this wording problem is restricted to one or two options, it is a local problem.

- A data entry field that requires a date does not indicate how to format the date. Participants try several alternatives before they find the correct format. Participants don't have problems like those with other fields.
- In a manual, a reference to another page in the manual is incorrect. Participants go to the page and do not find what they expected. Other cross-references are not a problem.

Global problems have a scope that is larger than one screen or page. The following are examples of global problems:

- The items in a menu hierarchy in an application are difficult to find. Participants spend time aimlessly looking through the menus for the item they want. In addition, the number of incorrect choices does not decrease during the second half of the test.
- There are no aids on any of the data entry fields to help users understand what formats are required.
- There are several places in a manual in which participants wanted a cross-reference to another part of the manual.

Usually, the global problems are the most important to address. People who are new to usability testing, however, and many designers tend to see the symptoms of a global problem as a series of local problems. In many cases, the connections between the local problems are not obvious to people without training and experience in human–computer interaction (see Figure 20–4).

Consider the following example (The findings are just part of the data from testing an electronic mail product.):

- Many participants complained that they did not know if what they wrote was actually sent, even though they had chosen the obvious menu option and what they had written disappeared from the screen.
- Several participants replied to the same message more than once. They were not sure that their reply had been successfully sent, even when it had been, and so they redid the task. In some cases, the original sender received three replies to the same message from the same person.
- Many participants stored the same message as many as five or six times in a row, because as one said, "I can't tell if it's stored. It's still on my screen and there's no message that it's saved now. I don't know if I'm doing the right thing or not."

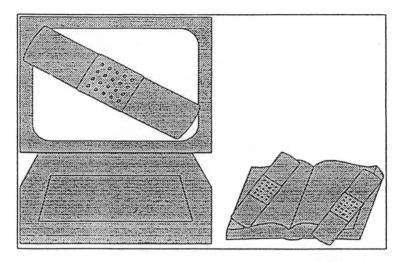

Figure 20-4.   Fixing some local problems that are symptoms of a global problem is like putting band-aids on a product that needs major surgery

Look carefully at every problem you find to make sure it is not part of a global problem.

These are not three local problems. They are symptoms of a lack of feedback for actions taken, and there are probably several more examples of it in the software. This lack of feedback is giving users the feeling that they are not in control, which makes the problem worse. They are not sure the software is doing what they tell it.

Organizing by Level of Severity

Sorting problems into local and global categories is helpful in understanding which problems have the widest scope. It is not, however, sufficient to identify which problems should be fixed first. For example, a local problem such as a missing step in a procedure can keep users from completing an important task. To organize problems into an order of priority, you also need to sort them by their severity.

We use this scale with four levels as a rough guide to the severity of problems:

- *Level 1 problems prevent completion of a task.* For example, users consistently select the wrong menu option and do not know where else to go, or participants give up after two tries to print an envelope because they can't figure out how to get the envelope into the printer correctly.
- *Level 2 problems create significant delay and frustration.* For example, a lack of feedback to users confirming what they have just done causes them to do the task over to make sure they have done it.
- *Level 3 problems have a minor effect on usability.* For

example, using the same word to mean two different actions causes users to question, for a moment, whether they are making the correct choice.

- *Level 4 problems are more subtle and often point to an enhancement that can be added in the future.* For example, after working with a new software application for an hour, a participant suggests that initial ease of learning would be improved if there was a short online tutorial explaining three or four basic concepts. But be careful here. If participants say, "It would be nice if this product had a spell-checker," you might put that as a Level 4 recommendation for future enhancements. But if participants say, "I wouldn't use this product without a spell-checker," or "My e-mail has a spell-checker and I consider it essential," getting a spell-checker into the product may be a Level 1 problem.

We call this method for sorting problems by severity a *scale*. But we do not want to give you the impression that it measures severity precisely. Many organizations that develop software have similar scales to identify the severity of software bugs. If your organization has such a tool, you may be able to modify it for use in determining the severity of usability problems.

Some companies with established usability engineering programs, actually rate severity of usability problems with the same tool used to rate the severity of software bugs. They then submit their usability problems to the same quality assurance process as ratings of software bugs. The designers then must treat a usability problem with the same care they would a software bug.

For most organizations, however, the severity rating is simply a convenient way to help organize usability problems.

Once you have sorted the problems by scope, into local and global, and by severity rating, you are ready to put the problems you found into their order of importance. Sort them first by level of severity, then by global and local. As you will see in the next chapter, you will use this order to organize the sections of your test report describing problems and recommendations.

This rough sorting of problems will help you communicate the problems you found to the design team. You will most often find that Level 1 global problems are the most severe and, therefore, those are the problems designers should be most committed to fixing.

There is an interesting dilemma, however, that sometimes occurs when you have sorted all of your problems—that the Level 1 *local* problems are much easier to fix than the Level 1 *global* problems. For example, adding a missing step in a procedure in a manual is easier to fix than reorganizing a manual that confuses users because it is organized around the product rather than user's tasks.

Because local problems are easier to understand and fix, there is a tendency for designers to focus on them. Fixing severe global problems usually involves a substantial redesign effort. If you are testing late in the design process, designers are likely to resist major changes. What the designers decide to do about the problems you find during the test should not keep you from describing the seriousness of problems according to the severity rating scale. Push to have the global problems considered. In the long run, they'll make the difference.

This resistance to redesigning late in development is another reason for testing early.

Common Usability Problems

In the final section of this chapter, we present two lists of the common problems we have found over the 7 or so years we have been testing products:

1. A list of global usability problems with software. (See Figure 20-5.)
2. A list of global usability problems with documentation. (See Figure 20-6.)

While these lists are quite long, they are not intended to be a complete list of the problems you will find with products. They do reflect our experience in testing software and documentation. Because we have seen many of these problems more than once, it is likely that you will see many of them when you conduct usability tests.

Almost all of these problems could have been avoided if designers were aware of the literature on human–computer interaction that we discussed in Chapter 4, "Basing Designs on Expertise in Human–Computer Interaction."

You might find it useful to use these lists in the form of a checklist when you are asked to review the usability of a user interface or a document.

Global Problems we have found with Software

Menus and function keys
Cannot find a task in menu hierarchy because
  Menus have no titles
  Menu titles not meaningful
  Menu options not grouped into categories
  Too many menu options
  Too much highlighting on menu screen
  Don't understand that there are more options than shown on the screen
Do not understand how to choose an option because
  Can't figure out how to move up or down options
  Can't figure out how to select option when at it
Do not understand which option to choose because
  Menu options use jargon
  Unavailable menu items not "grayed out"
  Menu options described in misleading noun strings
Cannot find the correct function to use because
  Function keys arbitrarily mapped to functions
  Function keys used inconsistently

Data entry fields
Cannot find data entry field because data fields not organized into groups
Waste time entering data because
  User must enter data already available to software
  User must enter dimensional units
  Required fields not indicated
Confused about what data to enter because
  Missing or misleading captions on data entry field
  No memory aids for formatting data fields
  Dates required in unfamiliar format
Cannot leave screen without entering data

Windows
Default size of some windows too small
Windows are hidden behind another window
Window titles do not describe contents

Messages and icons
Unsure what is happening because
  No message that action has been taken
  No confirmation that user intends action
  No message that system is working
  No cursor shape change to indicate system is working
  No message indicating where user is in screens
Confused about what went wrong because
  Error messages not specific
  Error messages do not describe what happened
  Error messages do not describe what to do
  Error messages assign blame
  Error messages need additional level of detail
Cannot identify the meaning of icons
Misunderstand meaning of icons

(continued on next page)

Figure 20-5 (continued)

Online help
Cannot find what they are looking for in online help because
   No synonyms
   Text too dense
   Paragraphs too long
   Not enough bullets, tables, and graphics
   Not enough examples
   Not enough cross-references
   No indication about where you are
Cannot understand what to do because
   Icons are described, but not shown
   Too much passive voice
   Too much conceptual information
   Too much past tense
   Too much jargon in online help

Displaying information and highlighting
Difficult to read text because
   Text displayed in all upper case
   Text displayed with right justification
   Acronyms not explained
   Font too small
   Font difficult to read on screen
Difficult to find information because
   Columns in table not labeled
   Too much blinking used for noncritical items
   Highlighting does not direct user's eye to critical information
   Poor choice of colors to highlight information
   Text in blue difficult to read

Figure 20-5. A list of global usability problems with software we found through usability testing

Figure 20-6 contains a list of the global problems with print documentation we have found in our usability tests.

Global Problems we have found with Documentation

Getting the big picture
Cannot understand what can be done with the product because
   No introduction that describes the product and its features
   No indication how product relates to other products
   No indication how manual relates to other manuals
   No description of audience(s) for manual
   No indication in introduction about what you can do with the product
   Introductory material written from system's point of view
   Introductory material filled with jargon

(continued on next page)

Figure 20-6 (continued)

Finding information
Cannot find the information I need because
  No tabs separating sections or parts
  No words on tabs
  Words on tabs are jargon
  Not enough tabs
  Not enough levels in the table of contents
  Too many levels in the table of contents
  Table of contents organized around system not tasks
  No parallel sentence structure in table of contents
  Table of contents entries incorrect
  Table of contents not at beginning of document
  No index
  Index too short
  Index entries not cross-referenced
  Index entries not listed in multiple orders of words
  Index entries incorrectly listed
  Missing headers or footers
  Headers or footers do not describe tasks
  Not enough levels of detail in headers or footers
  Headings do not describe user tasks
  Not enough levels of headings
  Levels of headings not shown consistently
  Levels of headings are not visually distinct
  Not enough white space on a page
  Line lengths too long
  Too much text – not enough lists, tables, and graphics
  Typeface not readable
  Highlighting not used effectively to help find information on a page
  Headings do not stand out on a page
  Page numbers not large enough
  Not enough cross-references within document
  Not enough cross-references between documents
  Cross-references that only go in one direction
  Formats and layouts inconsistent between documents

Understanding information
Cannot understand information when I find it because
  Ineffective or missing brief overviews of sections describing tasks
  Tasks described from the system's point of view
  Not enough examples
  Not enough illustrations
  Not enough illustrations showing the results of actions
  Illustrations have no captions when they need them
  Missing or ineffective callouts in illustrations
  Illustrations not near the text they relate to
  Technical terms not defined
  Too much jargon
  Procedures described in text paragraphs
  Action steps and text explanations not visually distinct
  Procedural steps have imbedded conditions

(continued on next page)

Figure 20-6 (continued)

Instructions in the third person
Instructions in the past tense
Instructions in the passive voice
Too many steps in procedures
Missing steps
Incorrect steps
Procedural steps not formatted consistently
Steps not described in the order they are performed
No glossary
Error recovery
Cannot recover from errors because
  No separate section on error messages or troubleshooting
  Cause of errors missing
  Description of solutions to errors missing

Figure 20-6. A list of global usability problems with documentation we found through usability testing

In the next chapter, we begin the discussion of how to communicate the results of the analysis of the data from the test.

21

Recommending Changes

When you uncover problems with the usability of a product, you will want to fix them or recommend that the developers fix them. When people come to a usability tester, they expect that person to not only conduct a test competently, but also be able to tell them how to solve the problems that the test finds. In this chapter, we discuss finding solutions to usability problems and recommending them to developers. In the three following chapters, we discuss how to communicate those problems and solutions and how to get the solutions implemented.

Back in Chapter 4, we noted that designing a user interface or a document is a creative process and that it is beyond the scope of this book to describe how to design products. Fixing user interfaces and documents is part of the same creative process. We do, however, have something to say about the process of finding solutions to usability problems, even if we cannot tell you how to fix every problem you find. We discuss

- understanding the complexity of usability problems
- solving problems as a team
- balancing effort for benefit
- testing the changes

Understanding the Complexity of Usability Problems

As we discussed in the previous chapter, usability problems often have many manifestations: that is why we use triangulation to find the real causes of problems. Likewise, you can usually fix usability problems in a variety of ways. Some solutions will only fix part of the problem by focusing on some of its symptoms, rather than the real cause. The best solutions attack the basic cause of the problem. When you make your recommendations for solving the problems a test uncovers, you need to

- consider the entire product
- focus on the global problems

Consider the Entire Product
The fastest and easiest solution may not be the best one.[1] "Explain it in the manual and online help," for example, is seldom the best

---

[1] Some of the material in this section has previously appeared in Redish, Dumas, and Hackos (1992).

recommendation when users cannot figure out complexities in the interface.

Many users do not work from the documentation. They only consult the manual when they have a problem. The point of testing should be to make sure that a product reduces the user's problems, not to accept those problems and suggest ways around them in the documentation. Adding explanations rather than changing the product increases the complexity and length of the documentation, making it even less likely to be used.

Consider this example:

To fix usability problems it is almost always better to change the product and the documentation, rather than just the documentation.

> We were testing a home entertainment center where users have a single remote control that operates several devices, including a TV, a VCR, and a cable box. Participants in the test had trouble understanding that the remote control is modal. To control the TV, you must first put the remote in TV mode by pressing the TV button; to control the VCR, you must put the remote in VCR mode by pressing the VCR button; and so on.

> When participants who had been using the remote to control the TV wanted to use the VCR, they spent many minutes aimlessly pressing buttons and paging through the manual. The manual mentions the modal nature of the remote only once, and that mention is buried in a paragraph and not highlighted in any way. The remote does not indicate the mode, nor does it make clear how many modes there are.

What should we have recommended that the developers change? The documentation could certainly be improved. We did suggest that the modal nature of the remote be brought out to the front of the manual and explained with highlighting and pictures. But is that enough? What about the many people who will never look in the manual or find the new material? The real problem here is that the modal nature of the remote is hidden. The solution is making it more obvious. That is the change we recommended, but only after we discussed it with the developers and made them feel they participated in creating the solution.

Focus on the Global Problems

The more local the problem, the easier it is to know what to do about it. Local problems can usually be fixed quite easily or not at all. For example, when you find that there is one dialog box that works differently from other dialog boxes, the most obvious solution is to change it so that all of the dialog boxes work the same way. But even here, you may need to consult with the designers to ask why they were inconsistent. Perhaps there is a reason that is not obvious to you.

Global problems require much more thought than local ones. There are two reasons why:

1. *Global problems affect many aspects of the user interface.* For example, to provide users of an electronic mail system with more feedback, we need to find a way to let users know that when they send a message, it actually goes where they send it. But how? We do not want to display a message such as "Message _____ sent to user JANERR" unless we are sure that it was. Do we use the same message when a user is *replying* to a message or *forwarding* a message? We need to think carefully about this problem before we recommend any solutions. As with most global problems, the solution may involve considerable redesign.

2. *Global problems have many symptoms; a usability test exposes only some of them.* For example, users might also want feedback to be sure that the distribution list they created actually exists, but this problem may not have occurred during the test. To use another example, if you found several instances of computer jargon in displays and messages during a test, how can you be sure that there isn't additional jargon in other places? Because testing is a sampling process, all you know from the test is what you found in your sample. From that sample, you can only make inferences about the parts of the product you didn't sample. Part of your recommendation should be to look for additional instances of jargon throughout the interface.

You can see from these examples that it takes just as much skill and experience to find solutions to problems as it does to create the product in the first place.

Solving Problems as a Team

As we noted in Chapter 6, developing usable products is a team effort. Finding solutions to usability problems is also a team effort requiring the collaboration of designers, usability specialists, and technical communicators. If you are the usability specialist on the team, you need to work with the designers and technical communicators. If you are a designer, you need to work with usability specialists and technical communicators. If you are a technical communicator, you need to work with designers and usability specialists.

Involving Product Designers
The people who designed the product you tested are almost always responsible for making modifications to it. When the product is

software, the designers understand how the software was put together and when changes are possible. You should include them, therefore, in discussions about solutions to problems. In addition to drawing on their knowledge of software design, you are more likely to get them to make changes in the product when they have partici- pated in the decisions about what solutions are needed.

You may encounter some resistance from designers about making changes, especially if testing is new to them. They often will interpret global problems as local ones and will want to change only some symptoms of the real problem. They also may insist that the changes you suggest will be too hard or take too long to make. You certainly want to listen to and verify their arguments, but you will, in some cases, need to stand your ground backed up by the data you have to support your recommendations.

If the test focused on documentation, you will have found problems with the user interface. Because usability is a characteristic that applies to the entire product, you can't help but find weaknesses in a product as well as the documentation. If you are a technical communicator, you need to get help from product designers to find effective solutions to usability problems with the user interface.

The recommendations you make to fix the problems will be more specific and authoritative when you have discussed them with the designers. You will also avoid a loss of credibility that can happen when a recommendation you make can't be implemented because of the makeup of the hardware or software behind the user interface.

Involving Technical Communicators
If the product tested was documentation, print or online, you should have had a technical communications specialist on the team. If, for some reason, you did not, you will need his or her help in finding solutions to usability problems. Many designers and even some human factors and usability specialists do not understand the role of document designers or communications specialists in product design.

The structure of menus, the words chosen for menu names and menu options, the messages, the design of online help all fall within the domain of technical communications. The typical software engineer and the typical human factors specialist do not receive training in this discipline. That is why they need to have someone who is a technical communications specialist help them fix usability problems.

Human–computer interaction is about communica- tion.

Involving Usability Specialists
Changes take time and cost money. Before you ask designers or their company to make changes, you need to feel confident that your recommendations are based on accurate information and are carefully considered.

If your test team does not include someone with training and experience in human–computer interaction, you may need expert advise from such a person to find solutions that actually improve the product. Consider this example, taken from Redish, Dumas, & Hachos et al. (1992):

> The software engineers who were developing a new product brought in a group of customers to try it out in a very informal test.
>
> When they saw that customers were having considerable difficulty with one part of the product, they ran back to their workstations and redesigned the difficult screen. They did no analysis of the data from the test. They did not confer with the design group or the documentation specialists. They did not involve the usability or human factors staff. They did not retest the new screen.
>
> Unfortunately the new screen made the problem worse, a fact eventually pointed out by the company's customer service people who were fielding phone calls from frustrated users after the product was released. The engineers, in their desire to help, had rushed the redesign without getting the help they needed to identify the real, underlying problem and arrive at a productive solution.

Even when you have a usability specialist on the team, you may want to draw on some additional help. As we mentioned in Chapter 5, research has shown that "double usability specialists" are better at finding problems than ordinary usability specialists. A double usability specialist is not only experienced designing user interfaces, but also is experienced with a particular technology domain. For example, if the product you tested is a spreadsheet, a double usability specialist would have experience designing the user interface to spreadsheets as well as experience designing other types of software.

Balancing Effort for Benefit

Global usability problems seldom have a single, obvious solution. In many cases, different solutions each with tradeoffs of effort (cost) for benefit, are possible.

Consider this example:

> In one of the first tasks in a usability test, participants have to install a program by copying files from a floppy disk to the hard drive. Some users do not close the latch on the drive and therefore get this message:
>
> *Cannot read from Drive A. **Abort, Retry, Ignore?***
>
> They spend an average of 5 minutes choosing different options, expressing great frustration, and then giving up and calling the help desk.

We could recommend solving this problem several ways. The following are four possibilities, in order from least to most helpful:

1. Change nothing. Plan to increase the help desk staff.
2. Add to the documentation. Put a line in the manual after the instruction to insert the disk in Drive A that says, "be sure to close the latch on the drive."
3. Rewrite the message. Make it more explicit, something like this:

    Cannot read from Drive A.
    Is there a disk in Drive A?
    Is the drive latch closed?
    Fix the problem and press Enter to try again.

4. Change the hardware so that users won't have the problem.

The hardware solution, of course, may not be an option for the software developers. This problem, however, certainly points out the importance of prototyping and testing hardware with applications and documentation, including messages, before the hardware gets too difficult to change. In fact, disk drives for 3½″ disks do not have latches.

Even if the hardware could be changed, eliminating this problem, you would still want to recommend changing the messages. This message might no longer be needed for this problem, but what other problems does this cryptic message cover? Is this message symptomatic of messages in this system? Would fixing this message be putting a band-aid on a much more global problem? What about other messages that did not come up in the test that are written in the same cryptic style?

Adding a sentence to the instructions in the manual may be the least expensive change to make. That might help users who are following the installation instructions avoid the problem and thus avoid getting the message. But would you be satisfied with that solution? If you have no way to influence the messages or the hardware, you may have to stop there; but ignoring problems that come up in a usability test just because they are not in the part of the product that is your responsibility does not serve the users.

Testing the Changes

How do you know that the changes you recommend actually solve the usability problems you found in the test? Do the changes create their own usability problems? Do the changes interact with what you have not changed in complex ways you did not expect? The only way to get clear answers to these questions is to conduct another test.

Whenever you have made major changes to a product, you should plan to retest. Fortunately, the retest will take less time than the previous test. Here's how you save that time:

- You know what the goals and concerns are.
- You have done the work of identifying the characteristics of the test participants and where to find them.
- You have the tasks, the scenarios, and the other test materials already prepared. It is critical that you have participants do many of the same tasks you included in the previous test.
- You know what you want to measure and have the tools to collect the data you need.

All you need to do is run a few more test participants through the test to check that your changes work.

There is an additional benefit when you retest a product: you can compare the performance of the participants on the two tests. If your changes are effective, the improved performance of participants reinforces the value of testing and the effort the team put into making those changes. Improved performance is a measure of success, and it can be very rewarding when it happens.

In the next chapter, we discuss communicating your findings and recommendations.

22

Communicating the Results

When you have completed the test, analyzed the data, and organized your list of the problems and recommendations for solving them, you have to communicate the results to those who need to know them. How you communicate the results—the media you use, the length and formality of the report, and the effort you need to put into communicating—will depend on the test and on your organization.

Consider these seven suggestions. One or more of these situations is likely to be relevant to your test and your organization.

1. If the people who need to know about the test results have been actively involved all along, they may already know about the changes that need to be made. You may need only a brief memorandum of findings and recommendations or a meeting at which you agree on the changes to be made. In early, rapid prototyping, you may be communicating recommendations and seeing changes made with a very fast turnaround, in which there is no time for a formal report.

2. However, even if the developers have been involved all along and need only a memorandum of findings and recommendations, you should still consider preparing a more complete and formal report. A test report can serve several other important purposes for you and for other audiences. The methodology sections can help other teams prepare for a test. The data sections can help other teams know what types of data are useful and perhaps see ways to improve their own products, even before testing them. The usability laboratory may need the report as evidence of the way that testing is done and as justification of its existence. Managers and other readers may be interested in more than just the findings.

3. If the development team is a "client" of yours, whether you are an internal usability department or an external independent testing group, you will probably want to prepare a more complete and formal report. The report would incorporate the findings and recommendations, but it would also describe the method and summarize the data. The extra information serves to show that the test was carried out with thought and method, that the users and tasks were representative, and that the data support the findings. The report not only meets contractual obligations, it can also be persuasive and educational for reluctant developers.

4. When time is critical and no one wants to wait even a few days for a complete report, you can prepare the findings and recommendations first so that the developers can get started fixing the product. You can then deliver the more complete report a week or two later. Even if few people read the

complete report, it serves both you and the client as a record of the test. The manager of your client group can deliver it to his or her managers.

5. If your findings lead to recommendations for changing both the product and the development process, you may want to prepare two separate reports or memoranda: one to the developers who are responsible for the product, and another to the managers who are responsible for the process.

6. If getting approval for the changes requires persuading managers that the product has problems, or if developers still need persuading, you may want to also prepare a brief videotape that drives home your conclusions visually.

7. If your organization has its own formal requirements for reporting usability problems, you will, of course, follow those requirements. For example, some organizations that integrate usability testing with other quality assurance functions use "usability bug reports" on the analogy of reports of problems that are found during function testing. These organizations have well-specified requirements and processes for who can (or must) initiate, respond to, and accept the responses to these reports.

Whichever of these situations is relevant to you, communicating quickly and clearly is a critical step in getting people to use your test results. In this chapter, we consider the issue of which media to use and then offer help on communicating in writing. The next chapter is about communicating visually by preparing a short videotape that highlights your critical findings.

Which Media Should You Use?

Consider how the three media—verbal, written, and visual—work together.

Communicating Verbally

Verbal feedback should always be part of your communications, but never the only medium you use. You should be talking with the developers throughout the testing process. Good teamwork and good client relationships require frequent and frank communications. If you want your findings and your written report to be accepted, you have to pave the way for them with talk.

In fact, even if they saw the test, you should still be talking with developers and managers before they get the report. They may not

The major points of your report should not come as a surprise to the readers. The readers should be prepared for the results because they saw the test or because you have been talking with them.

have reached the same conclusions you did, especially if they only saw some of the participants.

Even in organizations that have formal reporting requirements, like "bug" reports, verbal communications are important. Usability test specialists and developers often negotiate the severity level of the problems and the fixes that will be required.

Communicating in Writing

Plan on some level of written feedback from the usability test. Even if you deliver your recommendations verbally at a meeting, have someone take minutes and write up a memorandum that captures the agreements made at the meeting. Otherwise, you will have no record of the changes that you recommended, and the developers will have no document listing the changes that need to be made. It is extremely unwise for you or the development team to rely on everyone remembering what was said.

Communicating Visually

If you need to persuade people who did not attend the test that the product needs work, consider also producing a short videotape, highlighting the major findings of the usability test. For most tests, the tape is not a substitute for a written memorandum or report, but a supplement. In the next chapter, however, we also discuss ideas for using videotape for more extensive reports.

Writing a Report That People Will Use

In this section, we talk about communicating the test results in writing. Although we use the term "report" and describe preparing a complete, formal, test report, you'll find useful advice, even if you're only writing a memorandum of findings and recommendations. What you are really doing is writing one of the major sections of the report. Everything that we have to say here about planning, organizing, drafting, and formatting applies equally well to a memorandum as to a complete report.

Three Hints for Getting Started

As you prepare to write the report, it might help to keep these three general principles in mind:

1. People in the workplace are too busy to read. Think of your audiences as "users" not "readers." Don't prepare a long, rambling, prose report. Keep it short and simple. Use lists,

tables, and other techniques for helping people to grab the information off the page.

2. Expect to rewrite. Many people find it easier to start writing when they realize that everyone revises. It's OK to write a nonperfect draft and then fix it.

3. You can't write a clear report if you don't have agreement on the information to put into it. Working on the report may help you clarify what you want to say, but you do need to have analyzed the data, considered the nature and severity of the problems, and planned your recommendations before you can explain all that to other people.

Writing Documents is Just Like Developing Software

If you are not comfortable as a writer, it might help to realize that writing documents for the workplace is just like developing software. The concerns and the processes are very much alike.

In both, you go through a process of

- planning
- organizing (outlining, like writing specs)
- drafting
- formatting (like developing the interface)
- working with reviewers
- revising
- producing copies and distributing them

The process does not have to take a long time. In most usability tests, you will only have a week, or two at the most, to go through all these steps. In this chapter we show you how to plan and write a report quickly.

As you prepare your report, also think of it like a software product in this way: It must be both functional and usable. That is, think about what functions you want it to serve and how you will know if it works. Also, think about how you can make it easy for people to use.

Planning the Report

When you are planning a report, you have to think about

- who you want to read (use) it
- why you are writing it; what you want from that set of readers
- what they will do with it, and, therefore,
- what you will include in it and how you will organize it

These are the same questions that you have to ask as you plan any type of document for the workplace. They are also the same questions that you have to ask as you plan any type of product, including the hardware, software, or other product that you have just been testing.

It might help to build a chart like Figure 22-1 for your report. We've filled it in with likely answers about a usability test report. Change the information to match your situation.

Audiences Who will use it?	Purposes What do you want from this audience?	Readers' Tasks How will these people work with the report?	Scope and organization What content do they need? How can you make it easy for them to use?
Managers	You want support, buy-in, resources (time, money, staff).	They don't want to spend time reading. They want to only • read a summary • skim the rest	Content they need: • brief overview of test • high level report of major findings and solutions Making it easy for them: • Executive Summary • table of contents, in a full report • informative headings • headings that stand out on the page so they can be scanned easily • tables and lists, lots of white space

Designers
Developers
Programmers
Writers
	You want them to change the product or the documentation.	They don't want to spend time reading.
		
		They want to quickly
		• see the findings
		• grasp the solutions
			Content they need:
			• findings and recommendations
			
			Making it easy for them:
			• use a list format for
			  - findings
			  - explanation and supporting data
			  - recommendations
			
			• group the findings in a way that is logical for the people who have to make the changes.

Other product teams	You want to share information that can help them fix their products, too.	They don't want to spend time reading. They want to • skim the report • grab information quickly	Content they may need: • findings and recommendations Making it easy for them: .• same features as for others • white space, headings, lists
Other usability teams	You want to share information that can help them • prepare a test • report on a test	They don't want to spend time reading. They want to • skim the report • grab information quickly	Content they may need: • methods • entire report Making it easy for them: • same features as for others • white space, headings, lists

Figure 22-1. Sample chart for planning a usability test report

Audiences: Who Will Use Your Report?

Almost every document in the workplace has multiple audiences and multiple purposes. For your usability test report, you probably have two primary audiences: the managers who must agree to pay for the changes and the designers, developers, programmers, or writers who must carry out the changes.

If the product's potential users are an external group (public customers, for example), you probably don't want to share the usability test report with them. If you have user representatives on your development or test team, however, you will be working with them as you develop the report.

If the product's potential users are an internal group that is acting as a client of the development team, they will probably be very interested in the report. They may in fact be the "management" audience from whom the development team needs the "buy-in" and the resources to make the necessary changes.

Separating the Messages for Different Audiences

You may find that in some circumstances you cannot write one report for all your audiences. If you are going to tell managers that they need to change the process and people's roles in the process, the managers may not want to share that part of the report with the developers. Considering the impact that your report is likely to have, you may decide that it is more appropriate to write two pieces: a memorandum to managers, and a report that is meant primarily for developers.

Considering Other Audiences

As you write the report, keep in mind other audiences who might find it useful. These include:

- other product development teams who might learn from the problems you found and the way you solved them so that they don't repeat the same problems in their products
- other usability test teams who might learn from your methods for the test and who might find your report useful as a model

When we give workshops on usability testing, participants sometimes mention marketing people and training people as audiences for the test report. Their thinking is that these people need to know about the product's problems so that they can position it to its best advantage in the marketplace and so that they can know where the weak spots are that will need extra training.

If the usability testing has been left so late in the process so that nothing is going to happen as a result of the testing, that may be a realistic view. It would, however, be unfortunate. And it is certainly not the best use of usability testing.

Purposes: What Do You Want from Each Audience?

All documents in the workplace are meant to be functional. You write them to achieve goals, not just to pour out information onto paper.

Workplace documents have multiple purposes, just as they have multiple audiences. You'll be more likely to write an effective document if you think about those purposes before you write and make conscious choices of content, organization, style, and format to make the document work. This is exactly like thinking about quantitative goals for a product and then designing to meet those goals.

For each audience that you have identified, ask yourself: "What do I want to achieve by giving the test report to this audience?" "What do I want them to do when they have seen the report?"

Matching Audiences and Purposes

If managers are one of your audiences, you are likely to want them to make specific decisions: to accept that the product needs more work, to change the release date so that the product can be fixed, to pay for the changes that are needed, to agree to more testing after the product is changed, and so on.

How are you going to achieve those purposes? Where will you put the information you want managers to attend to, and how are you going to write it? You'll probably decide to put your points for managers right up front in the Executive Summary because that is what managers read. You'll probably decide to state the findings and recommendations sharply and succinctly, not beating around the bush, because managers look immediately for the "bottom line." You'll probably decide to put the recommendations in a bulleted list so that the busy managers can grab the information quickly without reading a lot of text.

If developers are another of your audiences, you are likely to want them to acknowledge the problems and make the specific changes that you recommend. Again, you have to think about where and how to give that information in the report. You'll probably decide to have a separate section on findings and recommendations. You'll probably decide to make that section look almost like a checklist, with very short paragraphs, bulleted lists, and lots of white space.

Understanding How Persuasive You Have to Be

To make the test report effectively achieve your goals with either managers or developers, you also need to know how baldly you can state your findings and recommendations, and how persuasive you have to be. You'll need to know how much you have to justify and motivate, not just report. That, of course, will depend on the particular situation and audience, which means you have to have some political savvy about the organizational environment in which the product you are testing is being developed.

This is exactly equivalent to saying to developers that they have to understand their users in order to develop a successful product. If you say, "I'm an objective scientist. I'm just reporting the facts," you are just like the developers who say, "I'm a professional programmer. I'm just coding the functions." We're not suggesting that you distort the facts but that you know what it will take to make your audiences believe them and want to act on them.

Deciding Whether to Include Positive Findings

Usability testing helps you find problems, so usability test reports usually focus on negatives. Educators know, however, that the best way to get someone to listen to negatives is to begin with positives.

Your usability test report may be the first direct feedback these managers, developers, or writers have had on the quality of their work. The impact can be devastating and demoralizing when the product needs major changes. In that case, you may want to provide feedback on what is right about the interface and the documentation as well as on what needs improving.

If there are good things to say about the product, say so. If the product is inconsistent and does things well in one part but not in others, talk about extending the aspects that work well. Remember, however, that the goal is to *improve* the product and the process. If you dwell only on the positives, if you minimize the problems, you aren't serving your audiences or their users.

Using the Report to Educate Your Audiences

One purpose to keep in mind as you write your test report is educating your audiences about usability and about good interface design and document design. Your report of a usability test may be the first introduction that some of the readers will have to these issues.

Use the opportunity to be persuasive about the values of usability, testing, and good design. Use the opportunity to educate readers about some specific points, such as the importance of bringing in actual users as participants, or the importance of having online help that people can find and understand, or the importance of being consistent in placing elements on the screen.

You won't achieve your educational purpose if you become long-winded and overly detailed, or if you take on a pedagogical tone, but you can add a relevant sentence in appropriate places or place the emphasis on relevant data or justifications for your recommendations.

Readers' Tasks: How Will These People Use Your Report?

People at work are always busy. They don't want to take the time to read anything. Managers are anxious to make decisions. Developers and writers are anxious to get on with the product. Deadlines are always looming.

Write your report for people to use. Don't expect them to read it from cover to cover.

Readers (users) want to find what they need quickly and grab the information off the page without reading extensive prose passages (Redish, 1989; Redish, Dumas, & Hackos, 1992; Redish, Battison, & Gold, 1985; Wright, 1987).

Scope: What Content Do These Audiences Need?

Your management audience wants a brief executive summary, very brief summaries of the data, and text that is easy to scan, so that they can skim the rest of the report, stopping at places that attract their interest. Your audience of designers, developers, programmers, and writers wants to quickly locate each finding, the data about it, and the recommendations. They need the findings organized in a way that will make their job easy.

While you do not want to ignore the numerical data, few of your readers will be interested in all the quantitative detail. The detail can go in a second volume of appendixes, if you include it at all.

Organizing the Report

Once you understand who will use the report, why you are writing it, how people use documents in the workplace, and what information your audiences want, you can outline the report.

The sample outline in Figure 22-2 may help you organize your test report.

The heart of the report is the list of findings and recommendations. This, plus a brief introduction, may be all that you are writing. These three principles will help you organize this critical section:

- Group findings for the people who must fix them.
- Order the findings by importance.
- Use the same organization and format for each finding.

Group Findings for the People Who Must Fix Them

Think about how to make this part of the report most useful to the people who have to make the changes. For example, if different

---

Report of the Usability Test of xxx

Executive Summary
  two or three pages, covering
      product tested; dates of test; who did the test
      goals of the test
      participants -- how many, what groups
      the major findings
      the business case for fixing the problems

Description of the Test
  two or three pages, covering
      product tested; dates of test, who did the test
      goals of the test
      participants (summary tables of who they were)
      tasks (a list; full scenarios probably go in an appendix)
      methods (only special points; This is not an academic paper!)

Summary of the Results
  a brief introduction and then a few pages of tables summarizing
      the data from your logging program for each task
      the data from your post-test questionnaires
      your list of findings (organized to match the rest of the report)

Findings, Explanations, and Recommendations
  the bulk of the report, covering
      findings, explanations with supporting data, recommendations

Appendixes
  including
      the scenarios
      the questionnaires
      data from the questionnaires

Figure 22-2.   Sample outline for a usability test report

groups will be taking care of different aspects of the product, you might divide the findings into sections for each of these groups. Logical groupings might be

- hardware problems; then software problems
- software problems; then documentation problems
- problems while installing; then problems while using

Order the Findings by Importance

Within each of these primary groups, put the findings in order of importance. Put the most severe problems before the least severe ones. Within each severity level, put global problems before local ones. That way, the first finding readers see will be the most severe of the global problems—the one that most needs to be fixed.

Use the Same Organization and Format for Each Finding

Report each finding in the same way. For example:

Finding:	a brief statement
Explanation:	numbers, examples, and users' comments
Recommendations:	what to do about it

If each of these headings stands out on the page, readers who are skimming the report will be able to locate the information easily. The people who have to use the report can return to it again and again, using it like a reference document, as they work on each problem.

Some groups use an even more formal organization for this section. Figure 22-3 is an example from the Usability Laboratory at American Airlines.

Problem #:	brief statement of the problem (The problems are numbered for easy reference.)
Scope:	global or local
Severity Level:	the appropriate number and what it means
Frequency:	how often the problem occurred how many participants had the problem
Explanation:	a paragraph or two of information about the problem, including examples of it, further supporting data, perhaps users' comments
Recommendations:	a bulleted or numbered list of ways to solve the problem

Figure 22-3. A sample organization and page layout for reporting each usability finding

Drafting the Report

Don't let writer's block hold up the test report. If someone on the test team is comfortable writing, you might let that person take on the task of putting the report into words. If you put off writing the report and hold up the iterative development process, you aren't helping the developers or the users of the product.

As you write the report, remember to keep it short, simple, clear, and easy to use.

Here are a few guidelines to help you write a readable report:

- Write in the active voice.
  - Talk about what you did.
  - Talk about what participants did.
  - Talk about what the product did.
- Write short sentences and short paragraphs.
  - Keep each sentence to one or two points.
  - Limit paragraphs to about three short sentences.
- Use lists and tables.
  - They hold down the prose.
  - They make it easy to see information on the page.
- Use parallel sentence structure.
  - Parallel sentences are easier to understand.
  - Parallel sentences reinforce each other.
- Include a table of contents in a full report.
  - The headings become the table of contents.
  - Therefore, make the headings informative.
  - The table of contents gets people to the right page.

A test report is not an academic paper. It is a functional document that people want to skim quickly and refer to later.

Figure 22-4 is a sample page from a usability test report. It exemplifies both the type of supporting evidence you might present and the type of writing style you might use.

Finding 1:	Participants couldn't find the menu options they needed.
Explanation	Participants searched aimlessly through the menus almost every time they looked for an option. Over the course of the test, the six participants selected an incorrect menu option **301 times**.
	Incorrect menu choices did not diminish over the one to two hours that participants used the product.
	Tasks **Incorrect menu choices** 1 to 9 125 10 to 18 176
	The current menu structure does not give new users a mental model that lets them figure out quickly where an option should be or remember where it is once they have seen it.
Recommendations:	1. Develop a new menu structure that is more intuitive for users. Find a metaphor that ties the structure together and that is meaningful to users. 2. Create quick prototypes of menu structures so that you can have users try a few different approaches.

Figure 22-4. Example page from a usability test report

As you write up the supporting evidence, consider using comments from participants. They often make the point vividly. Write the comment just as the participant said it. Indent it on a line by itself so it stands out, as in Figure 22-5.

Users were very frustrated by the online help. They said:
"This online help is useless!"
"I'd never read all of this. It's much, too much on one screen."
"I want help where I can just glance at the screen and the information I want is right there. I don't have time to hunt for it."

Figure 22-5. Example using participants' comments

Formatting the Report

The layout that you use for the pages of the report is almost as important as the words. If you want people to pick up the report and use it, you have to make it look inviting and easy to get through.

Format the report so that people can find what they need quickly and can grab the information off the page easily.

Here are a few guidelines to help you format a report that is easy to use:

- Make the headings stand out on the page.
  - The headings show the structure of the document.
  - The headings identify each piece of the document.
  - Use boldface type to differentiate headings from text.
  - Put the headings in the left margin to set them off.
- Use lists and tables to make each point stand out.
  - Report on questionnaire data in tables.
  - If you have several recommendations, consider putting them in numbered or bulleted lists.
- Leave white space on the page.
  - White space makes the separate pieces easy to find.
  - White space makes the page easier to digest.
- Use a readable typeface and type size.
- Include tabs if your report is large and has appendixes.
- Another idea: print the appendixes on a different color paper. To keep the text readable, use a light beige or off white, not a bright color.

For more help in planning the format for your report, consult these sources:

Benson, P. (1985). Writing visually: Design considerations in technical publications. *Technical Communication, 32*(4), 35–39.

Felker, D. B. et al. (1981). *Guidelines for document designers*. Washington, DC: American Institutes for Research.

Houp, K., & Pearsall, T. (1992). *Reporting technical information* (7th ed.). New York: Macmillan. Chapter 10 of the 7th ed. is a new chapter on document design.

White, J. (1988). *Graphic design for the electronic age*. New York: Watson-Guptill.

Working with Reviewers and Revising the Report

The other members of the test team should review the report before it goes beyond the team. Within your company, you may have other reviewers or want to seek advice from others as well.

- Does your manager need to see the report before it goes out?
- Are you a usability specialist working with internal or external clients? If so, would it be wise to share a draft with the client and negotiate some of the recommendations before the report becomes final? Being involved in the report might lower developers' and writers' resistance to making the changes.
- Do your clients need to take the report to their managers to get resources to change the product? If so, the clients may be able to advise you on how to best get your points across to meet your goal of reporting the test accurately and their goal of getting the product fixed.
- Are you sure you are speaking in the language that your readers understand? Sharing a draft with representatives of your readers may let you catch problems before they become misunderstandings.
- Does your team include people who are specialists in the areas of your recommendations? If you are recommending changes to the interface, have you worked with an interface design specialist? If you are recommending changes to the documentation, have you worked with a documentation specialist? Sharing a draft of your report with specialists like these may lead to improvements in the recommendations you are making.

Expect to revise the report. When you share the report with others, you must be open to suggestions for changes. That doesn't mean that you have to make every change any reader suggests. It does mean that you have to separate your ego as a writer from your purpose in writing a useful report.

A review of your report is just like a usability test of a product. It can be difficult to watch and listen as people point out that you haven't created the perfect report. Think of the product developers and make yourself be as open-minded about changing your report as you want them to be about changing their product.

Producing and Distributing the Report

Before distributing any version of the report, edit it carefully. Run it through a spell-checker. Have a human editor check it for you. Grammatical errors, spelling mistakes, and infelicities of style distract readers from the content. If your presentation gives the message that you don't do careful work, your readers may take your conclusions and recommendations less seriously.

Distribute the report through the appropriate channels, but make sure that everyone who needs to see it gets a copy.

If you need to convince managers or developers that the product must be fixed, you may also want to make an edited tape. That's what we cover in the next chapter.

23

Preparing a Highlight Tape

In addition to a test report, a highlight tape is a means for communicating the most important findings from a usability test. A highlight tape conveys, in about 20–30 minutes, the most global and severe problems with the product you tested.

A highlight tape is often just as important as the more detailed test report. Chances are that more people will see the tape than will read the report. Many of these people, especially senior managers, will be too busy to read the report, while others may simply prefer to "see the movie" than to "read the book."

Given its potential to influence more people, it pays to plan and prepare an effective highlight tape. If your educational experiences are similar to other people who conduct usability tests, you will have very little training on how to use the video medium effectively. An early lesson we learned was how ill prepared we were to produce a tape that had a pleasing visual appearance while conveying the information we wanted. Our solution has been to find members of our test teams who have some facility for video production and give them the responsibility for making the cuts and producing the tape.

In this chapter, we focus on

- why make a highlight tape?
- deciding what to highlight
- selecting the video segments for the tape
- making the tape

We end the chapter with a discussion of some other uses for the videotapes you make during a test.

Why Make a Highlight Tape?

We have already noted that some people prefer to watch a highlight tape than read a test report. That fact is enough to make the tape important to you. But there are other reasons for spending the time to create an *effective* tape:

For most of the people who watch the tape, it provides all the data they will ever see about the test. They will not read all the caveats and exceptions you mention in your report. They will not have the perspective you have gained from watching hours of testing. You will have only 20-30 minutes to convince them when there are serious usability problems with the product.

Pictures and sound convey images to people that are much more vivid and longer lasting than the words they read in a report. Because most of the people who watch a tape will not have observed a test, they will be easily distracted by the details of the testing situation and even the characteristics of the test participants. For example, we once prepared a section of a highlight tape showing a test participant who was unable to turn off the device we were testing. A designer who viewed the tape noticed that the test participant spoke with an accent and suggested that she may not understand English well. While the suggestion was incorrect and, in this case, irrelevant, the participant's accent was enough to distract attention away from the usability problem. In hindsight, we should have picked a different participant with which to make our point or have taped a preamble to the segment saying that the test participant they were about to see was typical of all of the participants.

In our culture, many busy managers will make the time to watch a short videotape, but will not read a report, even an executive summary. The highlight tape may be the only way you have to reach the people who make the final decisions about whether products are improved or released with major usability problems.

For these reasons, it pays to spend the time to create a tape that makes the points you want to convey about the usability of the product.

Deciding What to Highlight

Planning a videotape is no different from planning any communication. Just as with a test report, you need to consider:

- the scope of the videotape
- its objectives
- its audiences
- the constraints you will be working under

Let's consider each of these planning steps.

The Scope of the Highlight Tape
The scope of a highlight tape should be narrower than the scope of a test report.

Don't try to use the tape to teach your audience the details of how you conducted the test or to cover all the usability problems with the product. If you try to cover too much, you are likely to bore your audience and dilute your message.

A highlight tape should cover a few of the strengths of the product and the four or five most severe usability problems you found during the test.

The Objectives of the Highlight Tape
With very few exceptions, the objective of our highlight tapes has been to persuade the audience that there are global and severe

358 • *A Practical Guide to Usability Testing*

usability problems with a product. Because our lab is independent, most of the companies who come to us for tests do not have their own labs, and many do not have much experience examining usability systematically. Consequently, there is never any shortage of serious problems to discuss.

We start the tape by accentuating the positive by showing short segments about the strengths of the design. The video medium, however, gives you a very short time to make points about where the most important problems are. Select about five of the most severe problems, the ones you will discuss near the beginning of the findings section in a test report. Your objective is to illustrate these five problems clearly and effectively.

If your tape is effective, you hope that the audience will walk away from viewing it with the resolve to improve the usability of the product.

The Audiences for the Highlight Tape

You cannot always control who will see your highlight tape, but you typically create it for senior managers who control the development of the product and members of the design team who could not attend the test.

The Constraints You Will be Working Under

The constraints of the videotape medium are severe. First, you have to deal with the expectations of your audience about video. We live in a world where short, snappy, effective video is commonplace. We are so used to seeing well-made video that we immediately notice the shortcomings of amateur productions. We are especially susceptible to boredom from long sequences of action in which not much is happening visually. But, you may want to convey this very point, that is, that many test participants were confused and didn't know what to do. We will show you below how to do this effectively. But, you should not expect your videos to come close to the quality you see every day on Television. It is actually better if your videotape has an amateur look to it. It will help your audience to adjust their expectations. But, that does not mean you can bore or confuse your audience.

Second, the raw material you have to work with is limited. The video you shot during a test may be visually poor and the sound barely adequate. Even the best producer and editor could not make a high-quality highlight tape out of these materials.

Third, you have a limited time to get your points across. This is when the constraints combine against you. With the limited materials you have available and the expectations of your audience, you can only expect to keep their attention for 20–30 minutes. That's a short time to convey the serious usability problems with a product.

Fourth, as we have already mentioned, your skills at video production will be limited. Don't try to do too much with your first few highlight tapes.

The following is an example of the results of planning for a highlight tape for a test in which we compared our client's software application with a competitor's. In this case, our client was about to begin the design of a similar application and wanted to see the strengths and weaknesses of their current product and their competitor's.

> **Scope:** Illustrate the five most important recommendations for improving the current design:
> 1. Simplify the menu structure.
> 2. Add color to improve highlighting of information.
> 3. Do not use the touch screen approach of your competitor.
> 4. Allow users to access menu options in two ways, selecting from the screen and using function keys.
> 5. Add online help to explain how to accomplish basic tasks.
>
> **Objective:** Convince our client that these five recommendations are important for their new product.
>
> **Audiences:** Managers of the engineering design team and the marketing team.
>
> **What will they do with the information:** Discuss the design issues at an initial product design meeting.
>
> **Constraints:** We need to package the relevant segments into a 30-minute tape. We have two days to get the tape made.

From these planning steps, we went on to select the tape segments we wanted to show.

Selecting the Video Segments for the Tape

With your planning complete, you are ready to make the tape. This may not be an easy task, because you might have two or more full videotapes for each participant. For a test with 10 participants, there might be 40 hours of videotape. Unless you have some index marking on the tape, you will waste many hours finding the sections you want. The index may be as simple as the numeric counters that some camcorders can put on the tape. There are also time-code generators that will display the time and date on the tape. Some time code generators lay the codes visually over the video. Others put the codes on the video but also use an audio track to put markers on the tape. The generators that put markings on the tape allow you to move to the exact frame you want if you have an editor that can read them.

While you may not have written your test report before you make a highlight tape, you must have run all the participants and analyzed the data to know what the serious problems are. A highlight tape should illustrate four or five of the most global and serious usability problems with the product.

For each problem, look for sections of tape that illustrate the problem. The key to communicating the problem is finding an effective piece of video that illustrates it.

The most effective segments of video are those in which the problems with the product are illustrated clearly and dramatically. Often a comment, especially a humorous one, makes the point. For example, in one of our tests that involved a touch screen, a participant said, as he was having trouble hitting the touch area on the screen, "This is like trying to nail jello to the wall." Everyone who sees that segment laughs at the comment and gets the point about the problems with the touch screen.

During another test, a participant was trying to find a way to change the brightness of a display on a business telephone, which you adjust by finding the correct code number for that function. Based on his past experience when adjusting the brightness of screens, a test participant thought that he would find a hardware switch or knob to make this adjustment. While looking for the switch, he picked up the phone, turned it over, and looked underneath. This segment was an effective way to illustrate the test participant's difficulty in performing what should be an easy adjustment.

As you look for appropriate segments, there are several problems that you may have finding the right ones to illustrate your points:

A tape segment is difficult to understand without context. For example, if the problem is a menu hierarchy that is designed around the system rather than users' tasks, you look for segments in which participants pick the wrong menu option. In the segments you find, none of the participants say anything dramatic, and it is difficult to understand what the problem is without understanding the task the participants are doing. One way to deal with this problem is to tape a segment on which you make a comment about what is to come. You then copy this segment onto the highlight tape before you show what a participant is doing. For example, you might say, "In the following segment, the test participant is trying to find the menu option to archive a document."

The segments that show the problem are too long. This is a common problem. Many serious usability problems leave participants bewildered. They do not know what to do and they spend long periods of time paging through the manual or exploring incorrect alternatives.

It is not unusual for this to go on for 20–40 minutes. Watching this happen may be fascinating to you, but it will bore almost any audience. There is no way to show a segment of more than 2–3 minutes in which the participant is confused and nothing much is happening. The way to deal with this is to cut the segment up into smaller segments with an indication of how much time has passed. For example, you might show how the participant looked for an option in a menu and could not find it. You then insert a segment in which you say, "Ten minutes later, this participant was still trying to find where the option is." Instead of the words, you might insert a graphic that says, "Ten minutes later."

There are several segments that illustrate a problem, but none of them conveys the problem well. Reality is messy. People say things they don't mean, make irrelevant comments, and pick the worst times to decide to explore or be creative. We frequently find ourselves saying, "This segment would be great if . . . (she didn't mumble), (he didn't swear), (she hadn't said "I hope you are getting a kick out of this behind there"), (his hands hadn't gotten in the way), (she had just said that earlier), (the system hadn't crashed just then), (he hadn't said "I hope you are not going to show this to anyone"), (I hadn't interrupted), (she hadn't laughed), (I hadn't moved the camera then), (I hadn't had the wrong camera on)." In these cases, it may be more effective to cut several short sequences together in quick succession. You might take segments from the beginning of a task from four participants having the problem, cut them together, and record a preamble in which you tell the audience what they will be seeing.

As you make these decisions, try not to use too many segments from the same participant. In most tests we have run, there are one or two people who are very verbal and who make insightful comments throughout the test. You will be tempted to use these participants over and over to make your points. But, your audience will wonder whether the problems you are showing are generic and whether you are biased against the product. It is better to show a variety of participants on the highlight tape, even if you have to supplement the segments with preambles.

Rather than describe this process of selecting segments in abstract terms, let's look at two specific examples:

1. *Highlighting the important issues in the design of a software application.* In the previous section, we described our planning for a highlight tape to summarize the important issues in designing a new software application. The test itself compared the client's current application with a competitor's. Here are the segments we chose to show:
   * *Simplify the menu structure.* We chose two segments. The first one showed a participant who could not find a function using the client's current product. At the end of

this segment the participant says, "I need a map to find my way around here." The second one showed another participant who was unable to find the function he looked for without help from the test administrator. At the end of the segment, the participant blames himself for his failure.

- *Use color to highlight information.* Again we chose two segments. The first one showed a participant who was using the competitor's monochrome display and who was unable to complete a task because he missed an important piece of information on the screen. The second one shows a participant during the posttest interview who describes the advantages of color effectively.

- *Avoid the use of touch.* We chose a segment in which a test participant keeps missing the touch pads repeatedly and expresses frustration.

- *Use multiple ways to select items from menus.* We chose two segments showing two different participants quickly selecting items from menus with the two methods.

- *Add online help.* We selected two sequences. The first one showed a participant getting help from the online help feature of the competitor's application. The second one showed a posttest interview from a participant who had used the client's application, which did not have online help. She describes how she wished the application had been able to help when she didn't know where to find a function in the menu hierarchy.

2. *Highlighting user preferences for a prototype of a design.* In this case, we had conducted a test in which each participant had used 2 prototypes of a menuing system. Each of 10 participants attempted the same tasks with each of the prototypes. Nine out of 10 selected the same prototype. The one who preferred the other prototype said that he did so because he liked the challenge of figuring out difficult designs.

This would have been an easy test to prepare a highlight tape for. Unfortunately, we found out late on a Thursday afternoon that the marketing and engineering managers would be arriving the next morning to make the decision about which prototype to develop. There wasn't time to make a typical highlight tape. We decided to show the managers only the sequences in which each participant made the choice between prototypes. We advanced each tape to the point at which the participants were asked to pick between the prototypes. At the meeting, we simply put 1 of the 10 tapes into a VCR and played a minute or 2 of the participant choosing between the prototypes; put the second one in and did the same; and so on until we had shown all 10 tapes. We saved the tape of the one participant who preferred the other prototype until last. The contrast was striking. By the time we were done, the managers had no doubts about which prototype to develop.

Making the Tape

Making the actual highlight tape begins with finding the sections you want to copy. As we mentioned earlier, unless you have some index marking on the tape, you will spend many hours just finding these sections.

Whichever system you use to mark the tape, you will need to know about where in the tape you want to look for the beginning of the sequence you want to copy. For example, if you want to copy an important comment that participant #10 made, you need to know about where he or she said it. As we discussed in Chapter 13, "Deciding How to Measure Usability," you can simply have a written log of key events that occur, or the data recorder can make a notation in the data log. For example, in our data-logging software, we have a dedicated key labeled "Video." Whenever some event happens that we anticipate may become part of the highlight tape, we press this key. We can then look at the printout of the log to find the time for these events and fast forward to about where we want to begin the sequence.

The simplest way to make a highlight tape is to copy the sequences you have identified onto a blank tape and leave some blank space between the sequences. You could then play the tape for your audience, stopping before each segment to tell the audience what they are about to see.

The disadvantage of this simple method is that you or someone who understands the usability issues from the test needs to be present each time the tape is played. If managers take the tape home to view it, they will not have the benefit of the context and explanation you may want to give them.

You can avoid this problem by putting the narration onto the tape. The simplest way to do this is to say the words you want to record on a blank videotape or over some neutral section of tape, such as color bars. You then copy the narration onto the highlight tape before the sequence it describes.

Depending on your level of skill, you can do much more than just copy narrations and video from the test. For example, you can use a voiceover technique in which you comment on what is happening while the video is showing what the participant was doing.

Techniques such as voiceovers, however, require you to be able to edit pictures and sound separately. It is significantly more difficult to use any editing techniques other than just copying.

It is beyond the scope of this book to give you detailed instructions on how to operate a videotape editor. In concept, however, they are all the same. They require you to have a "source" tape, that is, the one with the audio or video you want to copy, and a "destination" tape, that is, the highlight tape. With each tape in a VCR and the editor in between, you follow whatever procedures are required by the editor to find and set the beginning point for the cut and the endpoint for the cut. You then copy the sequence.

Editing is a skill that takes some practice to learn. If you don't do editing on a regular basis, it is better to have someone who is practiced at the skill do the actual editing. If you find yourself with the task of making a highlight tape for the first time, plan on spending several days to create it.

There is a rule of thumb in the video industry that it takes 1 hour of editing to create 1 minute of finished video. Because the tapes you will make will not be broadcast quality, you will not have to spend quite this much time. But, plan to spend 1 to 2 days to create a 20–30 minute highlight tape, more if you have not made a highlight tape before.

Other Uses of a Videotape

A highlight tape aimed at managers is only one way to use the videotapes you produce during a test. You can make other types of tapes for other audiences and for other purposes. For example, you could make a videotape for a product's developers. A videotape would illustrate not only the global problems participants had with the product, but also how they got into trouble and what the consequences were. These segments may be too long and difficult for managers to follow, but just right for showing designers what happened.

We are so used to writing reports that we often do not consider that a videotape could be an effective way to communicate results even to designers. For every audience and purpose you consider for a written report, there is probably a comparable way to communicate your findings and recommendations on videotape. For example, instead of a test report consider a videotape with

- a preamble with the test administrator describing the objectives of the test and briefly showing the test method
- a quick view of the test participants while a narrator describes their characteristics
- a few graphics showing a summary of the quantitative values from the data analysis

- segments of tape from the test showing the major findings
- recommendations for changes to the product including hand- or screen-drawn graphics illustrating modifications to software or documentation

If you were skilled at producing and editing videotape, a tape such as this one could substitute for a written report and might be more effective at communicating what you want to say to your audiences. Perhaps, in the near future, as we learn more about the advantages of the video medium and as we become more skilled at using it, it will become more common to communicate test methods and findings on videotape.

In the next chapter, we discuss how to get the changes you suggest in your report or videotape into the product and the process.

24

Changing the Product and the Process

When you run a usability test, you will be focusing on identifying the strengths and weaknesses of the product. If you follow the procedures that we have discussed up to this point, you should by now have identified the product's strengths and its most important usability problems and have recommended ways to fix those problems. Your challenge now is to get the product's owners to fix the problems.

You can also do much more with the results of a usability test than just influence the usability of the one product that you tested. If you view yourself as a *change agent*, you can use the results of a usability test to change people's attitudes toward usability and to improve the *process* of design (Dumas, 1989).

We begin this chapter by discussing how to get managers and designers to improve the product. We then discuss how to get managers and designers to change the way that the organization designs and develops products.

Getting Changes into the Product

If changes are needed and don't get made, you can predict that users will have problems. If the product is sold, it may fail in the marketplace.

The point of a usability test is to improve the usability of the product and the process, not to check off a milestone on a product schedule.

This is so obvious that it shouldn't have to be stated. Unfortunately, however, budgets and schedules often drive managers' choices, and usability test results are too often dismissed with "We can't do it in this release; we'll do it next time."

It is important that managers understand the implications of not changing the product. If the implications are serious, you should emphasize that and be quite specific in the executive summary of your report. If you need to make a business case for time and money to improve the product, you can often do it by comparing the cost of the changes before release with the costs the unchanged product is likely to cause the company after release. Depending on the type of product and the problems that it has, these postrelease costs might be for customer support (toll-free lines and the people to answer them), for lost revenue and market share (if people don't buy the product), or for lost work time (if it is an internal product that people won't use or find hard to use). It is harder to quantify the loss of reputation that can happen with a poorly designed product.

Ignoring usability test results and going forward without making changes could be a very poor marketing strategy. Many of our clients have realized that. Based on usability tests we have done, clients have gone back to the drawing board with products, canceled products all together, changed planned release dates drastically, or made major changes and retested.

The first time that a group brings a product for usability testing, especially when they bring it for a single test late in the schedule, the number and scope of the problems that come out in the usability test may shock them. They may indeed be unable to cope with them all within the product's budget and schedule and may be unable to change either the budget or release date. What they get is a dramatic indication that they need to start usability engineering and usability assessment much earlier in the process. The most significant changes that come from the test may be in people's attitudes and in the group's design process, as we discuss in the next section of this chapter.

How can you be helpful to managers and developers who might be resistant to changing the product or overwhelmed by the task?

The first key is open communications throughout the project. You are much more likely to get willing cooperation if you have been working all along with the managers and developers, making them advocates of usability and getting them on the bandwagon with you.

A second key is to help them organize the changes that are needed. In Chapter 22 on "Communicating the Results," we recommended that you order the problems and recommendations in your report by scope and severity. That way, managers and designers can see which changes will have the greatest impact on the product. We also recommended that you present the problems and recommendations in a way that makes them easy to find, read, and use in the report.

A third key is to be realistic in your recommendations for changes. If you work with the developers in formulating the recommendations, you may increase their sense of ownership and willingness to make the changes, and you may in fact negotiate ways to fix the problems that are feasible given available time and money.

Product design at all stages is a matter of tradeoffs. In many cases, a problem can be alleviated in several different ways. Learning how to negotiate, how to serve as an advocate for the user while also being empathetic about the developers' difficulties and the company's need to minimize time and cost, is an important skill.

We aren't suggesting that you back off every time a developer says, "It can't be done." Push for changes. Make the business case. Point out the implications of not making changes. Show the edited tape to those who need to be convinced. Get support from upper management. Help developers figure out how it can be done.

Insisting that all changes have to be made, however, or that they have to be made in a certain way, is no more helpful than refusing to do a usability test in the first place because the client has too little time and not enough money.

Changes to the Process of Design

Almost all developers come to usability testing with a product orientation. They want to improve the product and do so quickly and cheaply. As we have discussed in several earlier chapters, however, the basic causes of usability problems may lie in a faulty design process or an attitude on the part of developers in that they already know what their users need. In these cases, you can do much more with the findings from the test than improve the usability of the product. You can change attitudes and organizations.

In this section, we discuss:

- changing attitudes about usability
- changing the process of design

Making these changes requires you to view your role as being more than a gatekeeper who fixes usability problems in products that pass through testing. If you look for the basic causes of problems, you will find that, in many tests, these causes lead you to problems with the attitudes of designers and problems with the way people are managed.

We are *not* suggesting that you in any way ignore the problems with the product that you find during a test. We are suggesting that you extend the process of looking for the basic causes of usability problems by considering that some causes may lie in the attitudes of designers and in a faulty design process. We describe examples of these causes of usability problems in this chapter.

You cannot fix process problems by focusing only on the part of the product you tested. Sometimes a problem that participants have on a particular screen is a global one that goes beyond that screen. In addition, sometimes the global problem lies in the process of design.

Viewing yourself as a change agent by seeking out the causes of problems that lie in the product development organization has important benefits. When you change an organizational problem, you are likely to improve the usability of all of the future products the organization develops.

Focusing on Changing the Process of Design

The most important skill in conducting a usability test is being able to diagnose the causes of a problem.

Throughout our discussions of interpreting data, we have stressed the need to think globally.

When you see a problem that a test participant has and realize that it is related to another problem, you are generalizing from a specific problem to a more global cause.

In our descriptions of this process, we have occasionally mentioned that some problems indicate causes that go beyond even the particular product you are testing. These problems indicate that the *way the product is being designed* is faulty. For example, when you find that the online help system for a software product is poorly designed, you may be seeing the result of a design process in which writers only work on the print documentation. This problem could be an indicator that the managers of product development have an outmoded view of documentation or that the management of the company had refused to consider documentation important enough to hire the staff it needs to create both online and offline documentation.

These organizational and managerial problems are the most important problems to fix, because they will affect many of the products the organization designs. It is frustrating to conduct a usability test and to find that a problem you identified during a previous test is recurring. When this happens, the cause of the problem is almost always organizational. These organizational problems can be difficult to correct, because they involve changing the people who manage products and companies. But it is worth the effort to identify and correct these problems. When you improve the process of design, you have the potential to make many products more usable.

Here are a few examples of the kinds of underlying problems a usability test can uncover, the probable causes for problems, and solutions you might recommend to solve the problems.

Finding:
A usability test shows that participants had problems finding the menu options they were looking for. They continually go to the wrong menu to look for an option and, when it is not there, they do not know where else to look.

Probable Cause:
This finding is usually caused by a lack of understanding of the tasks users want to accomplish with an application. Typically, you will find that the designers did not do a task analysis to identify users' tasks. Instead, the product is designed around the structure of the software modules. Because users have no knowledge of the software behind the interface, they have trouble forming a mental model of how the user interface is organized.

Solution:
The solution to this problem is to redesign the application around users' tasks. If it is early in design and the usability test was done on a prototype, there may be time to do a task analysis and create a new design. If the test was done near the end of design, it is probably too late to redesign the software without slipping the code freeze or release date.

Finding:
A series of tests of software applications or manuals shows that participants are confused by different formats, page or screen layouts, and inconsistencies in procedures.

Probable Cause:
This finding can be a symptom of the lack of a style guide for documen-

tation, the lack of local rules for the conventions used in a software user interface, or the lack of effective design reviews. It is almost impossible to create consistent products without a design team of programmers or writers agreeing on a set of standard ways to format and display information. The finding may also be a symptom of a laissez-faire management style.

Solution:
The writers should create a style guide through a consensual process and the software designers should establish local rules that specify screen formats and procedures. Writers and software designers should get together to agree on the wording and formatting of screen titles, menu options, prompts, status and error messages, and online help. In addition, managers should see that the rules are enforced once they are agreed to.

Finding:
A usability test shows a great deal of variability in the quality of the products tested. For example, in a library of user's manuals, many are well organized around the tasks people will perform, but some are poorly organized around the structure of the product. In these cases of inconsistency, you need to document the effects that the few very poor products have on both the performance of test participants and their attitudes toward the product.

Probable Cause:
This finding can be the result of a series of factors, such as the lack of clear guidelines for how to create effective software or manuals, a poor training program, or the ineffective screening and orientation of contract personnel who supplement full-time employees during peak periods.

Solution:
It may be tempting in these cases to elaborately criticize the poor manuals, software screens, and procedures. However, you can be more effective by telling the organization how to eliminate the worst cases of usability. This may involve the organization distributing clear guidelines so that developers know what types of practices are acceptable, setting up a training program for designers and for contract personnel, or doing a better job of screening new hires.

Finding:
A test of both a software interface and the manuals that accompany it shows that the messages displayed by the software are confusing and the manuals do not support the user by explaining what the messages mean.

Probable Cause:
This finding is often a symptom of the lack of cooperation between the people who make up a product development team. Confusing messages that frustrate users often indicate that the design team did not involve a human factors specialist in the design process. In addition, poor messages and/or online help may also indicate that writers were not part of the team or that their advice was ignored. Experience has shown that when human factors specialists and writers are not included in the design, the user interface suffers. When an organization has such people available, the problem is a lack of cooperation between groups in the organization. To solve a problem of this type, you may have to reach above the product manager's level and communicate your results to more senior-level managers.

Solution:
Creating a usable product is a team effort. It requires that the functionality of the product serve the user's needs, that the user interface to the product be designed for its users, and that the documentation also support the product when the user interface needs support. Getting all the people with relevant skills working together is essential to usability. This is clearly a management problem and only managers can solve it. You need to recommend that managers of the groups in question get together and cooperate for the good of the company.

These examples illustrate symptoms of a faulty development process, problems with poor methods, or poor management. The examples also show how you can stimulate changes that transcend the problems with individual products and how you can improve the design of all future products a company produces.

You may have noticed that some of these problems could be identified without a usability test. For example, an expert in document design may see the underlying problems with a manual. However, the empirical data and the pictures that are produced by a usability test provide systematic and sometimes dramatic evidence of the problems with a product. These data give credibility to your recommendations for change that even an expert does not have. An expert's judgment can be ignored in a way that the data from a test cannot.

Identifying these process problems is one of the hidden benefits of usability testing. We never turn down a request to conduct a usability test, because even in cases when the test will come too late to influence the product we are testing, it can help us to influence how all of the organization's products are being designed. In fact, it is worthwhile for an organization to conduct usability tests periodically just to see how it is progressing in improving the process by which it develops products (Dumas, 1989).

A usability test isn't just a way to make a specific product better. It's an opportunity to see how an entire organization is doing.

Iterative testing not only shows whether the product better meets its users' needs. It also shows whether management is being effective at producing usable products and whether the organization is improving its design process.

It is these organizational and managerial issues that you need to stress in your discussions with management, in your test reports, and in briefings you give on the finding of tests. Take advantage of the opportunity to be a change agent in addition to the opportunity to educate people about specific practices to improve human–computer interaction.

References

Apple Computer, Inc. (1987). *Human interface guidelines: The Apple desktop interface*. Reading, MA: Addison-Wesley.

Atlas, M.A. (1981). The user edit: Making manuals easier to use. *IEEE Transactions on Professional Communication, 24*, 28–29.

Bailey, R.W., Allan, R.W., & Raiello, P. (1992). Usability testing vs. heuristic evaluation: A head-to-head comparison. *Proceedings of the Human Factors Society 36th Annual Meeting*, pp. 409–413.

Beizer, B. (1984). *Software system testing and quality assurance*. New York: Van Nostrand Reinhold Co.

Benson, P. (1985). Writing visually: Design considerations in technical publications. *Technical Communication, 32*(4), 35–39.

Bock, R.D. (1975). *Multivariate statistical methods in behavioral research*. New York: McGraw-Hill.

Bowers, V., & Snyder, H. (1990). Concurrent versus retrospective verbal protocols for comparing window usability. *Proceedings of the Human Factors Society 34th Annual Meeting*, pp. 1270–1274.

Brockmann, R.J. (1990). *Writing better computer user documentation: From paper to hypertext*. New York: John Wiley.

Brown, C.M. (1988). *Human-computer interface guidelines*. Norwood, NJ: Ablex.

Brown, J.S. (1991, January-February). Research that reinvents the corporation. *Harvard Business Review*, pp. 102–111.

Calder, B. (1977, August). Focus groups and the nature of qualitative marketing research. *Journal of Marketing Research*, pp. 141–157

Case, J. (1991). Customer service: The last word. *Inc.*, pp. 89–93.

Carlisle, K.E. (1986). *Analyzing jobs and tasks*. Englewood Cliffs, NJ: Educational Technology Publications.

Carroll, J.M., & Kellogg, W.A. (1989). Artifact as theory-nexus: Hermeneutics meets theory-based design. *Proceedings of the ACM CHI'89*, pp. 7–14.

Chalupnik, K. (1992). A usability test of laptop computers. *Proceedings of the Usability Professionals Association, 1*.

Conover, W.J. (1980). *Practical nonparametric statistics* (2nd ed.). New York: Wiley.

Desurvire, H., Kondziela, J., & Atwood, M. (1992). What is gained and lost when using evaluation methods other than empirical testing. *Proceedings of HCI '92* (pp. 1–16). York, England.

Dillman, D. (1985). *Mail and telephone surveys: The total design method.* New York: John Wiley and Sons.

Drury, C., Paramore, B., Van Cott, H., Grey, S., & Corlett, E. (1987). Task analysis. In G. Salvendy (Ed.), *Handbook of human factors* (pp. 370–401). New York: John Wiley and Sons.

Drury, C.G. (1983). Task analysis methods in industry. *Applied Ergonomics, 14*(1), 19–28.

Dumas, J.S. (1988). *Designing user interfaces for software.* Englewood Cliffs, NJ: Prentice-Hall.

Dumas, J.S. (1989). Stimulating change through usability testing. *SIGCHI Bulletin, 21*, 37–44.

Dumas, J. (1990, February). *The current status of usability testing.* Paper from the Meeting of the Software Psychology Association, Washington, DC.

Dumas, J. (1991). Usability testing: Where are we and where are we going? *Proceedings of the Human Factors Society 35th Annual Meeting*, pp. 226–227.

Edmonds, E. (Ed.). (1992). *The separable user interface.* San Diego, CA: Academic Press.

Ericcson, K.A., & Simon, H.A. (1984). *Protocol analysis.* Cambridge, MA: MIT Press.

Federal Register. (1988). Notice of proposed rulemaking, *Federal Policy for the Protection of Human Subjects, 53*(218), 45661–45682.

Felker, D., et al. (1981). *Guidelines for document designers.* Washington, DC: American Institutes for Research.

Flower, L., Hayes, J.R., & Swarts, H. (1983). The scenario priciple. In P.V. Anderson, R.J. Brockmann, & C. R. Miller (Eds.), *New essays in technical and scientific communications: Research, theory, and practice* (pp. 41–58). Farmingdale, NY: Baywood.

Goldman, A., & MacDonald, S. (1987). *The group depth interview: Principles and practice.* Englewood Cliffs, NJ: Prentice-Hall.

Good, M.D. (1988). Software usability engineering. *Digital Technical Journal, 6,* 125–133.

Good, M., Spine, T., Whiteside, J., & George, P. (1986). User-derived impact analysis as a tool for usability engineering. *Proceedings of the ACM CHI'86,* pp. 241–246.

Gould, J.D., & Lewis, C. (1985). Designing for usability—key principles and what designers think of them. *Communications of the ACM, 28*(3), 300–311.

Gould, J.D., Boies, S.J., & Lewis, C. (1991). Making usable, useful productivity-enhancing computer applications. *Communications of the ACM, 34*(1), 75–85.

Gould, J., et al. (1987). The 1984 Olympic Messaging System—A test of behavioral principles in system design. *Communications of the ACM, 30*, 758–769.

Greenbaum, T. (1988). *The practical handbook and guide to focus group research.* Lexington, MA: D.C. Heath and Company.

Grudin, J. (1991). Systematic sources of suboptimal design in large product development organizations. *Human-Computer Interaction, 6*, 147–196.

Hackman, G.S., & Biers, D.W. (1992). Team usability testing: Are two heads better than one? *Proceedings of the Human Factors Society 36th Annual Meeting*, pp. 1205–1209.

Hays, W.L. (1973). *Statistics for the social sciences* (2nd ed.). New York: Holt, Rinehart and Winston.

Hewett, T., & Meadows, C. (1986). On designing for usability. *Proceedings of the ACM CHI'86*, pp. 247–252.

Hildebrand, D.K., & Ott, L. (1987). *Statistical thinking for managers* (2nd ed.). Boston, MA: Duxbury Press.

Hix, D., & Ryan, T. (1992). Evaluating user interface development tools. *Proceedings of the Human Factors Society 36th Annual Meeting*, pp. 374–378.

Horton, W. (1990). *Designing and writing online documentation.* New York: John Wiley and Sons.

Horton, W. (1991). *Illustrating computer documentation.* New York: John Wiley and Sons.

Houp, K., & Pearsall, T. (1992). *Reporting technical information* (7th ed.). New York: Macmillan.

Huchingson, R. (1981). *New horizons for human factors in design.* New York: McGraw-Hill.

Humphrey, W. (1989). *Managing the software process.* Reading, MA: Addison-Wesley.

IBM Corporation. (1991). *Systems application architecture: Common user access advanced interface design reference.* Cary, NC: IBM Corporation.

Jeffries, R., et al. (1991). User interface evaluation in the real world: A comparison of four techniques. *Proceedings of ACM CHI'91*, pp. 119–124.

Jeffries, R., & Desurvire, H. (1992). Usability testing vs. heuristic evaluation: Was there a contest? *SIGCHI Bulletin, 24*(4), 39–41.

Jorgensen, A.H. (1990). Thinking-aloud in user interface design. *Ergonomics, 33*(4), 501–507.

Karat, C.M. (1990). Cost-benefit analysis of usability engineering techniques. *Proceedings of the Human Factors Society 34th Annual Meeting*, pp. 839–843.

Karat, C.M. (1992). Cost-justifying human factors support on software development projects. *Human Factors Society Bulletin, 35*(11), 1–4.

Karat, C., Campbell, R., & Fiegel, T. (1992). Comparison of empirical testing and walkthrough methods in user interface evaluation. *Proceedings of ACM CHI'92*, pp. 397–404.

Kennedy, S. (1989). Using video in the BNR usability lab. *SIGCHI Bulletin*, pp. 92–95.

Labaw, P. (1981). *Advanced questionnaire design*. Cambridge, MA: Abt Books.

Lavidge, R., & Payne, M. (1986). The steps in a marketing research study. In V. Buell (Ed.), *Handbook of modern marketing* (2nd ed.). New York: McGraw-Hill.

Lewis, C., & Polson, P. (in press). Theory-based designs for easily-learned interfaces. *Human Computer Interaction*.

McCormick, E.J. (1976). Job and task analysis. In M.D. Dunette (Ed.), *Handbook of organizational and industrial psychology*. Chicago: Rand McNally.

Mantei, M.M., & Teorey, T.J. (1988). Cost/benefit analysis for incorporating human factors in the software lifecycle. *Communications of the ACM, 31*, 428–439.

Mayhew, D. (1992). *Principles and guidelines in software user interface design*. Englewood Cliffs, NJ: Prentice-Hall.

Melkus, L.A., & Torres, R. (1988). Guidelines for the use of a prototype in user interface design, *Proceedings of the Human Factors Society 32th Annual Meeting*, pp. 370–374.

Microsoft Corporation. (1992). *The Windows interface: An application design guide*. Redmond WA: Microsoft Press.

Mills, C. (1987). Usability testing in the real world. *SIGCHI Bulletin, 18*, 40–44.

Mundel, M. E. (1970). *Motion and time study*. Englewood Cliffs, NJ: Prentice-Hall.

Myers, G.J. (1979). *The art of software testing*. New York: John Wiley and Sons.

Nielsen, J. (1989). Usability engineering at a discount. *Proceedings of the Third International Conference on Human-Computer Interaction*, pp. 1–8.

Nielsen, J. (1990). Paper versus computer implementations as mockup scenarios for heuristic evaluation. *Proceedings of INTERACT '90*, pp. 315–320.

Nielsen, J. (1992). Finding usability problems through heuristic evaluation. *Proceedings of ACM CHI'92*, pp. 373–380.

Nielsen, J., & Molich, R. (1990). Heuristic evaluation of user interfaces. *Proceedings of the ACM CHI'90*, pp. 249–256.

Nisbett, R. E., & Wilson, T. D. (1984). Telling more than we can know: Verbal reports on mental processes. *Psychological Review, 84*, 231–259.

Norman, D. (1988). *The design of everyday things*. New York: Basic Books.

Open Software Foundation. (1991) *OSF/Motif style guide*. Englewood Cliffs, NJ: Prentice-Hall.

Ott, L., & Mendenhall, W. (1985). *Understanding statistics* (4th ed.). Boston, MA: Duxbury Press.

Payne, S.L. (1979). *The art of asking questions*. Princeton, NJ: Princeton University Press.

Philips, B., & Dumas, J. (1990). Usability testing: Functional requirements for data logging software. *Proceedings of the Human Factors Society 34th Annual Meeting* (pp. 295–299). Orlando, FL.

Polson, P., & Lewis, C. (1990). Theory-based design for easily learned interfaces. *Human-Computer Interaction, 5,* 191–220.

Prail, A. (1991). Suggestions on collecting observational data. *Common Ground, 1*(2), 3–4.

Price, J. (1984). *How to write a computer manual*. Menlo Park, CA: Benjamin/Cummins.

Redish, J.C. (1988). Reading to learn to do. *The Technical Writing Teacher, xv*(3), 223–233.

Redish, J.C. (1989, September). *It works, fine. But can people use it?* Keynote presentation for the testing stem, Technicom '89, Toronto.

Redish, J., & Dumas, J. (1991). Building usability into documentation. *Proceedings of the First Conference on Quality in Documentation* (pp. 40–55). Waterloo, Ontario, Canada.

Redish, J.C., Battisson, R.M., & Gold, E.S. (1985). Making information accessible to readers. In C.L. Odell & D.G. Goswami (Eds.), *Writing in nonacademic settings* (pp. 129–133). New York: Guilford Press.

Redish, J.C., Dumas, J.S., & Hackos, J.T. (1992, November). Finding the real problems: Making sense of what you see and hear in a usability test. *Proceedings of the Third Conference on Quality in Documentation,* pp. 139–160.

Redish, J.C., & Rosen, S. (1991). Can guidelines help writers? In E.R. Steinberg (Ed.), *Plain language: Principles and practice* (pp. 83–92). Detroit: Wayne State University Press.

Redish, J., & Schell, D. (1989). Writing and testing instructions for usability. In B. Fearing & W. Sparrow (Eds.), *Technical writing: Theory and practice*. New York: Modern Language Association of America.

Redish, J., & Selzer, J. (1985). The place of readability formulas in technical communication. *Technical Communication, 32*(4), 46–52.

Renegger, R.E. (1988). Exploring experimentally derived usability metrics by a laboratory evaluation of Electronic Paper, *National Physical Laboratory Report*, p. 119.

Rhenius, D. & Deffner, G. (1990). Evaluation of concurrent thinking aloud using eye-tracking data. *Proceedings of the Human Factors Society 34th Annual Meeting*, pp. 1265–1269.

Rosenbaum, S. (1987). Selecting the appropriate subjects: Subject selection for documentation usability testing. *Proceedings of the 1987 IEEE International Professional Communication Conference*, pp. 135–142.

Rosenthal, R. (1976). *Experimenter effects in behavioral research.* New York: Appleton-Century-Crofts.

Rowley, D., & Rhodes, D. (1992). The cognitive jogthrough: A fast-paced user interface evaluation procedure. *Proceedings of ACM CHI'92*, pp. 389–395.

Rubenstein, R., & Hersh, H. (1984). *The human factor: Designing computer systems for people.* Burlington, MA: Digital Press.

Schell, D. (1986). Testing online and print user documentation. *IEEE Transactions on Professional Communications, 29,* 87–92.

Schell, D. (1987). Laboratory-based usability testing of online and print computer information. *Bulletin of the Human Factors Society, 30,* 1–3.

Schrier, J.R. (1992). Reducing stress associated with participating in a usability test. *Proceedings of the Human Factors Society 36th Annual Meeting*, pp. 1210–1214.

Schriver, K.A. (1989). Evaluating text quality: The continuum from text-focused to reader-focused methods. *IEEE Transactions on Professional Communication, 32*(4), 238–255.

Schriver, K.A. (1991). Plain language through protocol-aided revision. In E. R. Steinberg (Ed.), *Plain language: Principles and practice* (pp. 148–172). Detroit: Wayne State University Press.

Shneiderman, B. (1992). *Designing the user interface: Strategies for effective human-computer interaction* (2nd ed.). Reading, MA: Addison-Wesley.

Simpson, H. (1985). *Design of user-friendly programs for small computers.* New York: McGraw-Hill.

Smith, S., & Mosier, J. (1986). *Guidelines for designing user-interface software.* Bedford, MA: Mitre Corp.

Soderston, C. (1985). The usability edit: A new level. *Technical Communication, 32*(1), 16–18.

Sudman, M., & Bradbum, A. (1972). *Asking questions: A practical guide to questionnaire design.* San Francisco: Jossey-Bass.

Teitelbaum, R.C., & Granda, R. (1983). The effects of positional constancy on searching menus for information. *Proceedings of the ACM CHI'83*, pp. 150–153.

Tetzloff, L., & Schwartz, D. (1991). The use of guidelines in interface design. *Proceedings of ACM CHI'91*, pp. 329–333.

Thovtrup, H., & Nielsen, J. (1991). Assessing the usability for user interface standards. *Proceedings of the ACM CHI'91*, pp. 335–341.

Virzi, R.A. (1989). What you can learn from a low fidelity prototype. *Proceedings of the Human Factors Society 33th Annual Meeting*, pp. 224–228.

Virzi, R.A. (1990). Streamlining the design process: Running fewer subjects. *Proceedings of the Human Factors Society 34th Annual Meeting*, pp. 291–294.

Virzi, R. (1992). Refining the test phase of usability evaluation: How many subjects is enough? *Human Factors, 34,* 457–468.

Whiteside, J., Bennett, J., & Holtzblatt, K. (1987). Usability engineering: our experience and evaluation. In M. Helander (Ed.), *Handbook of human computer interaction* (pp. 791–817). New York: North-Holland.

Whiteside, J., & Wixon, D. (1990). Improving human-computer interaction—a quest for cognitive science. In J.M. Carroll (Ed.), *Interfacing thought: Cognitive aspects of human computer interaction* (pp. 337–352). Cambridge, MA: Bradford/MIT Press.

White, J. (1988). *Graphic design for the electronic age*. New York: Watson-Guptill.

Wichansky, A. (1991). The future of usability testing. *Proceedings of the Human Factors Society 35th Annual Meeting*, p. 226.

Wiklund, M. (1991, February). Prototyping the user interface. *Medical Design and Material*, pp. 14–17.

Wiklund, M. (1993, March). Building a usability laboratory. *Medical Design and Diagnostic Industry*, pp. 68–77.

Wixon, D., Holtzblatt, K., & Knox, S. (1990). Contextual design: An emergent view of system design. *Proceedings of the ACM CHI'90*, pp. 329–336.

Wolfe, P., et al. (1991). *Job task analysis: Guide to good practice*. Englewood Cliffs, NJ: Educational Technology Publications.

Woodson, W.E. (1981). *Human factors design handbook*. New York: McGraw-Hill.

Wright, P. (1987). Writing technical information. In E.Z. Rothkopf (Ed.), *Review of research in education* (pp. 327–385). Washington, DC: American Educational Research Association.

Wright, R.B., & Converse, S.A. (1992). Method bias and concurrent verbal protocol in software usability testing. *Proceedings of the Human Factors Society 36th Annual Meeting*, pp. 1220–1224.

Yourdon, E. (1985). *Structured walkthroughs* (3rd ed.). Englewood Cliffs, NJ: Yourdon Press.

Additional Relevant Books

Beyer, H. & Holtzblatt, K., (1997), *Contextual Design: Defining Customer-Centered Systems*. San Francisco: Morgan Kaufmann.

Bias, R. & Mayhew, D., (1994), *Cost-Justifying Usability*. Boston: Academic Press.

Carroll, J. M. (Ed.), (1998), *Minimalism Since the Nurnberg Funnel*. Cambridge, MA: MIT Press in cooperation with the Society for Technical Communication.

Coe, M., (1996), *Human Factors for Technical Communicators*. NY: John Wiley & Sons.

Collins, D., (1995), *Designing Object-Oriented User Interfaces*. Redwood City, CA: Benjamin/ Cummings.

Cooper, A., (1995), *About Face: The Essentials of User-Interface Design*. IDG Books Worldwide, Inc.

Del Galdo, E. M. & Nielsen, J. (Eds.), (1996), *International User Interfaces*. NY: John Wiley & Sons.

Duffy, T., Palmer, J., & Mehlenbacher, B., (1992), *On Line Help: Design and Evaluation*. Greenwich, CT: Ablex.

Fernandes, T., (1995), *Global Interface Design: A Guide to Designing International User Interfaces*. Boston, MA: Academic Press.

Forsythe, C., Grose, E., & Ratner, J., (1998), *Human Factors and Web Development*. Mahwah, NJ: Lawrence Erlbaum.

Fowler, S. L. & Stanwick, V. R., (1995), *The GUI Style Guide*. Boston, MA: Academic Press.

Galitz, W. O., (1997), *The Essential Guide to User Interface Design*. NY: John Wiley & Sons.

Hackos, J. T. & Redish, J. C., (1998), *User & Task Analysis for Interface Design*. NY: John Wiley & Sons.

Hackos, J. T. & Stevens, D. M., (1997), *Standards For Online Communication*. NY: John Wiley & Sons.

Hix, D. & Hartson, R., (1993), *Developing User Interfaces: Ensuring Usability Through Product and Process*. NY: John Wiley & Sons.

Hoft, N. L., (1995), *International Technical Communication: How to Export Information About High Technology*. NY: John Wiley & Sons.

Horton, W., (1994), *The Icon Book*. NY: John Wiley & Sons.

Horton, W., (1994, second edition), *Designing and Writing Online Documentation: Hypermedia for Self-Supporting Products*. NY: John Wiley & Sons.

Jones, S., Kennelly, C., Mueller, C., Sweezy, M., & Velez, L., (1992), *A Digital Guide: Developing International User Information*. Bedford, MA: Digital.

Luong, T. V., Lok, J. S., Taylor, D. J., & Driscoll, K., (1995), *Internationalization: Developing Software for Global Markets*. NY: John Wiley & Sons.

Lynch, P. & Horton, S., (1999), *Web Style Guide : Basic Design Principles for Creating Web Sites*. New Haven, CT: Yale University Press.

Mandel, T., (1997), *The Elements of User Interface Design*. NY: John Wiley & Sons.

Marcus, A., (1992), *Graphic Design for Electronic Documents and User Interfaces.* NY: ACM Press/Addison-Wesley.

Mayhew, D., (1999), *The Usability Engineering Lifecycle: A Practitioner's Handbook for User Interface Design.* San Francisco: Academic Press/Morgan-Kaufmann.

Microsoft Corporation, (1996), *The Microsoft Manual of Style for Technical Publications.* Redmond, WA: Microsoft Press.

Microsoft Corporation, (1995), *The Windows Interface Guidelines for Software Design.* Redmond, WA: Microsoft Press.

Nielsen, J., (1993), *Usability Engineering.* Boston, MA: Academic Press.

Nielsen, J. (Ed.), (1990), *Designing User Interfaces for International Use.* Amsterdam: Elsevier.

Nielsen, J. & Mack, R. (Eds.), (1994), *Usability Inspection Methods.* NY: John Wiley & Sons.

Norman, D. A., (1998), *The Invisible Computer: Why Good Products Can Fail, the Personal Computer Is So Complex, and Information Appliances Are The Solution.* Cambridge, MA: MIT Press.

Pfaffenberger, B., (1997), *The Elements of Hypertext Style.* Boston, MA: Academic Press.

Rubin, J., (1994), *Handbook of Usability Testing: How to Plan, Design, and Conduct Effective Tests.* NY: John Wiley & Sons.

Sano, D., (1996), *Designing Large-Scale Web Sites: A Visual Design Methodology.* NY: John Wiley & Sons.

Schriver, K. A., (1997), *Dynamics in Document Design: Creating Text for Readers.* NY: John Wiley & Sons.

Shneiderman, B., (1997, third edition), *Designing the User Interface: Strategies for Effective Human-Computer Interaction.* Reading, MA: Addison-Wesley,

Tognazzini, B., (1996), *Tog on Software Design.* Reading, MA: Addison-Wesley.

Tognazzini, B., (1992), *Tog on Interface.* Reading, MA: Addison-Wesley.

Tufte, E., (1997), *Visual Explanations: Images and Quantities, Evidence and Narrative.* Cheshire, CT: Graphics Press.

Tufte, E., (1990), *Envisioning Information.* Cheshire, CT: Graphics Press.

Tufte, E., (1983), *The Visual Display of Quantitative Information.* Cheshire, CT: Graphics Press.

Wiklund, M. (Ed.), (1994), *Usability in Practice: How Companies Develop User-Friendly Products.* Boston, MA: Academic Press.

Wixon, D. & Ramey, J. (Eds.), (1996), *Field Methods Casebook for Software Design.* NY: John Wiley & Sons.

Wood, L. E. (Ed.), (1998), *User Interface Design: Bridging the Gap from User Requirements to Design.* Boca Raton, FL: CRC Press.

Appendix A
Setting up a usability laboratory

We have revised some of the material in this Appendix for the Revised Edition. We have included the seven lab layouts from the First Edition. Four of those labs are still in active use. We have updated the addresses of the active labs. We have kept the information about the other three labs from the First Edition because they still have unique features in their layout. If you are considering building a lab, you may find one or more of these layouts useful in your planning.

For the Revised Edition, we have added a list of usability equipment manufacturers at the end of this Appendix. They sell lab equipment for portable labs as well as permanent labs.

For each lab in the Appendix, we provide

- a short description of its unique features
- a floor plan
- a list of equipment

We have kept the equipment lists for the labs from the First Edition. With one exception, the equipment in labs in 1999 is not much different from the equipment we listed in the First Edition. That exception is a scan converter for showing the screen that the test participant sees by splitting the signal before it goes to the participant's monitor. One of the feeds from the split goes to the observation room so that testers and guests clearly can see what the participant is seeing. Most labs now have a scan converter. Converters vary widely in price from about $2,000 to as much as $10,000. The converters at the high end show a clearer image and have extra capabilities, such as being able to zoom.

We have not included information about the cost of building these labs. Comparing costs of construction is not useful. Construction costs are very different in different parts of the country. In addition, some organizations have their own maintenance groups that do part of the construction. These organizations may not know what the construction costs are. If you want more detailed information about building costs for specific labs, you can contact the organizations that provided the information for this appendix. In Chapter 6, "Establishing a usability program in your organization," we provide some information about the cost of audio-visual equipment for a lab although the equipment is usually not the largest cost item.

The seven layouts we describe provide a broad sampling of different types of labs. They include fully equipped, multi-room labs as well as simple labs that were built with small budgets. Here are the labs we describe:

- American Airlines/STIN
- American Institutes for Research
- A lab without a one-way mirror
- Lotus Development Corporation
- A lab with two test rooms
- University of Washington
- A lab with camera tracks

The Usability Laboratory at American Airlines/STIN

This laboratory is one of the best equipped and carefully planned labs we have seen. Figure A-1 shows the floor plan for the lab.

As you can see, there are two test suites. Each suite has a test room, an observation room, and an executive viewing area. There are three fixed cameras in each test room. Data logging is done in the observation room on a personal computer with data logging software.

Figure A-2 presents a side view of one of the test suites. The executive viewing room has a raised floor to allow visitors to look through the window, over the heads of the test team, and through the one-way mirror to see into the test room. There is also a large, 20-inch, monitor in the executive viewing room so that visitors can see the same camera view the test team is seeing.

The lab complex also has two conference rooms for planning tests and viewing videotapes. There is a room for editing tapes and additional rooms for storage.

Table A-1 lists the equipment used in this lab. In the table, we group the equipment into categories to make it easier to see what the

Figure A-1. Floorplan of usability laboratory at American Airlines/STIN

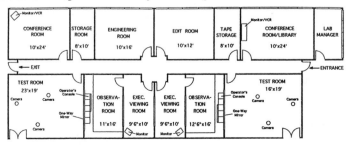

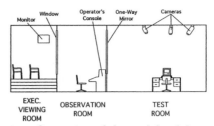

Figure A-2. Side view of a portion of the usability laboratory shown in figure A-1

equipment is used for. You can learn more about this laboratory by writing to:

Usability Laboratory - STIN,
American Airlines, Inc.,
4255 Amon Carter Blvd.,
Fort Worth, TX 76155

Test and observation room equipment	
Multicam color cameras	Mixer amplifier
Camera control units	Microphone preamp
Servo remote zoom lenses	Microphone preamp with volume
Pan and tilt tables	Microphone/headsets
Control panel	Graphic equalizer
Trolley assembly	Headphone console
Special effects generator	Custom control panel
Times six black burst generator	Hybrid coupler telephone
13" Monitors	interface
Rack mount frame	Audio distribution amplifier
S-VHS VCR	Wireless microphone system
Remote control	Conference microphone
Time-Date generator	Phase coherent cardioid
Personal computer	microphone
Data logging software	Speaker system
Talkback amplifier	Stereo double cassette deck
Editing System	**Executive Viewing Room System**
Editing VCR	20" Monitor
Editing controller	Speaker system
13" Monitor	
Routing switcher	**Conference Room System**
Remote switching panel	25" Monitor
Audio mixer	Speaker system
Cardioid microphone	S-VHS VCR
Phase compensated video patch panel	
Audio patch panel	

Table A-1. Equipment list for lab at American airlines/STIN

The Usability Laboratory at American Institutes for Research

In this section, we describe the usability laboratory located in American Institutes for Research's Concord, Massachusetts office. Figure A-3 shows the floor plan for the lab. The lab consists of two, good-sized rooms separated by a one-way mirror. There are three cameras, two of them fixed. We usually put the portable camera in the observation room to make the test room less intimidating. The portable camera provides a long shot of the test participant through the one-way mirror.

Table A-2 shows the equipment list for the lab. You can learn more about this laboratory by writing to:

Usability Laboratory
New England Research Center
American Institutes for Research
490 Virginia Road
Concord, MA 01742

Figure A-3. Floorplan of usability laboratory at American Institutes for Research

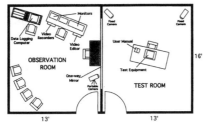

Customized audio/video console	Special effects generator
13" Monitors	Pan tilt joystick
Monitor receiver	Microphone/mixer
Audio channel mixer	Speaker
Mounted cameras	Desk microphones
Lens controllers	Lapel microphones
Motorized zoom lenses	Time/date generator
Portable color camera	Personal computer
VHS recorders	Data logging software
Editing VHS recorder	Printer
Editor	

Table A-2. Equipment list for lab at American Institutes for Research

A Usability Lab Without a One-Way Mirror

The lab we describe in this section has some interesting features. Figure A-4 shows the floor plan. From its shape, you can see that it was fit into the available space. The walls inside the lab, such as those that enclose the storage area, do not go all the way to the ceiling.

This lab does not have a one-way mirror. In fact, the people who built this lab believe that test participants are more comfortable when there is no one-way mirror. The low table provides a physical separation between the test and observation areas. The visitors sit in the observation area during the test. If they want to talk among themselves, they leave the lab.

There are three cameras in the lab, one of them fixed. The test administrator can see the entire lab from the console. While it does not show on the floor plan, the test participants' area has electrical connections that allow the equipment used in tests to communicate with the local area network.

Table A-3 shows the list of equipment in the lab.

Figure A-4. Floorplan of usability laboratory without a one-way mirror

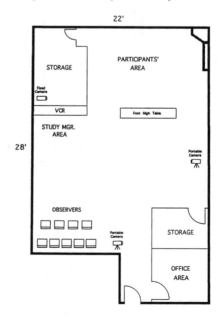

13" Monitors	Microphones
19" Monitors	Network drops
Key Stroke software	Portable cameras
Screen video pickup	Fixed camera
Video mixer	Videotape editor

Table A-3. Equipment list for the lab

The Usability Laboratory at Lotus Development Corporation

Figure A-5 shows the floor plan for this lab. The odd shape of the lab is the result of fitting the lab into the available space. The observation room has two areas: the area near the control panel where the test team works and a raised platform area where visitors can see the test by either looking through the one-way mirror or watching a 25-inch monitor.

There are three cameras, two of them fixed. The camera above the desk in the test room is recessed behind a clear piece of glass in the ceiling. This makes the camera unobtrusive and makes the test room less intimidating. The portable camera in the observation room is usually aimed at a monitor that shows what is on the screen in the test room. This arrangement provides a clearer and fuller picture than is provided by most scan converters.

Figure A-5. Floorplan of usability laboratory at Lotus Development Corporation

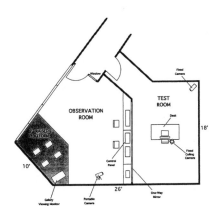

Fixed cameras	Speakers and amplifier for
Remote pan/tilt and focus/zoom controls	observation room
	VCR
Portable camera and lens with shutter speed adjustment for viewing computer monitors	12" Color monitor
	5" Camera monitor
	25" Color monitor
Microphones	Time/date generator
Intercom system	Personal computer
Sound board	Data logging software
	Special effects generator

Table A-4. Equipment list for lab at Lotus Development Corporation

Table A-4 shows the equipment list for the lab. You can learn more about this laboratory by writing to:

Usability Laboratory
Lotus Development Corporation
One Rogers Street
Cambridge, MA 02142

A Usability Laboratory with Two Testing Cells

This lab has two test and observation rooms. The floor plan is shown in Figure A-6. There is a one-way mirror separating each test and observation room. The test room on the left was planned as a software testing lab. In addition to the camera in this test room, there

Figure A-6. Floorplan of usability laboratory with two testing cells

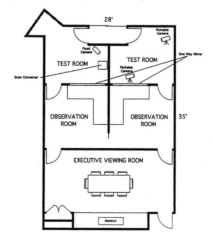

SVHS VCRs	Silicon Graphics 4D35™
Fixed cameras	workstation
Camcorders with tripods	Silicon Graphics VideoCreator™
Convergence editing deck	(takes RGB signals direct from
Video compression unit (allows	monitor to VCR)
picture within a picture from	Silicon Graphics Iris Indigo™
2 cameras and records it on a	workstation (audio, video
VCR)	capability)
12" Monitors	Silicon Graphics Iris Indigo
32" Monitor	Elan™ (for high-end graphics)
Microphones	Personal computers
Intercom system	Data logging software
Silicon Graphics 4D25™	Video editor
workstation	Video mixer

Table A-5. Equipment list for lab.

is a scan converter. An interesting feature of this layout is the
sliding door between the observation rooms. This arrangement
allows testers to move between the two observation rooms while tests
are in progress. There is a personal computer with data logging
software in each observation room. The executive viewing room does
not provide a direct view of the test room, but does have a large, 32-
inch monitor for viewing the test.

Table A-5 shows the equipment list for the lab.

The Usability Laboratory at the University of Washington

This lab was created with limited funds. Figure A-7 shows the floor
plan. It consists of a room divided into two areas separated by a
portable wall. In the test room, there are two portable cameras.

Figure A-7. Floorplan of usability laboratory at the University of Washington

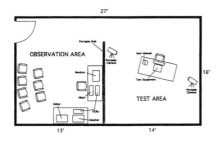

Camcorders
20" Monitors
Audio/Video mixer
Video cassette recorder in Hi-8 format
Video cassette recorder in VHS format
Editor

Table A-6. Equipment list for lab at the University of Washington

Table A-6 shows the equipment list for the lab. You can learn more about this laboratory by writing to:

Laboratory for Usability Testing and Evaluation
TC, Engineering, FH-40
College of Engineering
University of Washington
Seattle, WA 98195

A Usability Laboratory with Tracking Cameras

This lab has a test, observation, and executive viewing room. Figure A-8 shows the floor plan. There is a one-way mirror between the test and observation room and a counter separating the executive viewing room from the observation room.

There are three cameras in the test room, each on its own track. There is a personal computer with data logging software in the observation room.

Table A-7 shows the equipment list for the lab.

Figure A-8. Floorplan of usability laboratory with tracking cameras.

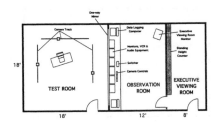

13" Monitors	Two-channel intercom
5" Monitors	Audio 8x2 stereo mixer
Scan converter	Video & Audio amplifiers
Sync generator	Speakers
S-VHS VCRs	Lapel and desktop microphones
Cameras	Edit Controller

Table A-7. Equipment list for lab

List of Usability Laboratory Equipment Manufacturers

As we prepare the revised edition, we are aware of five organizations that sell usability lab equipment, including portable labs for on-site testing. We do not endorse any of these companies. They are listed here for your information.

Noldus Information Technology
Innovative solutions for behavioral research
6 Pidgeon Hill Drive, Suite 180
Sterling, VA 20165
Phone: 703-404-5506
Fax: 703-404-5507
Email: info@noldus.com

Norm Wilcox Associates, Inc
Portable usability labs and data logging software
4574 Timbery Court
Jefferson, MD 21755
Phone: 1-800-A-LAB-2-GO
Or phone: 301-473-8124
Email: alab2go@aol.com

Systems Integration Group
Networked usability, real-time remote testing,
    recording and distribution
1184-A West Corporate Dr.
Arlington, TX 76006
Phone: 817-649-0088
Fax: 817-633-5920

Triangle Research Collaborative, Inc.
Multimedia research tools for the professional
100 Park Offices, Suite 115
Research Triangle Park, NC 27709-2167
Phone: 1-800-467-9093 or 919-549-9093
Fax: 919-549-0493
Email: 73227.3714@compuserve.com

Usability Systems, Inc.
Solutions for creating usable products
1150 Alpha Drive, Suite 100
Alpharetta, GA 30201
Phone: 770-475-4210
Email: ed@usabilitysystems.com

Appendix B
Becoming Active in the
Usability Profession

If you want to become active in the professional societies to which people who are concerned with usability belong, here is the up-to-date information you need to get started.

The Usability Professionals' Association

This is the organization that is most relevant to people who conduct usability testing. This association began as an informal group of people who were managing usability labs. It has broadened its focus to be concerned with all aspects of usability engineering. UPA holds an annual meeting each year in the summer.

The tutorials and sessions at this meeting are intended purposely for practitioners. You do not have to worry about being intimidated by the people at UPA. They are all practitioners.

UPA publishes an excellent newsletter, *Common Ground*, several times a year. Currently the dues are $75. A membership directory comes with membership. Also, its web site has useful links to other sites of interest to usability professionals. You can find out about joining UPA at:

http://www.upassoc.org

While it is not affiliated with UPA, there is a bulletin board in which many people in the usability profession participate. It is intended for active usability professionals, so don't join it unless you are willing to participate. Also be ready for a lot of activity. This bulletin board often produces long threads that generate more than 50 messages a week.

To subscribe, you must send a message to the list owner, Tharon Howard. His email is tharon@clemson.edu Tell Tharon that you are a usability practitioner and want to join the list. When Tharon puts you on the list, he also sends you information on how to use the list and the rules of participation. (This list is private and has rules about not advertising commercial products or workshops, not asking for jobs, not republishing messages from the list, etc.) If you are serious about usability, write to Tharon. The list is a great place to ask questions and get help from colleagues around the world.

The Society for Technical Communication

The Society for Technical Communication (STC) is the professional association to which most documentation specialists and documentation managers belong. For many years, STC's annual meetings have featured sessions on usability, usability research, and usability testing. STC has more than 23,000 members.

There are more than 100 local STC chapters and about 30 student chapters. STC members automatically become members of a local chapter and receive two journals, *Journal of Technical Communication* and the monthly, *Intercom*, from the national organization, as well as a newsletter from the local chapter.

STC sponsors Special Interest Groups (SIGs). STC established a SIG on Usability in 1992. To join the society, contact:

> The Society of Technical Communication
> Suite 904
> 901 N. Stuart Street
> Arlington, VA 22203
> Voice: 703 522 4114
> Fax: 703 522 2075
> E-mail:membership@stc-va.org
> Web: http://www.stc-va.org

You don't have to be a member of STC or the Usability Special Interest Group to get useful information for the SIG's web site. The site is full of useful resources for practitioners. Try it at

> http://www.stc.org/pics/usability

STC members who want to be part of the SIG on Usability should indicate that with their request for membership or renewal. Currently, STC dues are $95. Joining a SIG is $5 to STC members. Student memberships are less expensive.

The Human Factors and Ergonomics Society

Some of the people in the usability profession also belong to the HFES. At its annual meeting in the fall, there are several sessions and panels on usability issues. The annual meeting tends to be more research oriented than UPA. Many of the sessions at the annual meeting are of interest only to human factors professionals, so check out the advance copy of the meeting agenda before you go.

You can join the HFES in two different ways. You can become an Affiliate member, which requires no qualifications. You can become an Associate (voting) member with a bachelor's degree in an approved area, active participation in the field of human factors, and the endorsement of one Voting Member. To join the HFES, contact:

> The Human Factors and Ergonomics Society
> PO Box 1369
> Santa Monica, CA 90406-1396
> Voice: 310-394-1811
> Fax: 310-394-2410
> E-mail: 72133.1474@compuserve.com
> http://www.hfes.vt.edu/hfes/

Currently, the dues are $115. If you do join HFES, you may also want to join the Computer Systems Technical Group. The additional dues are $5. The Computer Systems Technical Group also sponsors a bulletin board that is relatively active. You can join it once you are a technical group member. There also are about 30 local chapters of the HFES located in major cities

The Association for Computing Machinery

The ACM is the professional society to which people in many computing professions belong. You can join it by contacting:

> ACM - The Association for Computing Machinery
> 1515 Broadway
> New York, NY 10036
> Voice: 1-800-342-6626
> Fax: 212-944-1318
> E-mail: acmhelp@acm.org
> http://www.acm.org/sigchi

Currently, the dues are $115. Membership also brings with it a subscription to *Communications of the ACM*, which is aimed at a general audience, not programmers, and sometimes has articles on usability issues.

Within the ACM, there is a Special Interest Group in Computers and Human Interaction, commonly referred to as SIGCHI. Many people who are active in the usability profession belong to SIGCHI. If you are an ACM member, you can join SIGCHI for $30. But you do not have to be an ACM member to join SIGCHI. You can become a member of SIGCHI only for $57. To join SIGCHI only, the address is:

ACM
PO Box 12115
Church Street Station
New York, NY 10257
http://www.acm.org/sigchi/

There is a membership application in the back of each issue of the *SIGCHI Bulletin*, which you also get for joining SIGCHI. The bulletin also has a list of local SIGCHI chapters.

SIGCHI sponsors an annual meeting in the spring. CHI is an exciting conference to attend. There are paper and panel sessions on usability issues, as well as demonstrations of new technology and a continuous loop of videotapes that illustrate what people around the country are doing at the time. But the audience for the conference is *not* practitioners. If you are new to the usability profession, UPA is the organization to join first.

Author Index

399

Subject Index

Scheduling
 a test, 100–105
 test participants, 145
Severity of problems, *see* Usability problems
Software, *see* Usability
Starting a usability program, 83–95
Statistics, 38, 318–321
Structured walkthroughs, 68, 69, 78–82
Subjects, *see* Test participants
Surveys, 24

T

Task analysis, 12, 24, 40–44, 49, 112
Task scenarios, 172–182
 characteristics of, 173–177
 definition of, 172
 dividing, 179–181
 stopping between, 181–182
Tasks to test, 10, 160–169
 estimating times for, 164
 finishing, 300
 organizing, 167–169
 resources for, 164–167
 selecting tasks, 160–164
Teams, *see* Usability
Technical communicators, 10, 12, 107, 335
TestLogr, 189, 228
Test administrator, *see* Test team roles
Test materials, 204–220
 checklist, 214, 291
 legal form, 204–208
 questionnaires, 208–212
 sample forms, 214–219, 291
 task scenarios, 213
 training script, 212
Test participants, 120–133, 135–152, 273–286
 attitudes towards, 274–276
 avoiding bias, 297–300
 caring for, 274–286
 defining, 120–133
 double booking of, 151
 feelings of, 285
 from advertising, 140
 from networking, 141
 from professional associations, 141
 from temp agencies, 139–140
 incentives for, 147–148
 interaction with, 295–297
 introduction to test environment, 276–277
 number of, 24, 26, 37, 127–129
 obtaining informed consent, 205
 recruiting of, 136–153
 refusing to participate, 282
 rights of, 207, 277–278
 sample forms, *see* Forms

 scheduling of, 145
 screening of, 141–144, 283
 sources of, 136–137
 telephoning of, 144
 thinking out loud, 278–281
 treatment of, 205–208, 281–286
 use in pilot test, 269
Test report, 25, 36, 340, 342–354
 audiences for, 344–345
 distributing, 354
 drafting, 350
 formatting, 352–354
 getting started, 342
 organization of, 348–350
 outline for, 249
 planning of, 343–348
 purpose of, 346
 revising, 353
 scope of, 348
Test team roles, 234–262
 briefer, 241, 242, 253
 camera operator, 241, 244, 255
 checklists, 214, 250–262, 291
 data recorder, 241, 245, 256
 help desk operator, 241, 247, 257
 narrator, 241, 249, 259–260
 number of people, 234
 product expert, 241, 249, 258
 test administrator, 241, 252
Testing at stages of development, 13, 22, 25, 32
Testing checklists, 214, 250–262, 291
Testing documentation, 53, 55–57, 61, 86
 usability problems, 328–329
Testing equipment for
 adjusting controls, 224
 audio adjustments, 227
 camera set-up, 226
 cost of, 94–95
 data-logging software, 227–229
 laboratories, 92–96, Appendix A
 set up, 222
 tapes and disks, 229
 viewing documentation, 225
Thinking out loud, 31, 77
 effect on performance, 279
 reminding participants about, 281
 retrospective, 279
 teaching participant to, 280
Training, 16, 17
 participants, 276
 reducing costs of, 16
 scripts, 212
 test team, 236–240
 in usability, ii
Treatment of test participants, *see* Test participants

M

M